The Legal Context of Education

MARVIN A. ZUKER

Monograph Series / 19

OISE Press–Guidance Centre

The Ontario Institute for Studies in Education

The Ontario Institute for Studies in Education has three prime functions: to conduct programs of graduate study in education, and to assist in the implementation of the findings of educational studies. The Institute is a college chartered by an Act of the Ontario Legislature in 1965. It is affiliated with the University of Toronto for graduate studies purposes.

The publications program of the Institute has been established to make available information and materials arising from studies in education, to foster the spirit of critical inquiry, and to provide a forum for the exchange of ideas about education. The opinions expressed should be viewed as those of the contributors.

In May 1988, the Institute's publications program was enlarged by the acquisition from the University of Toronto of the Guidance Centre. OISE Press and the Guidance Centre have merged to form a single unit presently known as OISE Press–Guidance Centre.

© The Ontario Institute for Studies in Education, 1988
252 Bloor Street West
Toronto, Ontario
M5S 1V5

Canadian Cataloguing in Publication Data
Zuker, Marvin A.
  The legal context of education

(Monograph series ; 19)
Includes bibliographical references.
ISBN 0-7744-0324-1

1. Public schools — Law and legislation — Canada.
2. Educational law and legislation — Canada.
I. Ontario Institute for Studies in Education.
Guidance Centre. II. Title. III. Series:
Monograph series (Ontario Institute for Studies in
Education) ; 19.

KE3805.Z78 1988   344.71'071   C88-095352-7
KF4119.Z78 1988

All of the royalties from The Legal Context of Education *are being donated to the Louis J. Zuker, Q.C., and Pearl H. Zuker Memorial Fund for needy visa and post-program thesis students at OISE.*

ISBN 0-7744-0324-1   Printed in Canada
  1 2 3 4 5 UTP 29 19 09 98 88

Contents

Table of Cases

Preface

Legislatures and our courts at both the provincial and federal levels are playing increasingly greater roles in the area of public education. Laws are being enacted that place additional responsibilities on schools to provide a range of services to meet the educational needs of students. Moreover, judicial interpretations of constitutional and statutory mandates impact on school policies and practices. It is important for all educators to be cognizant of this legal activity because ignorance of the law is not a defence for violating protected rights.

Few school personnel are aware of the burgeoning litigation and legislation and even fewer are familiar with the names of significant case law. Many teachers, administrators, and school board members harbor misunderstandings regarding the legality of the decisions they must make in the day-to-day operation of our schools.

This book is designed to provide basic information on the evolution and current status of the law as of 31 December 1987 pertaining to the organization and administration of our public schools. It will examine laws, regulations, and judicial opinions and their impact on our educational institutions. It will focus on the tension between academic autonomy and individual rights as they affect students' rights, faculty status, sanctions against discrimination, special education, and the current AIDS controversy. The work will also analyse school situations in terms of applicable constitutional and statutory provisions and the rationale for judicial interpretation.

Chapter 1 provides background to facilitate comprehension of succeeding chapters. Included in this chapter is a discussion of areas of underlying importance with which educators may be unfamiliar: an understanding of the legal significance of the sources of law under which educators operate; provincial legislation; applicable school board policies; and the importance of case law in establishing educational policy.

Chapter 2 examines the extent of the province's (in this case Ontario) and local school board's authority when individuals disagree with educational policy. A reading of the decisions in this chapter reveals the attempt to establish a balance between the legitimate demands or objections of individuals toward education policy and school authorities' perception of their responsibility to the greater population.

How does one become familiar with the law? One becomes familiar by studying it. To do this more effectively one must become familiar with the various techniques and tools of legal research. Chapter 3 introduces the reader to materials that are basic to law libraries and useful in researching education law.

Chapter 4 deals with the law of negligence, the notion that a person should be allowed to recover something, usually money, from the individual who harmed that person. The wrong grows out of harm to an individual by the unreasonable conduct of others. We cannot make the educational environment accident proof but we can take steps to reduce the number of factors which allow for successful actions. This chapter will focus on these factors.

Chapter 5 presents material pertinent to student interests, such as compulsory education, discipline, student records, child abuse, and the Young Offenders Act. Inclusion of particular legal decisions is based on several factors. These include most often selecting the case decided by the highest level court that had addressed the specific issue under consideration. In this way the case that best represented the majority of cases in areas where the law may not be well-settled, or perhaps the case that best illustrates the historic evolvement of the case law under consideration, is given the widest applicability.

Notes and questions occasionally follow the edited decisions. These notes are designed to provide helpful background material and information to the reader, additional citations for those interested in further pursuing the issue under consideration, the extent to which the law is well-settled, or other divergent views if the law is not well-settled. Provocative questions are intended to illuminate topics and foster discussion.

Edited verbatim decisions constitute a substantial portion of this book. Such decisions provide a rich source of information, enabling a reader to gain an insight and understanding of school law which cannot be obtained through secondary analysis. The reading of a judge's written opinion, majority, concurring, or dissenting, provides valuable philosophical underpinnings for a thorough understanding of judicial rationale. It also enables the reader to place a court's legal rationale within a specific factual context. Emphasis is on substantive school law issues. Not included in the edited cases are materials unrelated to the issues being examined, material pertaining to technical legal matters, and procedural legal issues which may be of more interest to lawyers.

Substantial controversy has focused on school attendance by students with acquired immune deficiency syndrome (AIDS). This is discussed in Chapter 6 with reference to several court decisions. The controversy of course is not limited to students but also as indicated to teachers and other school professional.

"Equal opportunity" is a principle that has not rung loudly or been translated into school policies and practices in Ontario for very long. Bill 82 in Ontario is the focus of Chapter 7, together with a discussion of special education in the United States which found its statutory roots in 1973. Case law references provide a useful tool in determining the development of the law in special education.

Chapter 8 presents an overview of provincial requirements pertaining to teacher employment, contracts, tenure, and related conditions of employment. Reference is made to teachers' evaluation of performance. There is also comment associated with teachers' rights, be it free expression, academic freedom, freedom of association, freedom of choice in appearance, and privacy rights, as well as of course the right to equal protection and due process.

The final chapter deals with the Canadian Constitution and its entrenched Charter of Rights and Freedoms. The potential effect of the Charter on education has yet to be determined, but cases to date have impacted substantially on the substantive rights of students and teachers, whether we speak again of equal treatment within the school setting, determinational rights in education, or the Charter's minority language education guarantees. Decided cases are referred to.

The book represents an attempt to convey to the educator a view of the law, whether emanating from common law, statute, or constitutional law. It was not written in a spirit of being for or against views espoused by school administrators, teachers, or students. Rather, its purpose is to provide those who are involved in public education with rudimentary knowledge basic for making educationally sound decisions within a legal framework. The work stresses the descriptive, not the prescriptive.

Finally, a book is not intended to serve as a substitute for competent legal advice should it be needed. However, in addition to learning about school law, an understanding of the materials should be of assistance in fostering a more fruitful exchange with a lawyer when that situation occurs.

The various topics are not intended to be rigid or all-inclusive; the law is dynamic, continually evolving from legislative enactments and judicial interpretations. I have attempted to be responsive to emerging issues of legal concern.

The divisions of topics are primarily for organizational purposes. No topic should be viewed in isolation because all areas are interrelated. For example, precedents from cases involving students may be relied upon in litigation pertaining to teachers' rights. Indeed, in analysing a given school situation, one may apply principles of law established in a variety of contexts that extend beyond the educational domain.

Understanding legal principles is a cumulative process. Discussion, debate, and analysis methods must be used to explore these complex interrelated topics.

I wish to acknowledge my many students at The Ontario Institute for Studies in Education (OISE) over the years. They deserve a special word of thanks not only for their penetrating questions, but also for sharing with me what school law topics they have deemed important as they carry out their school-related responsibilities. Of course, any failure or omission in this book is the sole responsibility of the author.

A number of individuals contributed to the completion of this book. Ted Humphreys and Anne Wilson of OISE provided excellent critiques of the chapters relating to Teachers and the Law and Special Education respectively. Irene Del Duca, of the Toronto Board of Education, was also most helpful on the chapter on special education. Susan Reid, University of Guelph, provided inciteful comments on the Young Offenders section. I am also grateful to Ann Morrison, Faculty of Law, University of Toronto, for the chapter on tools of legal research.

This book was based on a student manual designed and written with the assistance of Liz Burge, Head of the Instructional Resources Development Unit at OISE. Some of the introductions were written as part of the creation of a coherent and sequential course manual for distance-mode classes. I shall be forever grateful for IRDU's contribution to the original course manual.

Special thanks go also to Marion Morgan, Mary Howes, and Chris Elie, who helped with the typing, and especially Marion, whose late nights on Bloor Street could be blamed on me.

Finally, a special thank you to Hugh Oliver, Editor-in-Chief, OISE Press, whose encouragement was a great motivation and inspiration.

Marvin A. Zuker

1

The Legal Foundations of Education

Preventive Law for School Personnel

It usually costs less to avoid getting into trouble than to get out of trouble! Avoiding litigation and legal difficulties is a theme that cannot be underestimated. You need to know how the law operates, under what conditions, and how you can avoid meeting the law head-on in a court case. The following pages delineate problem areas that may create legal difficulties, school-based situations that are ripe for acquiring preventative measures, and some of the strategies for educators who are able to implement preventative measures.

Too often school officials find themselves in court defending causes that are not easily defended. Litigation in education has evoked an untenable relationship between schools and the courts that demands examination. In education, *preventive law is the voluntary revision of school policies and procedures to lessen or obviate potential litigation.* The concept of preventive law has one basic premise: the greater the use of the preventive law strategies in schools, the less the need for conflict resolution through litigation.

Disagreements amongst boards too often result in adjudication, that is, the intervention of the judiciary in conflict resolution. When a dispute moves to this level of decision-making, the legal system replaces educational administration as the key to the search for justice.

There are various problem areas that may contribute to wrongful actions by school boards and administrators in the context of legal liability:

- Board-owned vehicles;
- corporal punishment;
- teacher performance evaluations;
- inappropriate due process;
- inadequate duty of care through employment of untrained personnel;
- unsafe school buildings;

- overcrowded physical space in certain types of instruction;
- failure to correct identified hazards.

How do these problem areas relate to preventive law? Preventive law recognizes the transfer of risk through not only adequate insurance protection, but it also stresses the reduction of claims through the systematic review of operational policies and procedures. Putting a school's own house in order will not only lessen the number of legal wrongs but will also increase the capability of a board to obtain and maintain adequate insurance protection.

There are at least several situations that provide opportunities to improve prevention measures. These are:

- lack of school policy(ies),
- vague and unclear policies,
- disregard for affirmed policies
- inconsistent application of existing policies, and
- unwillingness to admit error.

Case law is full of litigation arising from poorly administered policies. Three essential dimensions relating to people that affect the implementation of preventive law are *commitment, communication,* and *compromise.* It is clear that before tangible benefits will fully accrue, a commitment to the proactive approach basic to preventive law is necessary. Communication is a major aspect of any plan to exercise increased prevention. To be effective, audiences of communication should include levels of faculty, staff, and parents. In the legal arena there must be give and take. Progress often must be incremental when changes are attempted. Compromise depends upon a willingness to engage in efforts to identify and accept trade-offs.

There are a number of strategies that are useful to educators ready to implement preventive law practice in schools. For example:

- increase communication on a regular basis among teachers, administrators, and parents;
- improved understanding of education law;
- consistent strengthening of the implementation of policies and procedures;
- periodic internal review of school district policy;
- development of systems for external preventive law audits.

Education law represents the intersection of two bodies of knowledge and practice, both absolutely integral to a flourishing society. It is necessary that institutionalized education function within bounds recognized as the law. The legal constraints are articulable as (1) prescriptions (something must be done — cause shown before terminating a contract); (2) proscriptions (something must not be done — employment decisions based on gender); (3) optional powers (something may be done — moderate corporal punishment administered to students). Value judgments essentially are derived not from the law but from considerations of educational expertise, public policy, and ethical considerations. Laws suggest what is mandatory and what is permissive, not what is wise or often feasible.

Even though some litigation is beyond the control of educators and even lawyers, certain areas for study and joint action can be identified. Many cases can be avoided simply by understanding the law pertaining to the relevant subject. What should be in writing? For example, poor teacher performance, pupil suspension, notice to terminate? How should a notice be worded to avoid misunderstanding? Appropriate prevention involves both knowledge of legal meanings and connotation of words that also are used in general communication, and knowledge of the subject area, including the types of problems that may arise under the policy.

It is in the area of resolution of disputes that perhaps the greatest challenges to ingenuity may lie. The resolution of disputes in an adversarial manner needs reassessment. Perhaps it has become too easy to activate complex mechanisms to deal with minor and idiosyncratic complaints. Light punishments for misconduct and trifling adverse academic decisions regarding students, as well as trivial matters related to employees, increasingly seem to be contested in courts. Are such matters the proper province of courts, or would other types of tribunals better serve society? The extent to which the issue is educational would seem to be the measure of the need for expertise in the decision. Although mediation or arbitration could provide this, selection and functioning of arbitrators frequently makes the process little different from the courtroom.

What Is Law?

- Is it a rule of action to which people are obliged in order to make their conduct comfortable?
- Is it a command?
- Is it a principle of conduct?
- Is "law" merely the expression for a uniformity of action which has been observed?
- What are human laws?

In its widest sense, law in general is a regime of adjusting relations and ordering human behavior through the force of a socially organized group.

With reference to its origin, law is derived from judicial precedents (*Stare Decisis*), from legislation, or from custom. That part of the law of England which is derived from judicial precedents is called **common law**, equity, or admiralty, probate or ecclesiastical law, according to the nature of the courts by which it was originally enforced. That part of the law which is derived from legislation is called the **statute law**. Many statutes are classified under one of the divisions mentioned, because they have merely modified or extended portions of it while others have created altogether new rules. That part of the law which is derived from custom is sometimes called the **customary law**.

The ordinary, but not very useful, division of law into written and unwritten rests on the same principle. The written law is the statute law, the unwritten law is the common law.

With reference to its subject-matter, law is either **public** or **private**. **Public law** is that part of the law which deals with the State, either by itself or in its relations with ordinary individuals. It is called constitutional when it regulates the relations between the various divisions of the sovereign power. The scope of constitutional law is emphasized and clarified by the existence of a written constitution.

It is called administrative when it regulates the business which the State has to do, its most important branches being criminal law and the law for the prevention of crimes, the law relating to education, public health, the poor, and so on, ecclesiastical law, and the law of judicial procedures (courts of law, evidence, and so on).

Private or **civil law** deals with those relations between individuals with which the State is not directly concerned or has some special relationship; as in the relations between husband and wife, parent and child, and the various kinds of property, contracts, and torts.

Even here, however, the courts take cognisance to a certain extent of the indirect effects or private conduct on the community in general. They accordingly refuse to sanction contracts which are immoral, or are otherwise against public policy.

The distinction between public law and private law must not obscure the fact that in many circumstances both public and private law may be relevant. Conduct may be both a crime and a tort.

Law is also divided by the Benthamite school into substantive and adjective. **Substantive law** is that part of the law which creates rights and obligations, while **adjective law**, a generic term, provides a method of enforcing and protecting those rights and obligations. In other words, adjective law comprises the principles and rules relative to the jurisdiction of particular courts, court procedure, pleadings, practices, evidence, and so on.

In a narrower sense, "law" signifies a rule of law, especially one of statutory origin. Hence, in its narrowest sense, "law" is equivalent to "statute."

Law is also sometimes used as opposed to equity, and then means the principles followed in common law courts in contradistinction to those which were administered only in courts of equity. Now in all our courts, effect is to be given to both legal and equitable rights. A court is a court of equity as well as of law in so far as it may do what is right in accordance with reason or justice.

Legal Foundations of Education

Today's educator must be aware of the legal foundations relating to the educational process. Fundamental is the concept that our laws are derived from many sources. The main sources in Canada can generally be divided into three levels of jurisdiction; namely, *federal, provincial,* and *local.* In addition, school administrators and teachers are subject to a large body of legal rules, principles, and policies established over the years.

While federal authority is based mainly on the constitutional provisions laid down in the Constitution Act of 1867, provincial authority relies on the statutes enacted by the legislatures and the regulations adopted by departments of education. At the local level, authority depends on policies established through resolutions of the local school boards. A federal system of governing in our country inevitably results in some conflict of power between the various levels of jurisdiction, and therefore leads to a continuous demand for the services of the courts to render decisions on constitutional questions.

Federal Role

The patriation of the Canadian Constitution in 1982 has not altered the federal position with regard to education. The Constitution Act of 1982 states clearly that the British North America (B.N.A.) Act is still in effect, and Section 29 of the 1982 Act preserves the rights and privileges guaranteed under the Constitution of Canada in respect to denominational, separate, or dissentient schools. Therefore, Section 93 of the B.N.A. Act, which specifically assigns responsibility to the provinces for making laws with respect to educational matters, is still of significance to education.

Does the federal government have the constitutional authority to challenge any provincial legislation which is, in its judgment, detrimental to the interest of Canada as a whole, or which is contrary to the Charter of Rights and Freedoms?

While education has been primarily a provincial responsibility, the federal government has maintained control in certain areas through federal departments.

Provincial Role

Aside from the limitations of our Constitution with respect to denominational, separate, or dissentient schools and minority language educational rights, the provinces have full authority to determine the educational structure within their boundaries. Provinces have the power to enact laws governing their educational system.

The basic legal framework for each province is provided by various statutes. Supplementary to these statutes are rules and regulations provided for under the acts. They are designed to allow for administrative details and are not so easily established in legislation. Generally, rules and regulations are intended to facilitate the practical application of the statutes.

Provinces have education departments responsible for education while adhering to the schools act, regulations, policies, and collective agreements. Although these departments maintain central control over such areas as teacher certification, curriculum, budget allocation, and textbooks, many responsibilities have been decentralized. Regardless, the ultimate responsibility for most public education continues to be that of the provincial government.

Local Role

Included in provincial power to control education is the prerogative to delegate authority. Provinces have established local boards to administer and supervise schools. The powers and duties of these boards are defined in the Education Act of Ontario. Boards act as agents of the province, and, within the limits of authority provided by the statutes, are the local legislatures in educational matters.

Through the Legislature, boards are assigned two distinct levels of power. The first is mandatory, which basically requires boards to exercise the will of the Legislature. The second is discretionary. It gives boards the right to enact rules and regulations pertaining to schools. These are considered administrative provisions. These rules and regulations must not be inconsistent with the law, and must apply equally to all. A board may not, under its rule-making powers, attempt to confer upon itself jurisdiction beyond the provisions of the law. Policies formulated by boards have the force of law and may well constitute part of the legal framework within which schools operate.

2

Boards and Trustees

In dividing the powers of the federal and provincial authorities, the Fathers of Confederation provided that the provincial legislatures would have the power to "exclusively make laws in relation to education." Although exclusive, the power is not absolute, but is "subject and according to the . . . provisions" relating to "separate, dissentient and denominational" schools, as enumerated in the remaining portions of section 93 of the Constitutional Act, 1867. This limitation does not, however, "purport to stereotype the educational system of the Province as it then existed. It expressly authorizes the Provincial Legislature to make laws in regard to education subject only to the provisions of the section."[1]

The law relating to education is for all practical purposes statutory. Present statutory provisions are the evolutionary result of both political pressure and educational theory developed over the last century.

Although some may consider that the existence of public education is for the benefit of either the child or the parent, the public interest of the Province is its dominant intention.[2]

Public education in Ontario is delivered in three systems: the public school system, the Roman Catholic separate school system, and the Protestant separate school system. The financing for all three comes from a combination of provincial government grants and municipal taxes levied on rateable property. To avoid inequities, tax levies on rateable property are made only on that property which is rateable, respectively, for public school purposes, Roman Catholic separate school purposes, or Protestant separate school purposes, depending upon the choice of the owner or tenant of the property concerned. Similarly, unless a person who has a municipal franchise is a supporter of the relevant system, that person does not have a vote for the school trustees of that system.

With respect to rateable property (property that is separately assessed for municipal tax purposes), every owner and tenant is a public school supporter unless he or she gives notice under section 119 of the Education Act (Roman Catholic separate schools), section 138 of the Education Act (Protestant separate schools), or section 14 of the Assessment Act, R.S.O. 1980, c. 31 (annual census undertaken by the assessment commissioner).

After such a notice has been given, and provided that a notice of withdrawal of support has not been given under section 120 of the Education Act (Roman Catholic separate schools) or section 139 (Protestant separate schools), the person becomes a separate school supporter.

A "public school elector" is defined in #43 of subsection 1(1) of the Education Act; "separate school elector" is defined in #60; and "separate school supporter" is defined in #61. Because of the cross-reference, regard must be had to the Municipal Elections Act, R.S.O. 1980, c. 308, in particular #31 and #36 of subsection 1(1), #5 and #6 of subsection 49(1), and subsection 49(4).

The School

To identify the nature of a **school,** #49 of subsection 1(1) of the Education Act reads as follows:

> "school" means,
>
> (i) the body of public school pupils or separate school pupils or secondary school pupils that is organized as a unit for educational purposes under the jurisdiction of the appropriate board, or
> (ii) the body of pupils enrolled in any of the elementary or secondary school courses of study in an educational institution operated by the Government of Ontario.
>
> and includes the teachers and other staff members associated with such unit or institution and the lands and premises used in connection therewith;

This may be contrasted with #40 of subsection 1(1) of the Education Act;

> **"private school"** means an institution at which instruction is provided at any time between the hours of 9:00 a.m. and 4:00 p.m. on any school day for five or more pupils who are of or over compulsory school age in any of the subjects of the elementary or secondary school courses of study and that is not a school as defined in this section.

The principal feature distinguishing a "private school" from a "school" is that the latter is operated by a board or by the government. One wonders whether the collective concept of the persons and facilities that characterizes a "school" is intentionally absent from the concept of "private school."

Section 15 of the Education Act deals expressly with "private schools." That section prohibits the operation of private schools unless notice of intention to operate has been given to the Ontario Ministry of Education in a form and containing particulars required by the Minister. In addition, someone on behalf of the private school is required to provide information regarding enrolment, staff, courses of study, and other information as and when required by the Minister. Inspections of private schools can be at the instance of the Minister, or on request of the school itself; similarly, teacher inspections may be provided on request. Offences are created for failure to comply with the requirements of the section.

An "**elementary school**" is defined in #20 of subsection 1(1) to mean a public school, a Roman Catholic separate school, or a Protestant separate school, but there are no definitions of those three terms. It may be presumed that a public school is an elementary school to which the provisions of Part III of the Education Act apply; that a Roman Catholic separate school is an elementary school to which the provisions of Part IV apply; and that a Protestant separate school is an elementary school to which the provisions of Part V apply.

The definition of "**secondary school**" is contained in #55 of subsection 1(1) of the Education Act to mean a school that is under the jurisdiction of a secondary school board, but there is no definition of a "secondary school board." To assess the jurisdiction of a secondary school board, it is necessary to examine, in particular, four definitions contained in subsection 1(1).

Subsection 42(1) of the Education Act contemplates that a pupil who has been promoted from elementary school shall be admitted to secondary school, or if not promoted, the principal of the secondary school must be satisfied that the applicant is competent to undertake the work of the secondary school.

There are several specific provisions that apply to secondary school boards, in particular, sections 152 and 153 (relating to vocational courses); subsection 166(3) (a special provision related to transportation); and sections 260 through 277 (related to French-language instruction at the secondary-school level).

Reference should also be made to sections 8 and 9 of Ontario Regulation 262, R.R.O. 1980, as amended, dealing with courses of instruction that may be offered or must be offered at the grades 9 and 10 level in elementary schools, and continuing education classes.

The People Associated with Schools

"**Pupil**" is not defined as such in the Education Act, and, with some exceptions, is likewise not defined in the Regulations. What is more significant is whether a person is a "resident pupil," for rights of attendance are dependent upon whether a person is a resident pupil of the board that operates the school in question, whether public school board, Roman Catholic separate school board, Protestant separate school board, or secondary school board. Sections 31 through 48 of the Education Act provide a series of formulae for determining both the concept of "resident pupil" and eligibility of attendance.

One place where there is a definition of "pupil" is *Ontario Regulation 532/83*, "Supervised Alternative Learning for Excused Pupils," where the term is defined to identify a child for whom a program has been prescribed under this Regulation.

With the approval of the Lieutenant Governor-in-Council, the Minister of Education has the power, under section 10 of the Education Act, to make regulations under the Act. One of the powers thus given to the Minister is the power to prescribe duties of pupils. Pursuant to that power, section 23 of Ontario Regulation 262 provides a list of responsibilities for pupils of all ages.

Parent/Guardian

The term "**parent**" is not defined in the Education Act, nor (except to include "guardian") in the Regulations.

Notwithstanding the definition of the term under The Child and Family Services Act, S.O. 1984, c.55, the term is most likely given the usual meaning of the biological parents, or in the case of adoption, the adoptive parents. For practical purposes, the issue of whether a person is a parent will arise in matters involving access to the pupil or the pupil records, the right to participate in teacher interviews or in interviews respecting exceptional pupils, or in truancy prosecutions.

Until recently "**guardian**" was defined as a person who had been appointed by order of a court as the legal guardian of a child in place of a parent. The present definition, found in #22 of subsection 1(1) of the Education Act means "a person who has lawful custody of a child, other than the parent of the child." The term "guardian" is given an extended meaning in section 17 (for the purposes of compulsory attendance and its enforcement, and for the suspension and expulsion of pupils) to include any person who has received into her or his home another person's child who is of compulsory school age and who is resident with him or in her care. The term is given a further meaning under subsection 239(11) for the purpose of access to and control over pupils records.

Teachers

Subsection 1(1) of the Education Act defines five kinds of teachers: *teacher* (#66); *permanent teacher* (#35); *part-time teacher* (#33); *temporary teacher* (#67); and *occasional teacher* (#31).

Many sections of both the Education Act and Regulations deal with teachers. Reference may be made to Part IX of the Act, comprising sections 230 through 248; sections 17 through 20 of Ontario Regulation 262, as amended; Ontario Regulation 269, as amended (teacher qualifications); and Ontario Regulation 277 (teachers' contracts) amongst others.

One particular section of the Education Act provides a unique prohibition against teachers, supervisory officers, or other employees of either a board or of the Ministry of Education itself. Section 93 prohibits such persons from receiving compensation, other than their salary, from promoting, offering for sale, or selling — directly or indirectly — any book or other teaching or learning materials, equipment, furniture, stationery, or other article, not only to the board of which he or she is the employee, but to *any* board, provincial school, teachers' college, or to any pupil enrolled therein. Royalties are excluded from such prohibition where paid to the teacher or other employee who is the author. A parallel prohibition is imposed upon other persons, organization, or agents to prevent any of them from employing a teacher, supervisor, or other employee for such a purpose.

Principals

The term "**principal**" is defined in #39 of subsection 1(1) of the Education Act to mean "a teacher appointed by a board to perform in respect of a school the duties of a principal under this Act and the regulations." The definition prefigures, in part, other sections of the Act that specify qualifications. Section 149, #12, of the Education Act requires that a principal must be appointed for each school that a board operates.

Qualifications for a principal are set out in O.R. 269 and are referred to in section 10 of O.R. 262.

Duties of a principal are enumerated in section 236 of the Education Act, sections 12 and 14 of O.R. 262, and throughout the Act and Regulations.

The term is defined in #65 of subsection 1(1) of the Education Act to mean a person who is qualified in accordance with the regulations governing supervisory officers and who is employed by a board or by the Ministry to perform duties as required of supervisory officers by the Act and the Regulations.

Part X, sections 249 through 257, and Ontario Regulation 276 (R.R.O. 1980), as amended, contain the main provisions relating to the duties and responsibilities of supervisory officers.

Supervisory officers whose responsibilities extend to supervisory and administrative functions related to the academic program must be qualified as teachers. Supervisory officers whose responsibilities are related to the business aspects of board operations must also be qualified in business administration.

Several of the sections deal with the office of " **Director of Education**" who is by section 253 both the chief education officer and the chief executive officer of the board. Since he or she is the chief education officer, the person must hold the qualifications of a supervisory officer on the academic side, and must therefore be qualified and experienced as a teacher.

Trustees

There is no formal definition of the term "**trustee**" contained in the Education Act. Most uses of the term are found in Part IV of the Act.

Assuming a person is both eligible and qualified to be elected as a trustee, a person becomes a trustee in one of the following ways:

.01 if no more candidates are nominated at the end of a nomination day for the office than the number to be elected, the clerk as returning officer declares that the candidate is duly elected (Municipal Elections Act, s.40(1));

.02 after having tallied the total number of votes cast at an election, the clerk as returning officer publicly declares as elected, at noon on the Thursday following the polling day, the candidate or candidates having the highest number of votes, and at the same time the clerk has posted the statement showing the number of votes for each candidate (Municipal Elections Act, s.79(2)); or

.03 the person is elected or appointed to fill a vacancy in the office of trustee in the manner contemplated in sections 198 through 205 of the Education Act.

The person is deemed by subsection 185(2) of the Education Act to have resigned unless, on or before the day fixed for the holding of the first meeting of the board after his or her election or appointment, or on or before

11

the day of the first meeting that he or she attends, the person makes and subscribes to the following solemn declaration of office:

> 1. I am not disqualified under any Act from being a member of (name of board).
>
> 2. I will truly, faithfully, impartially and to the best of my ability execute the office of trustee, and that I have not received and will not receive any payment or reward or promise thereof for the exercise of any partiality or malversation or other undue execution of the said office and that I will disclose any pecuniary interests, direct or indirect, as required by and in accordance with the Municipal Conflict of Interest Act.

Section 185 also requires that the person take the oath of allegiance to the Crown.

Several sections of the Education Act (see subsection 59(32)) provide that election of trustees shall be conducted by the same officers and in the same manner as elections of members of municipal councils. Notwithstanding any other general or special Act, the Municipal Elections Act, section 2, applies to and governs all elections to the offices of members of the local board whose members are to be elected at elections required by law. These elections are to be conducted by the same officers and in the same manner as elections of members of the council of a municipality. That Act provides, in section 34, that any person who is qualified to hold an office as designated under the Act may be nominated as a candidate for the office.

Although the mechanics of the election process are determined under the Municipal Elections Act, qualification and eligibility of candidates must be determined under the Education Act. Eligibility and qualifications will be determined on the nomination date,[3] and must continue for as long as the person remains in office (see Education Act, subsection 197(4)).

A person who does not retain the qualifications to act as a member of the board becomes disqualified; this is the effect, already examined, of subsection 197(3). If a person were to qualify as a candidate for more than one seat on a board, and were elected to hold one or more of those seats on the board, that person would not be entitled to sit as a member of the board by reason of the election, and even the seat to which she or he was elected would thereby be vacated.

Section 206 of the Education Act states that trustees must attend meetings of the board; as noted earlier, the seat of a trustee is vacated if he or she is absent from three consecutive regular meetings of the board without being authorized to do so by a resolution of the board entered into the minutes. Similarly, a trustee has a duty to remain in office throughout the whole of his or her term, unless, with the consent of a majority of the other members, he or she is permitted to resign the seat; it is to be noted that this obligation is abrogated where the reason for resignation is to become a candidate for some other office (see subsection 197(4)).

School trustees have a "public duty" to act as reasonable business people, and are required to take precautions against the loss of public money. Failing this they can incur personal liability.[4] Even if trustees exceeded their powers, but acted on behalf of the school board in good faith, they would not incur personal liability.[5] This may be the effect of the Public Authorities

Protection Act, R.S.O. 1980, c.406, where persons such as trustees acting illegally but in supposed pursuance of, and with the bona fide intention of, discharging a public duty are sheltered under its protective umbrella.[6]

The Board

For most of its activities, a board will act in a **legislative** or **administrative capacity.** For example, it will appoint its officers, establish and maintain its head office, provide instruction and accommodation for its pupils, appoint principals and other staff, establish programs, provide school books, establish its own procedures, and so on. Where it establishes policy, it is acting in the legislative capacity; where it is carrying on the "business" of a school board, it is generally acting in an administrative capacity.

Occasionally, the board will act in a **judicial capacity**, because it is required to hear an appeal, or to make a decision where the parties before it have problems in resolving disputes. Thus, for example, a board will be acting in a judicial capacity when it hears a pupil suspension appeal under subsection 22(2); or where it conducts a hearing before making a decision whether to expel a pupil under subsection 22(3); or hearing an appeal under clause 236(m) of a person whom the principal has refused to admit to a school or classroom on the grounds that the person's presence would be detrimental to the physical or mental well-being of the pupils; and perhaps also when the board is considering the report of an Appeal Board under subsection 7(11) of Ontario Regulation 554/81 regarding the identification of placement recommendation of a special education pupil.

The Education Act contains numerous sections that impose duties upon boards. Section 149 imposes those duties very directly: appointment of a secretary and a treasurer; the establishment of its own internal procedures; the establishment and maintenance of head office, the provision of instruction and adequate accommodation for pupils; the appointment of principals and teachers; the provision of textbooks; and so on. Other provisions, although more indirectly expressed, similarly impose duties on boards: subsection 8(2) obliges boards, at the instance of the Minister, to implement early and ongoing identification of learning needs of pupils.

Boards are creatures of statute; they thus have the power to perform any duties imposed upon them, and, in addition, only those powers expressly granted to them. Boards are not "endowed with capacity by the common law."[7]

The Education Act contains a number of provisions that give to boards certain powers; the principal section, of course, is section 150, containing a list of forty-six powers.

Every board is required under section 149 of the Education Act to "fix the times and places for meetings of the board and mode of calling and conducting them, and ensure that a full and correct account of the proceedings thereat is kept." The Ontario Court of Appeal has held that this gives to the board, within the scope of its statutory powers, inherent jurisdiction to regulate its own meetings.[8] But this imperative duty will not authorize the adoption of a rule by which the power of the majority at a meeting will be hampered or restricted.[9] This is consistent with the provisions of section 26(a) of the Interpretation Act, R.S.O. 1980, c.219, which provides that, unless a contrary intention appears, words in any

Act making any number of persons a corporation vests in the majority the power to bind the others by their acts.

Although as a public body, a board must, pursuant to subsection 183(1) of the Education Act, conduct its proceedings in public, there is a recognition in subsection 183(1a) that there may be need, for the protection of the interest of the board, for certain matters to be closed to the public. Different boards will adopt somewhat different formulae in order to ensure that the record of proceedings undertaken in private will not prematurely disclose the very interest intended to be protected.

Notes

1. Hirsch v. Protestant Board of School Commissioners of Montreal (1928) A.C. 200 (P.C.), also [1928], 1 D.L.R. 1041.
2. Ottawa Separate School Trustees v. City of Ottawa [1915], 24 D.L.R. 497 (Ont. C.A.)
3. See R. ex. rel. Mitchell v. McKenzie (1915), 33 O.L.R. 196, and Kennedy v. Dickson (1915), 7 O.W.N. 769.
4. See School Section Number 24, Vaughan v. Scott (1932), 41 O.W.N. 149.
5. Township of Toronto v. McBride (1869), 29 U.C.Q.B. 13.
6. West Nissouri Continuation School (1917), 38 O.L.R. 207, 33 D.L.R. 209, where the township counsellors who refused to obey a court order to nominate school trustees were required personally to pay costs.
7. See MacKay v. City of Toronto (1919) P.C. 208, Radio Chum 1050 Ltd. v. Toronto Board of Education [1964] 2 O.R. 207 and Law v. Ottawa Public School Board (1928), 63 O.L.R.1.
8. Radio Chum 1050 Ltd. v. Toronto Board of Education [1964] 2 O.R. 207; 44 D.L.R. (2d) 671.
9. Law v. Ottawa Public School Board (1928), 63 O.L.R. 1; (1928) 4 D.L.R. 483.

3

Tools of Legal Research

Legal bibliographies invariably refer to primary and secondary sources of law. A primary source of law is one that is itself an authority for the enforcement of the law it expresses. Traditionally, a common law system, such as in Canada, has two primary sources of authority: **decisions of the courts** and **statutes** enacted by the duly constituted legislatures. These two sources are grounded in traditions that reflect the refinement of the doctrines of **precedent** and **stare decisis**, and the political development of England. A third source of primary law that has increasingly provided its own category is the **regulations** and **decisions** that flow from administrative bodies. Although their authority is derived from statues, their influence on the legal system requires separate mention.

Secondary sources of law, on the other hand, are alternatively said to be "everything else," that is, all legal material other than primary material, or, more informatively, those works which comment on, criticize, and describe the law for the practitioner, the judge, scholars, and the student. Such material circumscribes the writings that have a persuasive influence in the law-making process, as compared to the mandatory influence of the primary authorities.

The doctrine of precedent and the need of the legislature effectively to inform those concerned with the laws it passes make necessary some means of access to the massive body of law represented by the legal publishing industry, which includes digests of decisions, citators, encyclopedias, annotations, indexes, and loose-leaf services. This third category of legal material, which merely provides the means of locating the primary sources of authority, may be called finding-tools, reference books, treatises, or periodicals.

Case Citations

As a preliminary issue, what is a "**case**"? In legal literature, a case is simply a record of an individual legal dispute that has been decided by a court. The body of it is the decision, written by a judge or judges, in which the parties to the dispute are identified, the facts of the dispute are reviewed for the purpose of providing a record of them and making the decision comprehensible, the arguments presented by the parties to the court are sometimes summarized, and the court's decision is rendered. As each case is decided, it may become an example to which later courts in cases can refer when confronted with a similar situation, a possible precedent.

Four basic elements make up a complete case citation:

1. The style of cause, which identifies the parties to the dispute. (The style of cause is always underlined or italicized.)

In civil cases, the name of the party who has instituted or commenced an action, the **plaintiff**, appears first, separated from the name of the defendant by "v." If the government is a party, it is represented by the reigning monarch.

In criminal cases, the state is always a party and, as in civil cases, is represented by the monarch. As the initiator of the action it is referred to first in the style of cause by the abbreviation "R." for Rex (King) or Regina (Queen).

In the appeal of either a civil or a criminal case, the party requesting the appeal is referred to as the **appellant**, the other as the **respondent**. Practice regarding the order of the names of the appellant and the respondent in the style of cause is different in the Supreme Court of Canada from that of other courts. In the Supreme Court, the name of the appellant appears first, whether it is the plaintiff or the respondent who initiates the appeal. For example, the case of Stein v. Lehnert, as it was referred to at the trial and in the Manitoba Court of Appeal, became Lehnert v. Stein in the Supreme Court of Canada, as it was the defendant who brought the appeal. In other Canadian appeal courts, the style of cause remains as it appeared at the trial, notwithstanding that the defendant brought the appeal.

In a criminal case in the Supreme Court of Canada where the names are reversed upon an appeal by the accused, the reference to the monarch is changed from "R." to "The King" or "The Queen," whichever is appropriate. This practice is not universally followed, however, particularly in the Canadian Abridgment, where one infrequently sees "R." in the second place of a style of cause.

In some cases the plaintiff/defendant dichotomy is absent, and the style of cause must reflect the fact. In re Smith and Re Smith both mean "in the matter of a party named Smith," while Ex parte Smith means "on an application of a party named Smith." These forms are used in cases involving applications to a court for some order or declaration, rather than the more common disputes involving a plaintiff and defendant. The full names of the parties involved in a case will be found at the head of the official report of the case, and often they will be much longer than is necessary to identify them unambiguously. It is acceptable to shorten the names in the second and later references to the same case for brevity and ease of reading. Thus, for example, while the first citation of the case of H.F. Clarke Ltd. v. Thermidaire Corp. would necessarily be printed in full, it could be referred to as Clarke v. Thermidaire thereafter.

2. The location of the case in the law reports. The essential components

of this element of the citation are the **name of the law report**, usually abbreviated in conformance with general usage, and the **relevant volume and page number**. The way these components are combined varies among law reports, and the best guide is usually the report itself, as it will often have a comment such as "Cite as . . .", or will contain citations of other cases reported in the same series.

In general, the accepted way of combining these components depends on the method adopted by the publisher for identifying the volumes in its report series. There appear to be two basic ways in which this is done:

2.1. The first is consecutively from the beginning of the series. All American and most Canadian reports use this method, with only slight variation. When this is the method used by the publisher, a citation's reference to a particular volume is in the following form:

volume number report name (abbreviated) series number page number

For example, 14 D.L.R. (4th) 229 and 392 P.2d 209.

The first example refers to a case found on page 229 of the fourteenth volume of the fourth series of the Dominion Law Reports, a major Canadian report series. The second identifies a case on page 209 of the three hundred and ninety-second volume of the second series of the Pacific Reporter, which is part of the Reporter System published by West Publishing. Note that the series number of the Canadian report is in round brackets and is separated from the report's name by a space, while that of the American report is unbracketed and no space separates it from the report's name. A "series" of a report is simply a set which the publisher has numbered consecutively from volume 1. When the volumes reach some arbitrarily high number, a new series is started from volume 1 again, so the series number is necessary to distinguish volumes assigned the same number.

2.2. The second method publishers use to identify their volumes is by referring to the year in which it was published, and, if necessary, the volume number within that year. This method is common in British reports and is used by some Canadian publishers. When this is the method used by the publisher, a citation's reference to a particular volume is in the following form:

(year) volume number report name (abbreviated) page number

For example, (1947) 2 D.L.R. 141, and [·1961] 3 All E.R. 822.

The first example identifies a case found at page 141 of the second volume of the Dominion Law Reports published in 1947. The second identifies a case at page 822 of the third volume of the All England Reports published in 1961. Note that the date in brackets refers to the publication date of the report, and not to the date of the case itself. A case may be published any number of years after its hearing.

3. The third element of a complete case citation is an indication, which may be implicit in the name of the report, of **the identity of the court**

in which the case was heard. This is an important factor in determining the relevance and importance of the case, and should be communicated to the reader. Some law reports include only cases from a particular court. In Canada, only the Supreme Court Reports fall into this category.

4. The fourth element is **the year** in which the case was decided. This is another important factor in assessing the weight of an authority.

There is considerable lack of uniformity on this point. In Canadian and English reports, the date of the case is not always included in the citation. When the report series uses its own publication date to identify the volume, the date of the case is omitted; otherwise, the case date follows the style of cause in round brackets. Examples of these alternative form are:

> **Morgentaler v. The Queen** [1976]1 S.C.R. 616, and R. v. Morgentaler 33 C.R.N.S. 244.

The comma following the style of cause clearly separates it from the reference to the report of the case, which includes the square-bracketed date essential to a Supreme Court citation.

It is practice, in some instances, to provide more than one source in which a case may be located, since it may be assumed that not all readers have ready access to all reports. In Canadian Supreme Court and Federal Court cases, the official report is generally accompanied by a reference to a **commercial report** of the case. In cases from other Canadian jurisdictions, only a single reference is usually given, although it is certainly permissible to provide several. Consecutive references are generally separated by a comma, although a semi-colon may improve clarity. Examples are:

> **Ontario Mushroom Co. v. Learie** (1977), 15 O.R. (2d) 639, 76 D.L.R. (3d) 432 (Div. Ct.);
>
> **Lloyd's Bank v. Bundy** [1975] Q.B. 326; [1974] 3 All E.R. 757 (C.A.); and
>
> **Roe v. Wade,** 410 U.S. 113, 93 S. Ct. 705, 35 L. Ed. 2d. 147 (1973).

Statute Citations

The three basic elements in a statute citation are the **title** of the statute, its **location** in the statute books, including its chapter number, and the **section numbers** of any provisions of the statute specifically referred to.

Traditionally, statutes had long titles, although an alternative **short title** by which it is permissible to cite the statute is now invariably given in the act itself. In the three forms in which researchers generally deal with the Statutes of Canada, namely, the revised and sessional volumes and in Part III of the Canada Gazette, the short title is found in the first section.

In the annual volumes of the Statutes of Ontario, the short title is given in the last section, while in the Revised Statutes of Ontario no short title is given as part of the statute, so the title in the heading of the Act should be used.

If the citation is to the statute as a whole, and it has been amended, the citation of the amending act should be appended. Thus, the **Shoreline Property Assistance Act,** R.S.O. 1980, c. 471, which was amended in 1983, should be cited as follows:

> Shoreline Property Assistance Act, R.S.O. 1980, c.471, as am. S.O. 1983, c. 8, s. 18.

Periodical Article Citations

Legal literature uses a citation method for periodical articles that differs considerably from that used in most other disciplines. Its elements are:
(1) the author's surname;
(2) the full title of article;
(3) the year of publication of the article; and
(4) the name of the journal in which the article is published. Journals, like law reports, number their volumes either consecutively or by year, and when the latter form is used, the date appears in square brackets as an essential component of the reference to the volume which contains the article. Examples of these alternative citation forms are:

> Mirfield, "Shedding a Tear for Issue Estoppel," 1980 Crim. L.R. 336, and
> Leff, "Law and" (1978), 87 Yale L.J. 989.

If the article cited in the last example was referred to in a journal of another discipline, it would probably be cited as follows:

> A. A. Leff, "Law and," *Yale Law Journal* 87 (1978), 989-1011.

For detailed discussions of the technicalities of writing style, see the following publications:

> J. W. Samuels, *Legal Citation for Canadian Lawyers* (Toronto: Butterworth, 1968).

> J. A. Yogis and I. M. Christie, *Legal Writing and Research Manual,* 3rd ed. (Toronto: Butterworth, 1987).

> *A Manual of Style for Authors, Editors and Copywriters,* 12th ed. (Chicago: University of Chicago Press, 1969).

> *A Uniform System of Citation,* 13th ed. (Cambridge: Harvard Law Review Association, 1981).

> J. M. Jacobstein and R. M. Mersky, *Fundamentals of Legal Research* (Mineola: Foundation Press, 1981).

> M. Price, H. Bitner, and S. R. Bysiewicz, *Effective Legal Research.* 4th ed. (Boston: Little, Brown, 1979).

> Chin-Shih, Tang, *Guide to Legal Citation: A Canadian Perspective in Common Law Provinces* (Toronto: Richard DeBoo, 1984).

> McGill Law Journal. *Canadian Guide to Uniform Legal Citation* (Toronto: Carswell, 1986).

Primary Sources and Their Finding-Tools

Canadian Legal Material

1. Canadian Law Reports

The British North America Act, now the Constitution Act, 1867, and the Constitution Act, 1982, provide for the establishment of provincial and federal courts. Provincial courts administer the common law as well as statute law, including the Criminal Code. There are two federal courts, both created by an Act of Parliament in 1875.

The Supreme Court of Canada provides a court of general appeal from any of the provincial courts, and has jurisdiction in all common law and statutory issues. As a result, common law and federal statute law is administered consistently in all the provinces and territories of the country.

The other federal court was originally known as the Exchequer Court of Canada, and since 1971 has been called the **Federal Court of Canada.** It consists of a trial division and an appeal division, and has jurisdiction in cases involving suits against the Crown at the federal level, as well as matters such as copyrights, patents, and interprovincial railways. Appeals from decisions of federally created regulatory agencies and tribunals are generally made to the Federal Court.

It is important to understand the hierarchy within the provincial court system, and its relation to the federal courts, in order to evaluate the weight of authority that should be attached to any particular decision. In Ontario, the hierarchy ascends from the **Provincial Courts** whose judges are appointed by the province. Above them are the **District Courts**, which hear "intermediate" civil cases (usually up to $25,000) and most criminal cases. The highest trial court in the province is the **High Court of Justice**, which is the trial division of the **Supreme Court of Ontario**. It is the court with unlimited power and authority to administer the laws of the province, and its judges are federally appointed.

In Ontario, appeals from any court, including the High Court, go to the **Ontario Court of Appeal**, which is the appellate division of the Supreme Court of Ontario. Statutes which create administrative tribunals and empower them to make binding judgments often provide for an appeal to the **Divisional Court**, which comprises a panel of three High Court judges. Appeals from decisions of the Divisional Court may go to the Ontario Court of Appeal. Appeals from the Ontario Court of Appeal are, by leave, to the Supreme Court of Canada.

A provincial court may reach decisions that are consistent with those that have been given in courts to which an appeal could be taken. These higher court decisions, together with statutes, are sometimes referred to as mandatory authorities. A provincial court may allow itself to be influenced by a decision of a higher-ranked court of another province, or another country, but these decisions are persuasive only. The importance, then, of identifying the court in which a case was heard is clear. For brevity, courts' names are often abbreviated, using their initials, but care should be taken to ensure that the identity of the court is clear.

Canadian Law Reports

Reports of Cases from Federal and Provincial Courts

The general Canadian law report series reporting cases from both federal courts and provincial courts is the *Dominion Law Reports*, which is cited D.L.R. Sometimes a case which is not reported in the *Supreme Court Reports* (cited S.C.R.) or *Federal Court Reports* (cited F.C.) will be found in the D.L.R. Any cases decided by the superior and lower courts of the provinces are also included.

The D.L.R., which began publication in 1912, is currently in its fourth series, and the manner in which it is properly cited has changed somewhat in its four series. Currently, it is cited with reference to its volume and page number, noting the series. The same form of citation is used for cases reported in the second series, published from 1956 to 1968. The first series has two forms of citation: from 1912 to 1922 (that is, volumes 1 to 70) the same citation form as that used in the second and third series is used, and between 1923 and 1955 citation is with reference to the year of publication, volume number in that year, and page number. Examples of each of the four forms are:

58 D.L.R. 386	first series
1928 2 D.L.R. 170	first series
39 D.L.R. (2d) 114	second series
110 D.L.R. (3d) 725	third series
21 D.L.R. (4d) 210	fourth series

Statutes

Federal Statutes. The *Statutes of Canada*, cited S.C., are the sessional volumes of statutes enacted by Parliament. A single session may extend over years, in which case the sessional volume is identified with reference to each of the years in which the session was active. Bills which become Statutes are assigned consecutive chapter numbers, for example, the *Canada Ports Corporation Act,* which was passed in 1983, is cited as:

S.C. 1980-81-82-83, c. 121

Periodically, most of the existing Acts and their subsequent amendments, which are scattered throughout the sessional volumes, are consolidated in the *Revised Statutes of Canada*, cited R.S.C., of which R.S.C. 1985 is the most recent (although not yet proclaimed or published). Acts which are of very limited impact, because they affect only a limited number of persons, or because they have become superseded by other Acts, may be omitted from revisions. When a statute reappears, the most recent revision should be cited from that source rather than from the sessional volume in which it first appeared, since the enactment of the revised volumes makes it the formal, primary authority.

Federal Regulations

Regulations are made under the authority of a statute, for the purpose of specifying the detailed implementation of the provisions of the statute. The statute becomes known, in relation to its regulations, as the "enabling statute," or the "enabling act." It is important to note the difference in the origin, status, and judicial treatment of statutes and regulations. Statutes are enacted by bodies of elected officials. They supersede common law doctrines with which they may be in conflict, and disputes that arise out of violation of them are dealt with in accordance with standard procedures established by other statutes and are administered by the courts.

Regulations are made by the Lieutenant-Governor in Council, under a provincial statute, the Governor-General in Council, under a federal statute, a government department, or a statutorily created administrative body. They are, once removed from direct political procedures, unlike statutes. Disputes that arise out of their administration are initially dealt with by procedures that may be established by the regulations themselves, and appeals to the judicial system are channelled through a special court (in Ontario, the Divisional Court; when a dispute involves federal regulations, the Federal Court of Canada). The ultimate appeal in disputes involving relations may be, like disputes involving statutes, the Supreme Court of Canada.

Thus, although references to regulations frequently coincide with references to statutes, the significant differences between the two should be borne in mind.

In most Canadian jurisdictions, a statute provides for the publication of regulations. The relevant statute for federal regulations is the Statutory Instruments Act, S.C. 1970-71-72, c. 38. In Ontario, the relevant statute is the Regulations Act, R.S.O. 1980, c. 446.

Provincial Regulations

Some provinces follow the federal policy of publishing regulations in a separate part of the Gazette: Alberta, British Columbia, Newfoundland, Nova Scotia, Prince Edward Island, Manitoba, and Quebec now publish regulations in Part II of their official Gazettes. (Acts of the National Assembly are also published in part II of the **Gazette officielle du Quebec/Quebec Official Gazette**.) Saskatchewan publishes its regulations in both Parts II and III of the **Saskatchewan Gazette.** A note at the beginning of each part explains the difference. Those printed in Part II are regulations or amendments to regulations included in the **Revised Regulations of Saskatchewan**, a loose-leaf service now in course of publication, which, when completed, is expected to consist of four or five volumes. Amendments to existing regulations that have not yet been revised are printed in Part III. Ontario regulations are printed at the back of each issue of the **Ontario Gazette**. Double pagination is used, so all regulations for a year can be separated from the issues of the **Gazette** and bound together if desired. New Brunswick issues annual volumes of regulations, which are part of the **New Brunswick Royal Gazette,** published weekly as part of the Gazette.

The regulations of the Yukon Territory are published in Part II of the **Yukon Gazette**, but Parts I and II of each issue are contained in the same booklet and pagination is continuous. Part II of the **Northwest Territories Gazette** containing regulations is, on the other hand, paged separately.

There is much variation from one jurisdiction to another as to a policy of issuing revised or consolidated regulations.

Carswell published the R.R.O. 1980 and has an annual loose leaf service called *Ontario Regulation Service*. These, in fact, are reprints of the *Ontario*

Gazette where the regulation first appeared. Each year's volumes contain a *Table of Regulations* which lists alphabetically, under the appropriate enabling Act, all regulations in force at the time of publication. The table shows whether the regulation was published in the last consolidation of regulations or first appeared in a later year.

Regulations

The federal regulations were last consolidated in 1978. The citation of the regulations for that series is as follows: C.R.C. 1978, C.# Regulations of Canada after 1978 are cited: Orders-in-Council are cited: P.C. 1971-100.g.S.O.R./79-109.

Regulations of Ontario in the Revised Regulations are cited: R.R.O. 1980, Reg. 892. Regulations after the R.R.O. are cited: O.Reg. 26/81, orders-in-Council are cited: O.C. 191/71.

Unlike the Rules of Practice, the numbered items in each regulation are called "sections, subsections, etc." as in the statutes. (For the proper wording to use in connection with federal and provincial statutes see the notes under statutes.)

Digests are volumes containing collections of decided cases organized by subject matter. They vary in the amount of synthesis and commentary they provide. *The Canadian Encyclopedic Digest*, for example, is a general treatise on Canadian case law with cases cited as footnotes to a continuous text. *The Canadian Abridgement*, however, is a collection of case summaries with no commentary. There are also a number of loose-leaf services.

Digests and Encyclopedias

In Canada, the terms *digest, encyclopedia,* and *abridgement* are used interchangeably to refer to a *subject-based indexing and summary of the law*, which can be relied upon by a research for a researcher for a reasonably comprehensive survey of a particular subject. In the United States, legal bibliographers generally reserve the term **encyclopedia** to a work that deals with both case and statute law, and takes the form of essays or articles, with footnotes citing the primary sources on which it is based. The term **digest** is reserved for works dealing with case law, which generally take the form of brief summaries of individual cases. A similar distinction is maintained in England, with the term **abridgement** used synonymously with "encyclopedia."

(i) *The Canadian Abridgment, Second Edition*, cited Can. Abr. (2nd), contains the case law affecting the common law provinces, from 1809 to the present, organized according to a comprehensive table of classifications known as the *Canadian Abridgment Key*. It includes 128 different subject titles, each broken down into suitable conceptual headings. The *Canadian Abridgment* and *Canadian Current Law* and *Canadian Citations* are important because of their extensive coverage of jurisdictions and report series. They do not, however, provide any commentary or analysis, but simply digest or summarize cases.

The following alternative research tools are designed for a different phase of research: the encyclopedic digests (*Canadian Encylopedia Digest*) (Ont. 3rd), *Canadian Encyclopedia Digest* (Western 3rd) and *Canadian Charter of Rights* (Annotated) are helpful starting points for research when the researcher is less than thoroughly familiar with the topic, since they provide *editorial overviews* of the various subject categories. In any case, most research will probably involve reference to several of these finding-tools.

(ii) The *Dominion Report Service*, cited D.R.S., is a loose-leaf reporter, published monthly, which digests reported cases from all the Canadian Courts, as well as selected unreported cases. It provides prompt coverage of recent cases, often before the cases appear in the law reports. Cases are indexed under thirteen general subject headings. There is a *Criminal Code* citator, *Bankruptcy Act* citator, *Quebec Civil Code* citator, and detailed topical index.
Publisher is C.C.H.

(iii) *Canadian Weekly Law Sheet* is a weekly publication of digests of Canadian cases, as well as some unreported family law cases. A cumulative table of cases is published. Digests are indexed by subject, so that an overview of recent decisions on a particular topic can be quickly obtained.
Publisher is Butterworth.

(iv) *Butterworth's Ontario Digest,* cited B.O.D., is a quarterly digest of reported Ontario cases, including a case citator that refers to all subsequent references to each use. Volume 12 has a list of subject categories, each of which includes the corresponding *Canada Weekly Law Sheet* reference. Volume 11 has a "consolidated Case Table," and each volume has a statute citator.
Publisher is Butterworth.

(v) *Canadian Encyclopedia Digest (Ontario) Third Edition,* cited C.E.D. (Ont. 3rd) summarizes in essay form case and statute law originating in Ontario, and provides citations of relevant cases. The C.E.D. (Ont. 3rd) *Key* is a useful starting point for entry into the 34-volume *Main Work,* which is organized by subject-heading. The *Key* provides the following indices upon which research can be based:

(1)   the *Contents Key* lists the Table of Contents of each of the 151 major subject titles; a perusal of the Table of Contents of a title provides a researcher with an overview of the topics reviewed;

(2)   the *Statute Key* is a list of Ontario statutes, with references to paragraphs in the *Main Work* provided for various sections of each statute;

(3)   the *Key-words Index* is designed to assist the user who is starting research without a particular statute in mind and unsure under which subject title his search should proceed; and

(4)   the *Title Key*, which lists all the subject titles published in the C.E.D. (Ont. 3rd), as well as the title number and volume location of each.

Publisher is Carswell.

In addition to those already mentioned, other examples of digests and encyclopedias are the *All Canada Weekly Summaries* (A.C.W.S.), *Butterworth's Ontario Digest, Canadian Current Law,* now called C.C.L., and

Canadian Citations, Canadian Weekly Law Sheet, Weekly Criminal Bulletin, and the *Supreme Court of Canada Report Service.*

These works are not primary sources of the law. Their purpose is to summarize the law and direct you to the primary sources. Something should be said about the difference between a legal encyclopedia and a digest. The term "abridgment" should also be mentioned, as you will find references to it from time to time. In a sense, both digests and encyclopedias are abridgments of the law; they summarize it under subject headings. The subjects are arranged alphabetically, and there is a wide range of headings, some general, others more specific. You will find, for instance, a section dealing with tort and other sections relating to specific torts such as negligence. If you look up a subject that is not dealt with separately, you may find a reference to the section of the work in which information on it is included.

Encyclopedias generally deal with both case and statute law. They state the law in the form of essays or articles, with footnotes citing the cases and/or statutes on which it is based. Digests are usually restricted to case law, though they may include references to statutes, if a case involves statutory interpretation. They give brief summaries of individual cases, together with citations, so that you can look up the reports if you wish. If a case is very similar to one already digested, a summary of it may not be included: in this instance, only the citation is given. One useful feature of a digest is that if a case is reported in more than one series of reports, all sources are listed. Thus, if your library does not have one of the series of reports, or if the volume you need is in use, an alternate citation may lead you to a report of the case in another series.

American writers on legal bibliography usually make a definite distinction between encyclopedias and digests. In England, a similar distinction is made, though it does not seem to be quite so clear cut. The term "digest" is generally used in the same sense as in the United States, while either "abridgment" or "encyclopedia" denotes the essay type.

The following are the most important Canadian series:

- Administrative Law Reports (Admin, L.R.)
- Alberta Law Reports (Alta. L.R.)
- Alberta Reports (A.R.)
- British Columbia Reports (B.C.R.)
- Business Law Reports (B.L.R.)
- Canadian Cases on Employment Law (C.C.E.L.)
- Canadian Cases on the Law of Insurance (C.C.L.I.)
- Canadian Cases on the Law of Torts (C.C.L.T.)
- Canadian Criminal Cases (C.C.C.)
- Canadian Human Rights Reporter (C.H.R.R.)
- Canadian Insurance Law Reports (C.I.L.R.)
- Canadian Labour Law Cases (C.L.L.C.)
- Canadian Labour Relations Boards Reports (Cdn. L.R.B.R.)
- Canadian Native Law Reporter (C.N.L.R.)
- Canadian Rights Reporter (C.R.R.)
- Carswell's Practice Cases (C.P.C.)
- Criminal Reports (C.R.)
- Dominion Law Reports (D.L.R.) This series has an annotation service.

- Federal Court Reports (F.C. or C.F.)
- Immigration Appeal Cases (I.A.C.)
- Insurance Law Reporter (I.L.R.)
- Labour Arbitration Cases (L.A.C.)
- Legal Medical Quarterly (L. Med. Q.)
- Maritime Provinces Reports (M.P.R.)
- Motor Vehicles Reports (M.P.R.)
- National Reporter (N.R.)
- Nova Scotia Reports (N.S.R.)
- Ontario Appeal Cases (O.A.C.)
- Ontario Appeal Reports (O.A.R.)
- Ontario Labour Relations Board Reports (O.L.R.B.Rep.)
- Ontario Law Reports (O.L.R.)
- Ontario Municipal Board Reports (O.M.B.R.)
- Ontario Reports (O.R.)
- Ontario Weekly Notes (O.W.N.)
- Quebec Court of Appeal (Que. C.A. or C.A.)
- Quebec Queen's Bench (Que. Q.B. or B.R.)
- Real Property Reports (R.P.R.)
- Reports of Family Law (R.F.L.)
- Supreme Court Reports (S.C.R.)
- Western Weekly Reports (W.W.R.)
- Workmen's Compensation Report (W.C.R.)

Canadian Loose-leaf Services

Annotated Insurance Act of Ontario (Weir Carswell)

Bankruptcy Law of Canada (Houlden and Morawetz; Carswell)

Canada Corporations Manual (De Boo)

Canada Income Tax Guide (C.C.H.)

Canada Labour Service (De Boo)

Canada Regulations Index (Canada Law Book)

Canadian Charter of Rights Annotated (Canada Law Books)

Canadian Charter of Rights Prosecution and Defence of Criminal and Other
    Statutory Offences (McLeod, Takach, Morton and Segal; Carswell)

Canadian Labour Law Reporter (C.C.H.)

Canadian Law of Landlord and Tenant (Williams and Rhodes: Carswell)

Canadian Tax Reporter (C.C.H.)

Crankshaw's Criminal Code of Canada (Rodriques; Carswell)

Family Law Reform Act of Ontario (Revised Ed.) (MacDonald, Weiler,
    Mesbur, Perkins and Wilton (Carswell)

Holmestead and Watson Ontario Civil Procedure (Watson and Perkins,
    Carswell)

Manual of Motor Vehicle Law (Third Ed.) (Segal: Carswell)

Matrimonial Property Law in Canada (Bissett-Johnson and Holland;
    Carswell)

Ontario Limitation Periods (Butterworth)

Ontario Regulations Service (Carswell)

Organized Advocacy A Manual for the Litigation Practitioner (Manes,
Carswell)

Canadian Periodicals

Administrative Law Journal (Admin. L.J.)
Advocates Quarterly (Advocates' Q)
Business Quarterly (Bus.Q.)
Canadian–American Law Journal (Can.-Am.L.J.)
Canada–United States Law Journal (Can.-U.S.L.J.)
Canadian Bar Association Papers (C.B.A. Papers)
Canadian Bar Journal (Can.Bar.J.)
Canadian Bar Review (Can.Bar.Rev.)
Canadian Business Law Journal (Can.Bus.L.J.)
Canadian Computer Law Reporter (C.C.L.R.)
Canadian Journal of Criminology (Can.J.Crim.)
Canadian Journal of Criminology and Corrections (Can.J. Crim. & Corr.)
Canadian Journal of Family Law (Can.J.Fam.L.)
Canadian Journal of Insurance Law (Can.J.Ins.L.)
Canadian Lawyer (Can.Law.)
Chitty's Law Journal (Chitty's L.J.)
Criminal Law Quarterly (Crim.L.Q.)
Dalhousie Law Journal (Dalhousie L.J.)
Family Law Review (Fam.L.R.)
Health Law in Canada (Halth L.Can.)
Journal of Business Law (J.Bus.L.)
Law Quarterly Review (L.Q.Rev.)
Lawyers Weekly (Lawyers Wkly)
Legal Alert (Legal Alert)
Modern Law Review (Mod.L.Rev.)
Osgoode Hall Law Journal (Osgoode Hall L.J.)
Ottawa Law Review (Ottawa L.Rev.)
Provincial Judges Journal (Prov.Judges J.)
Queen's Law Journal (Queen's L.J.)
Saskatchewan Bar Review (Sask.Bar.Rev.)
Special Lectures of the Law Society of Upper Canada (Spec.Lect.L.S.U.C.)
Supreme Court Law Review (Sup.Ct.L.Rev.)
University of British Columbia Law Review (U.B.C.L.Rev.)
University of New Brunswick Law Journal (U.N.B.L.J.)
University of Toronto Faculty of Law Review (U.T.Fac.L.Rev.)
University of Toronto Law Journal (U.T.L.J.)
University of Western Ontario Law Review (U.W.O.L.Rev.)
Windsor Yearbook of Access to Justice (Windsor Y.B. Access Just.)

American Reports

Most Canadian Law libraries do not possess a complete series of all the American State Reports. Most, however, subscribe to the National Reporter System published by the West Publishing Company. This has several series some of which include the following:

Atlantic Reporter (A)
California Reporter (Cal.Rptr.)
Federal Reporter (F.)
Federal Supplement (F.Supp.)

New York Supplement (N.Y.S.)
Northeastern Reporter (N.E.)
Northwestern Reporter (N.W.)
Pacific Reporter (P)
Southeastern Reporter (S.E.)
Southern Reporter (So)
Southwestern Reporter (S.W.)
Supreme Court Reporter (Sup.Ct.)

The official reports of the U.S. Supreme Court are published in a series cited as U.S. and the reports of the State Supreme Courts are published in a series referred to by abbreviations of the names of the States, for example, Mich., N.Y., and so on. There is a series of annotated reports called the American Law Reports (A.L.R.). Shepard's Citator lists subsequent references to reported cases. Contents for the complete revision, a copy of which is also published at the end of each sessional volume of the *Statutes of Ontario.*

4

The Law of Negligence

Standard of Care of Boards

In today's complex society duties and expectations are unprecedented. Nowhere is this more evident than in an examination of liability issues affecting schols boards.

Educators have arguably more responsibilities and obligations imposed, in addition to the common law, than most comparable professions or occupations. When one combines such considerations as a demand for more diversified non-academic programs, increased expectations and standards of performance, diverse community backgrounds, and the ever expanding role of government as the protector, it is easy to understand the onerous load of legal obligations on a teacher.

School boards may be required by the courts to pay damages for personal injuries, or may incur liability for negligence, because of a number of relationships. As a legal entity, a corporation, and an employer, the board owes a duty of care, which varies in extent, to all those with whom it comes into contact through the course of its business. The board's business being, of course, education, the greatest source of concern is with pupil injuries. In fact, teacher and school board liability emanating from school accidents, particularly in sports and field trips, has attracted more legal scrutiny (by both educators and lawyers) than any other incident or aspect of the employment relationship.

Secondary concern also exists for potential liability to others, to teachers and other employees, and to the parents and the public who anticipate a safe visit to school premises.

Yet school boards are seldom directly in contact with students or others. Rarely then, is the question one, as would be true of other corporate employers, of school board's personal liability for its own acts and defaults. Rather it stems from what is established as a principal incident of the employment relationship, or vicarious liability, liability for the acts of employees carried out in the course of their employment. Besides this common law liability, for which negligence must be proved, strict or absolute liability for the breach of any statutory duty may be imposed on the school board by the Education Act, or other Act of the Legislature, or regulations.

Sports are as American as apple pie, they used to say, and so are lawsuits. Many high school students are injured each year in gyms and on various playing fields across Canada. Those injuries are a source of concern to school administrators and coaches alike, not only because of the human costs they create but also because of potential litigation costs. Injuries in schools increasingly have become a fertile ground for litigation. Boards are not the only potential defendants. Coaches, physical education instructors, teachers, and principals are also being sued and may be held personally liable for injuries incurred in sports-related activities.

Because the danger of being sued is real, school officials must make every effort to structure and conduct their programs so as to minimize both the risk of injuries occurring in the first place and the risk of being found liable for injuries that do occur. That in turn requires some working knowledge of the basic legal claims that are generally available to injured students.

The most likely claim is a negligence claim. Like so many legal concepts, negligence is sometimes a vague concept and the question of whether someone acted negligently is more a function of the facts than simply a legal formula.

There are several elements that an injured person must prove in order to prevail on a negligence claim. Those elements are: (1) duty, (2) breach of duty, (3) causation, and (4) damages.[1] The second element, breach of duty, is generally referred to as negligence. There are a variety of verbal formulations of what constitutes negligence. Here is one such formulation:

> Where an act is one which any *reasonable man* would recognize as involving a risk of harm to another, the risk is unreasonable and the act is negligent if the risk is of such magnitude as to outweigh what the law regards as the utility of the act or of the particular manner in which it is done.[2]

In other words, negligence is failing to anticipate and eliminate unreasonable risks of injuries to others when a reasonable person would have anticipated and eliminated those risks. As the term "reasonably prudent person" suggests, the standard used in determining whether someone was negligent is an objective, not a subjective, standard.

The standard of conduct imposed by the law is an external one, based upon what society generally demands of its members, rather than upon the actor's personal morality or individual sense of right and wrong. A failure to conform to the standard is negligence, therefore, even if it is due to clumsiness, stupidity, forgetfulness, and excitable temperament, or even sheer ignorance. An honest blunder, or a mistaken belief that no damage will result, may absolve the actor from moral blame (but not from liability).

While terms like "negligence" or "foreseeable risk" can always be defined in the abstract — a foreseeable risk is a risk that a reasonable person would have anticipated — the only way to develop some sense of what those vague terms actually mean is to see them at work in a variety of specific factual settings. Take, for example, the case of **Ehlinger v. Bd. of Educ. of New Hartford Cent. School Dist.**[3] In that case, a student dislocated her elbow while running a speed test in gym class. As she neared the finish line, the student lost her balance and was unable to come to a stop before crashing into an unpadded wall eight feet from the finish line. The instructor put the finish line eight feet from the gym wall even though the state physical fitness testing manual recommended leaving fourteen feet of unobstructed space beyond the line "so that pupils will be able to run at top speed past the finish line without danger of running into the gymnasium wall."[4]

Under these circumstances, should the instructor — and, through her, the school board — be held liable to the student? Yes. All four elements of a cause of action for negligence are present.

Elements of a Cause of Action

1. Duty. A school board and its employees are under a duty to exercise reasonable care to protect students from reasonably foreseeable risks of injury. More specifically,

> The duty owed an athletic takes the form of giving adequate instruction in the activity, supplying proper equipment, making a reasonable selection or matching of participants, providing non-negligent supervision of the particular contest, and taking proper post-injury procedures to protect against aggravation of the injury.[5]

Common sense suggests that a student running at full speed may have trouble coming to a complete stop before smashing into a wall eight feet away. In other words, the risk was foreseeable, especially because the manual put the instructor on notice that the finish line should be at least fourteen feet from the wall in order to prevent the very kind of accident that occurred. Because the risk of injury was foreseeable, the instructor had a duty to take reasonable steps to minimize that risk.

2. Breach of Duty (negligence). The instructor breached that duty by placing the finish line where she did. Doing what she did exposed the student to a risk of serious injury. Admittedly, there are risks of injury in any athletic events. Negligence is not a failure to eliminate all risks of injury by the failure to eliminate unreasonable risks of injury.[6] What made the risk in **Ehlinger** unreasonable was that it could have been eliminated or at least reduced had the teacher used common sense. Among other things, she could have set up the course differently to leave more space between the finish line and the wall.

The teacher argued that she had no choice but to set the finish line where she did because the girls' gym was smaller than gyms in general. That argument didn't hold water. Even if the course could not have been set up differently with careful planning, there were obviously other steps that she could have taken to protect her students. The risk of injury could have been reduced by using spotters or placing pads against the wall. At the very least, the instructor should have and could have warned the students of the risk and given them some safety tips on how to protect themselves. The instructor did not even do that, however. As the court said,

> . . . the recommendations in the (state) manual were sufficient to put the instructor on notice of a possible safety hazard created by the proximity of the finish line to the wall and she was under a duty to warn students of that danger and instruct them to take the necessary precautions.[7]

There were therefore a number of steps that the instructor could have taken to reduce the risk of injury to her students. Taking those steps required nothing more than using common sense. Whatever else may be said, the failure to use common sense is negligence.

3. Causation is the determination as to whether there is a sufficient causal link between the defendant's negligence and the plaintiff's injury. This actually involves two separate inquiries: causation in fact and proximate cause. The first is relatively straightforward: would the injury have occurred but for the defendant's negligence? The second, however, is more complex. Even if there is a causal link between the defendant's conduct and the plaintiff's injury, is the link so attenuated or bizarre as to make it unfair to hold the defendant liable for the injury?

Both aspects of causation — causation in fact and proximate cause — were present in **Ehlinger.** Had the teacher used her common sense, the accident would most likely not have happened. The reason it happened is because of what the instructor did — set up the course as she did — or, alternatively, what she failed to do — warn the students, provide them with safety tips, and use pads or spotters. In other words, her negligence in fact caused the student's injuries. Also, the connection between the instructor's negligence and the student's injury was direct and foreseeable. In other words, her negligence was the proximate cause of the student's injuries.

4. Damages as a result of the injury. The student suffered actual damage. She incurred medical bills and endured pain. The dollar amount of those damages was recoverable from the board.

As stated before it is again important to note that a Board is vicariously liable for all acts of negligence performed by its employees and volunteers acting within the scope of their employment or within the scope of their authority.

It should also be noted that in most cases liability "flows" from the teacher to the principal to the Board.

Reasonably Prudent Parent

The common law view is that negligence or careless conduct which injures another does not, by itself, give a right of action. Any right of action is dependent upon a legal duty to assume responsibility for the safety of another. As such a duty rests on a parent that duty of care is transferred first to the school board and then to the teacher. At the close of the last century Lord Esher stated in Williams and Eady: "The school master was bound to take such care of his boys as a careful father would take care of his boys and there could not be a better definition of the duty of a school master."[8] While the statement may now show an archaic sexist preference, it raises the initial critical question: What is the extent of the duty? Its answer permits the determination of a breach.

The standard of care expected of the school board and of its teachers is first then basically conceptualized as equal to that of the careful or prudent parent. The parental duty of care is a duty personally imposed upon the parent irrespective of the wrong-doing or the liability of a child. The duty is to supervise and control the activities of the child and, in doing so, to use reasonable care to prevent foreseeable damage to others. The extent of the duty varies with the age of the child. The degree of supervision and control required of a young child may be very different from that required of a child approaching the age of majority. As the age of the child increases and the expectation that he will conform to adult standards of behavior also increases, the parental duty to supervise and control his activities tends to diminish.

Within schools the careful parent concept has been regarded as neither wholly adequate nor accurate. This has been primarily due to the recognition of the large number of students that require teacher supervision. The careful parent is therefore often said to have a rather large family.

It is not a standard which can be applied in the same manner and to the same extent in every case. Its application will vary from case to case and will depend upon many factors: the number of students being supervised at any given time; the nature of the exercise of activity in progress; and the age and the degree of skill and training which the students may have received in connection with such activity. The nature and condition of the equipment in use, the competency and capacity of the students involved, and other matters which may be widely varied but which, in a given case, may affect the application of the prudent parent standard to the conduct of the school authority in the circumstance.

A comparison to the concept of the "reasonable man," or the law's enjoining on everyone to exercise reasonable care in the circumstances, is that all are expected to guard against foreseeable risks. Warding off such risks is part of the prudent parent duty, as such might well be the circumstances in which we could find the reasonable man.

The apparent vagueness of "reasonableness" and "foreseeability" necessitates the observation that each case will turn on its own peculiar facts. A basic assumption is that breach of the duty to supervise has contributed to the accident. If no such duty existed at the time of the accident or if the accident would have occurred despite supervision, there is no liability. Reasonableness does not mean that teachers must watch every pupil all the time, or in taking all reasonable measures to minimize risks be successful in eliminating all of them. School boards are not insurers in regard to school accidents.

A reasonable presumption is that a teacher will be on duty wherever there is a likelihood of an accident. Therefore, the absence of the teacher from such an activity station shifts the usual burden of proof to the defendant school board to show that adequate supervision was in place. However, adequate supervision does not mean constant surveillance. Thus where students and teachers moved from room to room, and a fifteen-year-old sustained an eye injury from a chalk throwing incident prior to the teacher's arrival, no liability was found. The system of teacher rotation was held adequate and appropriate in the circumstances.

Perhaps the most critical consideration deemed to arise from the concept of foreseeability is the known predilections and tendencies of children. These, of course, vary with a child's age. Recent expectations, for example, were that risk of injury should have been foreseen where an obese and inexperienced thirteen-year-old boy expressed anxiety about making a vertical jump of seven feet in a gym class, and where a fifteen-year-old had climbed to a gym gallery to retrieve a ball and the teacher failed to warn him to come down the staircase and not jump. Particularly relevant in the supervision of a young child is the concept of an allurement or enticement, such as his being drawn to a construction site. In the presence of such enticing hazards the board's responsibilities or its duty of care increases, and any warning given must be timely.

Yet risk is inherent in living and learning. A balance therefore must be struck to prevent any activity with a modicum of risk from being prohibited. In fact some of the most desired learning accrues from the higher risk activities in schools. Supervision *per se* must be weighed against the value of the child acquiring self-responsibility and independence. While it must be recognzied that teachers have a duty to supervise certain school activities — a duty that of necessity bears some relation to the age of the pupils, the special circumstances of each case, and, in particular, the type of activity engaged in — nevertheless it must also be recognized that one of the most important aims of education is to develop a sense of responsibility on the part of pupils — personal responsibility for their individual actions, and a realization of the personal consequences of such actions.

The natural corollary here is that the duty of care is often commensurate with the risk, and the caveat that the emphasis on independence and individual responsibility does not displace the need at times for supervision and instruction to match that risk.

The case of **Myers v. Peel County Board of Education et al.,**[9] enunciated the test as follows:

The standard of care to be exercised by school authorities in providing for the supervision and protection of students for whom they are responsible is that of the careful or prudent parent, described in **Williams v. Eady**. It has become qualified in modern times because of the greater variety of activities conducted in schools, with larger groups of students using more complicated and more dangerous equipment. It is not, however, a standard which can be applied in the same manner and to the same extent in every case. Its application will vary from case to case and will depend upon the number of students being supervised at any given time, the nature of the exercise or the activity in progress, the age and the degree of skill and training which the students may have received in connection with such activity, the nature and condition of the equipment in use at the time, the competency and capacity of the students involved, and a host of other matters which may be widely varied but which, in a given case, may affect the application of the prudent parents-standard to the conduct of the school authority in the circumstances.

McIntyre, J., in Myers, stated that the standard of care is not the same in every case and depends upon the following:

   (i)   the number of students being supervised at any given time;
   (ii)   the nature of the exercise or activity in progress;
   (iii) the age and degree of skill and training which the students may have received in connection with such activities;
   (iv) the nature and condition of the equipment in use at the time, the competency and capacity of the students involved, and
   (v)   a host of other matters which may be widely varied.

The British Columbia Court of Appeal in **Thornton et al. v. Board of School Trustees of School District No. 57 (Prince George) et al.,**[10] held that the following code should be applied in all cases when deciding whether the school authorities were negligent:

(i) Was the attempted exercise suitable to "his" age and condition (mental and physical)?
(ii) Was "the student" progressively trained and coached to do this exercise properly and voice the danger?
(iii) Was the equipment adequate and suitably arranged?
(iv) Was the performance, having regard to its inherently dangerous nature, properly supervised?

The Classroom, Gym, and Science Lab

What about cases concerning the negligence of teachers within the classroom other than those concerning physical education, science, or shop classes? In one case a teacher left her special education class unattended in a classroom and one student was injured by another in a scuffle. A U.S. Court held that the teacher's absence was not negligence. The teacher had only left for five minutes and had instructed a neighboring teacher to supervise the class. (See **MacDonald v. Terrbonne Parish School Board.**[11])

In another case, where a grade 4 student was accidentally hit and injured by another when the teacher left the room during calisthenics, the teacher was not found liable. The Court stated that the injury was not a reasonably foreseeable result of the absence of the teacher and was not caused by the absence of the teacher but rather by the other student. The accident would have occurred whether or not the teacher was there and therefore no causal connection was proven. (See **Segerman v. Jones.**[12])

The **Myers** case, previously mentioned, concerned an accident suffered by a fifteen-year-old boy in attempting to dismount from the rings in a gymnastics class at high school. The Supreme Court of Canada upheld the trial judge's findings that the school board and the teacher had not provided that degree of supervision which it was encumbent on them to provide and that there had been insufficient protective matting available and in place beneath the rings at the time of the accident. The teacher was conducting a class in the gymnasium and had given permission to Myers and others to go to the exercise room to practise their routines. This he permitted without his direct supervision. The evidence at trial also disclosed that there were more protective mats available than those provided.

Thornton concerned a similar accident in which Thornton, a grade 10 student, was injured while doing an aerial form somersault off a springboard in a gymnastics class. The British Columbia Court of Appeal held that there was an inherent and readily foreseeable element of risk or danger in gymnastics, but that this did not mean that Thornton exclusively assumed the risk nor that the Board was strictly liable.

Sidestepping the basic fundamentals is an open invitation to disaster, a lesson that the defendants in **Larson v. Indep. School Dist. No. 315,**

Braham[13] learned too late. Larson, an eighth grader, broke his neck while attempting to perform a head spring in gym class and subsequently sued, among others, his instructor, his principal, and the board itself.[14] The trial court found all three negligent and awarded the plaintiff slightly over $1.1 million in damages, a judgment later affirmed by the Minnesota Supreme Court.

According to the plaintiff, the instructor required the boy to do a running head spring before "that class had participated in the necessary preliminary progressions of less advanced gymnastic exercises, progressions designed in part for safety."[15] Perhaps the most damning evidence that was introduced was a physical education curriculum guide published by the Minnesota Department of Education. The evidence established that the instructor varied from the sequence of activities suggested by the curriculum guide by introducing head springs when he did. The evidence further established that the instructor made the activity even more complex than it might otherwise have been by adding an element — running to the mat — that was not included in the curriculum guide.[16]

Although the curriculum guide did not establish any mandatory requirements, the guide was nevertheless relevant to the question of whether the instructor had been negligent because so many schools followed the guide in structuring their physical education classes.[17] In many ways, the reason why the curriculum guide was relevant is more important than the facts of that case. It not only helps to explain how lawyers go about proving negligence but also suggests one way in which coaches can minimize the risk of liability.

Because negligence is a function of what a reasonable person would have done under the circumstances, evidence of how other schools and coaches approach their physical education programs may well be relevant to the question of whether the defendant was acting reasonably. If other coaches structure their programs in a particular fashion, the inference is that a reasonably prudent coach would have also structured his program in that fashion. From a litigation standpoint, that means that a lawyer attempting to prove that a coach acted negligently will often call other coaches or any other professionals as expert witnesses to compare what they do with what the coach in question did and to explain why, in their opinion, what he or she did was wrong.

Duties of a Coach

An interesting case dealing with a coach's duties is **Vendrell v. School Dist. No. 26C, Malheur Co.**[18] The plaintiff Vendrell was a high school running back who fractured his spine after running into a tackler headfirst. According to the plaintiff, the school's coaches were negligent in failing to provide proper instruction and in failing to warn him of the dangers involved in lowering his head when first making contact with a tackler. The court rejected those claims, explaining:

> No one expects a football coach to extract from the game the body clashes that causes bruises, jolts and hard falls. To remove them would end the sport. The coach's function is to minimize the possibility that

36

the body contacts might result in something more than slight injury. The extensive calisthenics, running and other forms of muscular exercise to which the . . . coaches subjected the squad . . . were intended to place the players in sound physical condition so that they could withstand the shocks, blows and other rough treatment with which they would meet in actual play. . . . Each player was taught how to handle himself while in play so that a blow would fall upon his protective equipment and not directly upon his body. . . . (E)very player was instructed in the manner of (1) running while carrying the ball, (2) tackling an opposing player, and (3) handling himself properly when about to be tackled.

All of the football coaches who testified upon the subject swore that the instructions and practice which were given to the defendant's football squad were adequate and were similar to that which they gave to their own players. No criticism was offered of the instructions and the practice. Had the plaintiff followed the instructions that were given to him about holding his head up, his injury would not have occurred, assuming, of course, that the failure to hold up his head was the cause of his injury.[19]

The court's description of a coach's basic duty — to take reasonable steps to minimize the possibility of serious injury — is accurate. To the extent Vendrell suggests that a coach discharges that duty by doing what the coaches in that case did, simply instructing players to run with their heads up may no longer be accurate. Coaching techniques have changed and the law along with them.

That was the central theme of the celebrated case of **Thompson v. Seattle School District No. 1.**[20] Thompson was a fifteen-year-old fullback who played for his high school's varsity football team. After catching a pass during an inter-school game, Thompson ran toward the sidelines and lowered his head to run through a tackler. As a consequence of running through the tackler, Thompson severed his spinal cord and instantly became quadriplegic.

Thompson later sued the district, claiming that his coach had been negligent both in failing to instruct him on how to handle himself when coming in contact with a tackler became inevitable and in failing to warn him of the inherent dangers in attempting to bull through a tackler for a few extra yards. The jury agreed and awarded Thompson $6.4 million in damages. While the case was on appeal, the board in question settled the case for slightly less than $4 million.

The evidence indicated that while the coach instructed his players to keep their hands up while running, he did not instruct them on what to do when they made contact with a tackler. Furthermore, he did not warn his players that using the helmet to make initial contact can lead to catastrophic injuries, including quadriplegia. Even though the rulebook published by the National Federation of State High School Athletic Associations urged coaches to warn players of the danger, the coach decided that giving his players such a warning would be to take too negative an approach.

Coaches called by the plaintiff as expert witnesses testified that they put their players through repeated drills designed to teach them the proper technique for confronting a tackler at the sideline. The plaintiff also introduced evidence that safety movies and brochures discussing the dangers of head-first contact were readily available from a variety of sources but were not used at Thompson's high school. Finally, the plaintiff introduced evidence that the school board employed a trained safety expert who routinely examined all school activities — for example, shop, physical education, and chemistry classes — that posed a risk of serious injury, except for one: interscholastic sports.

Improper Equipment

A board's legal obligations include more than a duty to provide adequate supervision and instruction. A board also "has an affirmative duty, where students are engaging in school activities, whether they are extracurricular, or formally authorized as part of the school program, to furnish equipment to prevent serious injuries."[21] Merely because proper equipment may not be on hand is no excuse.

In **Leahy v. School Board of Hernando Co.,**[22] the plaintiff shattered his front teeth while participating in an agility drill during football practice. Although helmets had been issued to most of the players, a few of the players, including the plaintiff, had not yet been issued helmets because there were not enough helmets in their sizes to go around. Despite the fact that he had no helmet the plaintiff was nevertheless required to participate in the drill. The drill did not involve tackling or blocking but did involve some physical contact. Ten players all wearing helmets arranged themselves in a straight line while on their hands and knees. The remaining players were then instructed to approach the first lineman, hit the lineman's shoulder pads with both hands, fall on the ground and roll over, get up as quickly as possible, and then repeat the process with each of the remaining linemen. As the drill went on, the players became more aggressive with some of the linemen raising their heads to make contact and also hitting the other players while they were down. When the plaintiff hit the first lineman, the lineman raised his head so that his helmet hit the plaintiff's face and shattered his teeth.

In holding that the evidence was sufficient to support a finding that the board had been negligent, the court emphasized that the coaches themselves admitted that they encouraged the players to move through the drill as quickly as possible, which increased the risk of physical contact. The courts further noted that some of the players were inexperienced and were therefore not expected to perform the drill properly, and that the coaches knew that the players tended to become progressively more aggressive during the drill.[23] Nevertheless, the coaches did nothing to lessen the intensity of the drill and had placed no limitations on participation by those players who had not been issued helmets. No instructions or warnings were given to any of the players about making contact, especially contact with those without helmets.

Although these three factors — the failure to issue the plaintiff a helmet, the failure to supervise the drill closely, and the failure to warn the players against making contact — all combined to support the conclusion that the coaches had been negligent, the judgement suggests that the crucial factor was allowing the plaintiff to participate in that kind of drill, a drill that involved physical contact and a correspondingly foreseeable risk of injury without a helmet.

Because football helmets with their attached faceguards and mouthpieces are used as safety or protective devices, calculated to protect the player against head or facial injuries, the evidence that (the plaintiff) was permitted to participate without a helmet was a sufficient basis upon which a jury could conclude that the school (through its employees) failed to exercise reasonable care under the circumstances for the protection of the (plaintiff).[24]

The lesson to be learned is that coaches should think twice before conducting any practice sessions in which the students participate without protective gear. Protective equipment may be necessary even in touch football scrimmages, assuming of course that more than the customary type of bodily contact is allowed.[25]

Failing to furnish proper equipment to athletes engaged in sports is a fairly obvious source of potential liability. A less obvious but very real source of potential liability is failing to provide proper equipment to students in gym classes[26] or in intramural sports. Intramural sports are perhaps the most neglected school activity from the standpoint of protective equipment.

To summarize, therefore, before allowing students to participate in a team practice, in an intramural league, or in gym class activities, a careful determination should be made of the kinds of injuries that students might incur and whether there is any protective equipment available on the market that would minimize the risk of those injuries occurring. If there is any such equipment available, the students should be provided with that equipment or not be allowed to participate irrespective of what other schools may do or what athletic associations may require.

Transportation Facilities

A Board will be vicariously liable for any negligence occurring with respect to transportation facilities owned and operated by it.

Where transportation is provided by a company not affiliated with the Board but the Board retains a substantial degree of control over the bus company and over the discipline of the pupils while they are on the bus, the Board's duty to the pupil continues until the child arrives home. The bus company acts as a servant of the Board in the circumstances and not as a true independent contractor.[27]

The issue is whether the bus company is truly an independent contractor or in reality an employee of the Board. The distinction depends on the degree of control by the Board over the bus company in what the bus company does as well as the manner in which it does it.

In **Baldwin et al. v. Lyons,**[28] it was held that the bus company was clearly an independent contractor, and the judge stated that it would require cogent and unequivocable evidence to demonstrate that the parties had in fact changed the relationship into one of master and servant.

The Court found that on the evidence the bus company was an independent contractor. The analogy the Court used was that the relationship of the Board to the bus company was that of a passenger who hires a taxi. The passenger may instruct the taxi cab driver on where to go but he does not have control over the manner in which he gets there.

The distinction between Mattinson and Baldwin was that in Mattinson the Board had issued a policy statement with respect to transportation which was given to the bus company with instructions to follow it. The policy gave the Board a substantial amount of control over any matter concerning the safety of the pupils. The evidence of both the Board and the bus company indicated that the Board considered it could exercise a substantial degree of control over the bus company in implementing its policy.

Field Trips

Moddejonge et al. and the Huron County Board of Education et al.[29] concerned two girls that drowned while on a school field trip. The supervising teacher as well as one of the girls that drowned were unable to swim. No life-saving equipment was available. The teacher permitted the children to swim in an area that was close to a dangerous drop-off point. When the children drifted into the dangerous area, the teacher did nothing. The Court held that the duty owed by a teacher or supervisor towards children in his charge is to take such care of them as a prudent father would of his children. Since the teacher was acting within the scope of his employment both the Board and the teacher were found liable.

Some injuries will inevitably occur in activities. As long as a board and its employees acted reasonably under the circumstances, providing, for example, adequate supervision and training, proper equipment, and reasonably safe premises there may be no liability. As with all generalizations, however, that statement must be qualified. Even though an injury may have occurred through no fault of a board, it may nevertheless be liable if it fails to provide the injured athlete with prompt medical treatment (provided that such treatment is reasonably necessary under the circumstances and the failure to provide such treatment aggravates the original injury).

That was certainly the case of **Mogabgab v. Orleans Parish School Board.**[30] Mogabgab involved a negligence action brought by the parents of a boy who died of heat stroke after his high school football practice. Shortly before practice ended, the player became nauseous, vomited, and was unable to walk without assistance. Following the coaches' instructions, a few of the other players undressed the boy, gave him a room-temperature shower, and laid him on a blanket in the high school cafeteria. The coaches subsequently put a blanket over the boy, massaged his arms, and unsuccessfully attempted to have him drink salt water. While all this was going on, the boy was extremely pale and unable to talk.

The boy's condition grew steadily worse over the next hour, with his mouth hanging slightly ajar and his skin turning grayish blue. Even then the coaches did not call a doctor, but instead called the boy's parents to ask them if they had a preference for any particular doctor. The boy's mother then called the family physician who arrived shortly thereafter, or about two hours after the boy collapsed. The doctor concluded that the boy was suffering from extreme heat exhaustion and had the boy transported to the hospital where he died seven hours later.[31]

The jury found that the coaches had been negligent in failing to seek medical treatment for the boy sooner than they had and that their negligence was the cause of the boy's death. On appeal, the coaches argued that there was insufficient evidence of a causal link between their failure to secure medical treatment and the boy's death. The Court of Appeals disagreed.

> (T)he negligence of Coaches O'Neill and Mondello actively denied Robert access to medical treatment for some two hours after symptoms appeared. When he did see a physician, it was too late and he died . . . it was not proved that (Robert) would have certainly lived if brought to a doctor sooner or for what precise period of time the condition remained reversible. We do not think, however, that the law demands such flawless precision. . . . Taken as a whole, the record supports the premises that it is more likely than not that Robert would have survived with reasonably prompt medical attention.[32]

This does not mean that a coach is negligent whenever he or she either fails to secure medical treatment for an injured player or mistakenly concludes that an injury is insufficiently serious to warrant medical attention. The coach will be deemed negligent only if a reasonable layperson under the same circumstances would have concluded that the student's condition was sufficiently serious to warrant prompt medical attention.[33]

What really happened in Mogabgab is that coaches failed to exercise common sense. While perhaps only a doctor might have been able to diagnose that the player was suffering from extreme and potentially irreversible heat exhaustion, a reasonable person with no formal medical training could not help but conclude that something is very seriously wrong with a young man who is growing progressively more pale and who cannot walk, talk, or undress himself. When something is seriously wrong, the time has come to seek medical treatment. The law does not expect coaches to be fully trained physicians but it does expect them to exercise common sense.[34]

Inside and Outside of School Hours

Ontario Regulation 617/81

> "s.3(3) On and after the first day of September, 1982 the instructional program of the school day for pupils of compulsory school age shall consist of not less than five hours excluding recesses or scheduled intervals between classes and shall begin not earlier than 8:00 a.m. and end not later than 5:00 p.m. except with the approval of the Minister.
>
> s.3(8) Every board shall determine the period of time during each school day when its school buildings and playgrounds shall be open to pupils during the period beginning 15 minutes before classes begin for the day and ending 15 minutes after classes end for the day.
>
> s.12(3)(d) In addition to the duties under the Act and those assigned by the board, the principal of a school shall make provision for adequate supervision for the period of time during each school day when the school buildings and playground are open to the pupils, and for the supervising and conducting of any school activity authorized by the board."

If a school teacher acting as a coach holds a practice before or after school hours and a student is injured as a result of the teacher's lack of proper supervision the Board and the teacher may be liable to the student.

In **Lataille v. Les Commissaires D'Écoles de la Municipalité Scholarie de Farnham et Mercier,**[35] the Board was held not to be liable when an eleven-year-old girl lost her eye when struck by a hockey stick being used by a sixteen-year-old boy while using the school facilities at night. A senior member of the teaching staff of the school voluntarily supervised a rink and a basement adjoining the rink after school hours for use by the public. The Board tolerated this use but did not authorize it. The Supreme Court of Canada affirmed the Court of Appeal, which held the Board had no duty to provide for the entertainment of the public or to make the school or any of its facilities available to the public outside of normal school hours.

Principals and Teachers

In addition to the common law standard of care of a reasonably prudent parent, principals and teachers also have statutory duties pursuant to the Education Act, R.S.O. 1980, c. 129, s.235 and s.236, and Ontario Regulation 617/81, s.12, s.17, and s.21.

Section 236(j) is included in the general principle of reasonably prudent parent or is a statutory description of some of the components of the common law principle. It is the responsibility of every parent to give assiduous attention to the health and comfort of his or her child and to the cleanliness, temperature, and ventilation of the home environment.

The following guidelines should assist in assessing the degree of supervision required by a teacher to reduce the risk of liability which one can choose to employ in assessing potential liability in any given circumstances:

(i) The number of students being supervised at any given time. The greater the number of students, the less the required supervision of each individual student.

(ii) The age, competency, and capacity of the students involved in relation to the activity. The lower the age and experience as compared to the increasing sophistication of the activity, the higher the expectancy of close supervision.

(iii) The nature of the activity engaged in. The higher the degree of difficulty or risk of injury, the closer the supervision that is required.

(iv) The nature and condition of the equipment used. Obviously, the poorer the condition and the greater the unsuitability, the greater the risk of injury.

(v) One that comes in handy very frequently is: What would you permit or do if these were your children? This is especially useful in assessing risks associated with field trips and the like.

Volunteers

If a school board enlists the services of a volunteer, such a volunteer may be said to be an agent of the Board. If a volunteer acts within the scope of his authority as an agent, the Board may be vicariously liable for any tort committed by the volunteer.

Occupiers' Liability Act

In Ontario, since the coming into force of the Occupiers' Liability Act, R.S.O. 1980, c. 322, the distinction between the duty of care owed to an invitee, licensee, or trespasser no longer exists. An occupier of premises under the Act owes a duty of care to "persons entering on the premise." (s.3(1)) However, an occupier does not owe such a duty of care to persons who willingly assume risks. All persons on the premises with the intention of committing a criminal act are deemed to have assumed all risks. (s.4)

The standard of care under the Act is that of reasonableness, and the traditional principles of negligence require that all of the case be considered, including the likelihood of injury to others, the seriousness of the injury, and the burden of avoiding the risk.

An "occupier" is defined as follows:

> "Occupier includes
>
> (i) a person who is in physical possession of premises,
> or
> (ii) a person who has responsibility for and control over the condition of premises or the activities there carried on, or control over persons allowed to enter the premises, notwithstanding that there is more than one occupier of the same premises;"

Pursuant to subsection 149(8) of the Education Act, a Board may be an "occupier" under the Occupier's Liability Act.

A principal of a School is in charge of the organization and management of the school pursuant to Ontario Regulation 617/81, s.12(1) (b). Thus, a principal is an "occupier" under the Act. However, as long as the principal is acting within the scope of his employment, the Board is liable for any violation of the Act committed by the principal.

In **Boryszko v. Board of Education of Toronto,**[36] an eight-year-old boy playing on a pile of blocks after school hours was injured when an unidentified child pushed a block off the pile onto the child's foot. The children had been warned by the school principal not to play on the blocks and a guard had chased the children away from the area many times. The Court held that a neat pile of blocks put there by a contractor for the purpose of construction on the school was not a trap and therefore the Board was not liable.

The general test here was whether there is a concealed danger on the premises which the occupier knows or ought to have known existed which danger is unusual in the circumstances.

Limitation of Actions

Section 11 of the **Public Authorities Protection Act,** R.S.O. 1980, c. 406, limits the period within which an action may be brought against various public authorities.

> "No action, prosecution or other proceeding lies or shall be instituted against any person for an act done in pursuance or execution or intended execution of any statutory or other public duty or authority, or in respect of any alleged neglect or default in the execution of any such duty or authority, unless it is commenced within six months next after the cause of action arose, or, in case of continuance of injury or damage, within six months after the ceasing thereof." (Subsection 1 of s. 11.)

The Courts have ruled that the six-month limitation period provided in Section 11 applies to actions against boards.[37] This section would also apply to actions against trustees in cases where the acts complained of were not *ultra vires.*

In **Moffat v. Dufferin County Board of Education,**[38] a teacher asked a pupil to help the janitor move a piano and the pupil was injured in doing so. The Court held that the teacher's action was in pursuance of a public duty and the limitation period in Section 11 was applicable.

In **Urzi v. Board of Education for the Borough of North York, (1981),**[39] R. E. Holland, J. held that the **Moffatt** and **Levine** cases were no longer good authority with respect to s. 11 in view of the decision of the Supreme Court of Canada in **Berardinelli v. Ontario Housing Corp. et al.**[40] Mr Justice Estey, writing for the majority, held that based on the wording ". . . an act done in . . . the execution . . . of any statutory or other public duty or authority . . .", s. 11 provides protection only for those activities which have a public aspect as distinct from a private connotation.

In spite of decisions of the Supreme Court of Canada that interpret s. 11, there is still some difficulty in applying it. But what the Supreme Court said in **McGonegal v. Gray**[41] is significant. There, the plaintiff was a twelve-year-old pupil who was asked by his teacher McGonegal to light a gasoline stove for the purpose of heating soup. In the course of doing so, he was severely burned. An action was brought by the pupil against the teacher and the trustees of the school, but only after six months had passed following the accident. The defendants said that s. 11 should bar the pupil's action.

Three members of the Supreme Court panel of seven said that the trustees of the school could not successfully plead s. 11 because the act in question was a private act that did not relate at all to the direct public duty of the teacher or the trustees to the children. A fourth member agreed that s. 11 did not apply but only because he found that the soup was to be heated for the teacher alone. If it had been an act for the benefit of school children, Locke J. said that s. 11 would apply. The remaining three members said that the trustees had provided the stove in the execution of their public duty to teach and to attend to the health and comfort of the pupils. Because it was in the course of executing this public duty that the accident occurred, the plaintiff was required to bring his action within six months of his injury or to lose the right to do so.

The questions of the actual definition of the public duty and how wide such a definition should be were both relatively clearly answered. Any matter that could be considered to be within the broadest scope of duties that public officials were involved in was considered a public duty. Section 11 afforded a defence for those public officials if they committed wrongful acts when carrying out such public duties.

The test generated by **Berardinelli** was to differentiate between the primary purpose and matters incidental to the primary purpose. These again are often very difficult to distinguish. For example, the clearing of snow from sidewalks around a school has been held to be incidental to the primary purpose of a school board's activities as mentioned in **Urzi**.[42] The dismissal of a finance manager by a school board was held not to be in the execution of a public duty or authority.[43] But the repair of entrance steps to a school has been held to be a public duty: **Danis v. Nipissing Roman Catholic Separate School Board**.[44]

In Danis the court distinguished Urzi by means of the authority/duty analysis. In Urzi, the defendant school board had not had a specific statutory duty to keep sidewalks clear of snow, and so the board was liable to a plaintiff who had fallen on icy steps and who had brought an action more than six months after the fall. In Danis, where the issue revolved around steps that were in disrepair, the trial judge found that there was a positive statutory duty to keep the school "in good repair," and so the defendant was protected from suit by s. 11 and the passage of more than six months after the accident. Section 11 was also applied to bar an action by a student against a Board of Education, a principal, and a teacher for similar reasons in **Eddington v. Kent County Board of Education**.[45] The Court based its decision on the fact that there is a positive duty in the Education Act on principals and teachers to supervise pupils and on the school board to provide suitable furniture and equipment and to keep it in proper care combined with a general statutory duty to provide instruction for pupils in prescribed or approved courses of study.

The concept of a private contract has in some cases included the hiring and firing of employees. The case of **Lacarte v. Board of Education of Toronto**[46] stands for an opposite proposition with respect to contracts of employment between a school board and teachers. Decided well before Berardinelli, the case established that the hiring and dismissal of teachers by a school board proceeded from the board's general duty of management, and was protected by s. 11. The following cases dealing with teachers' employment were decided before Berardinelli, and followed Lacarte: **Stewart v. Lincoln County Board of Education (H.C.)**,[47] and **Wright v. Board of Education for the City of Hamilton**.[48]

It could be argued that Berardinelli overruled the decision in Lacarte by making a distinction between what is incidental to the primary purpose of the public authority and what is central. The private contracts of employment with each teacher could be seen to be merely secondary to the more direct regulation of school curriculum and facilities. But these cases, decided after Berardinelli, have followed Lacarte: **Riddle v. University of Victoria; Goodwin v. Oxford County Board of Education; and Re Gallant and Roman Catholic Separate School Board of District of Sudbury**.[49]

The case of **Clarke v. Ottawa Board of Education**[50] established that

e interpretation of the contract between a school board and a teacher
ith respect to sick leave benefits was a private matter, and not limited
⌐ s. 11.

Conclusion

It should be fairly clear that there is no all-encompassing definition of
negligence that everyone can mechanically apply to determine whether
they are acting negligently. Most of the cases discussed here were chosen
because they — hopefully — provide some sense of what the law expects.
Developing that sense is far more important than developing a checklist
of do's and don'ts.

It should also be fairly clear that be they coaches, instructors, and principals, they cannot afford to operate in isolation. Safety requires a team
effort. Furthermore, keeping up what others are doing is something whose
importance cannot be overstated. In so many cases plaintiffs rely heavily
on expert testimony from others to establish negligence on the part of, for
example, the coach at issue. If others are taking certain safety precautions,
the inference is that a reasonably prudent coach would have taken those
precautions as well. Attending seminars, workshops, clinics, and the like
is an indispensable component of minimizing the risk of liability.

Continually re-evaluating instructional techniques and safety procedures
is also something whose importance cannot be overestimated. There is no
substitute for routinely sitting down and carefully evaluating what kinds
of injuries might occur, why they might occur, whether they can be
prevented, and, if so, how.

Although the risk of litigation and the corresponding risk of liability are
ever-present in schools, the same is true of almost everything. We all run
those same risks every time we drive a car. Just as there is no need for
people to stop driving cars, there is no need for schools to eliminate programs from curricula. There is a need, however, for everyone, drivers and
high school personnel alike, to use their common sense. And in many ways,
that is really all the law expects of us.

Ways to Avoid Being Negligent

One way, of course, to avoid negligence is to institute policies to evaluate
school programs to determine the areas where dangerous conditions exist
and to develop safety measures to avoid injuries. Although litigation cannot always be avoided, boards might avoid losing cases where the courts
find that they could have done nothing to avoid the injury because it was
simply not foreseeable. Thus, in the following examples:

Student "flip" from the top of a fence. Two students left the cafeteria
during lunch and went to a grassy area near the track to practise gymnastics. One was injured while attempting to do a "flip" from the top
of a chainlink fence, which collapsed. The appellate court agreed with
the lower court that there is sufficient evidence to go to trial.[51]

Lesson: Not all injuries can be avoided. But we must teach athletes to use only those facilities that are designed for the particular athletic activity.

Assault against another student by a student with a history of violence. During a wiffleball game two eighth graders got into a dispute. When the gym teacher started to separate the boys, Hornbeck, the defendant, hit the plaintiff, Hanley. Years earlier, Hornbeck had assaulted two students on a bus trip.

At that time the school referred the child to the committee on the handicapped because of his behavior traits. The committee ruled that he should remain with regular students. A jury found for the plaintiff and apportioned liability 20 percent to Hornbeck and 80 percent to the school board. The appellate court reversed this decision, holding that the action was not *foreseeable* and pointing out that immediately upon seeing the altercation the teacher had intervened, thus fulfilling any *duty* which the school had toward the plaintiff.[52]

Lesson: (1) When a student displays behavior traits which may result in injury to others, you might want to discuss the matter and review the student records with behavioral experts. (2) Advise teachers to intervene *immediately* when altercations between students arise.

Assault and rape on school grounds. A student's mother let her off at school an hour before class. She was beaten and raped as she was about to enter the school. Plaintiffs charged that the school should have warned students after similar attacks had occurred in the neighborhood and should have instituted security measures. The trial court ruled that the injury was not foreseeable and found for the school board. The state supreme court reversed stating that the jury should determine whether the prior events made this assault foreseeable. The court would then determine what the school should have done to prevent the injury.[53]

Lesson: Schools are not responsible for everything that might happen to a student inside or outside the school. However, when schools become aware of potential hazards, whether animate or inanimate, they should notify students or their parents of the hazards. Should boards consider hiring security personnel to monitor the building when students are likely to be on the premises? Here the plaintiffs' argued that just cutting down the bushes around the school might have left the assailant with no place to wait for his victim.

Student had convulsions on a school bus and sustained injury. An elementary student with cerebral palsy suffered a mild convulsion when she was pushed into some chairs and sustained a head injury. The teacher did not send her to the nurse. Later she suffered severe convulsions on the bus. The bus driver contacted his supervisor and asked that a school nurse be provided at the next stop, but none was provided. The driver took her to the next day care centre, where she received medical attention. The state supreme court affirmed the dismissal of the suit against the board because of immunity granted under Texas's Tort Claims Act.[54]

Lesson: Not all schools have nurses, and few have them every day of the week. Schools should develop procedures for assuring prompt medical treatment, or referral for treatment, where nurses are not available or the child requires specialized care. Parents should also be notified. In the case of handicapped children, the child's records should contain provisions for care where the child might be expected to suffer particular symptoms.

Student electrocuted in a whirlpool, modified by the football coach. A football coach modified a single person whirlpool so that more students could use it. Two students were injured, one fatally, while using the enlarged whirlpool. There was a conflict of testimony as to whether the original installation was faulty. However, the state appellate court ruled that the failure of the coach to properly ground the device was the sole causative factor. The school district was not joined in the suit.[55]

Lesson: Employees should be instructed to call in experts to make alterations and repairs in equipment, including athletic, laboratory, shop, and other types of equipment.

Injuries in shop class. In **Barbin v. State,**[56] a twelve-year-old student at the Louisiana School for the Deaf, who lost her right index finger on the blade of a table saw, charged the woodworking teacher with negligence in allowing the saw to be used without a safety guard in place. The court awarded $185,000 in damages because the teacher violated posted shop rules as to the age of students to be allowed in the shop and manufacturer safety procedures that recommend that the machine not be operated without a safety guard.

In **Velmer v. Baraga Area Schools,**[57] a student caught his hand in the unguarded rotary cutting mechanism of a milling machine. School employees were unaware that a cutting head guard was available to protect against such injuries. The machine was donated to the school by its former owner, who had used it for some twenty-five years. At the time of manufacture no guard was available for the machine. The court held that the board was immune under the state's governmental immunity law.

Lesson: Some injuries cannot be anticipated or avoided by the school. But school shops are potential spots for serious injuries and special care should be taken to develop and follow safety measures.

- Train employees well in the use of the machines and instruct them to maintain careful supervision of students in the shop.
- Post shop rules in a conspicuous place and **insist** that employees follow the rules.
- Limit use of hazardous machinery to older students.
- Restrict entrance to the shop to students in the class.
- Provide for proper supervision, which may necessitate keeping class enrollment low.
- Require in-school policies that directions for operation and safety precautions be obtained with the equipment upon purchase and be followed scrupulously.
- Consult safety standards, even if not technically applicable to the school board. The plaintiffs in **Velmer** accused the board of

violating federal standards, including those of the National Safety Council and the Occupational Safety and Health Administration, which called for the use of safety guards.

Appropriate Equipment

The parents of a third grade student sued the school board alleging negligence in failing to provide safe equipment for use in the physical education class. The student was the catcher in a softball game, when he was struck in the face by a bat. The appellate court ruled that the school has a duty to provide safe equipment. It sent the case back to the lower court to determine whether the school breached that duty by failing to provide a mask or other protective device to the catcher, by allowing students of this age and inexperience to use regulation size wooden bats, and by failing properly to mark the area around the base to indicate where the catcher and batter should stand.[58]

> *Lesson:* Consult with experts as to the appropriate equipment to be used for each sport at each grade level. If there is insufficient funding available for the equipment, consider developing fund-raising mechanisms, trading equipment among schools or school districts, alternating the sports offered, or sponsor sports not requiring expensive equipment. The safety precautions here would not have been expensive.

Student injured in fall down wet steps. A student entered the school through the gym entrance. It had been raining and there was a large puddle of water inside at the entrance. No mat was at the entranceway. The student proceeded to the down stairway on which there was no railing, slipped on the top step and fell to the bottom of the flight sustaining severe injuries. The school district was held to be immune from suit under Georgia's sovereign immunity law.

> *Lesson:* This is the type of accident which could easily have happened even if the stairs had a railing and a mat had been placed on the floor. However, actions arise because a school fails to take reasonable precautions that *might* have prevented the accident. In this case procedures should have been in place to assure that every time it rains certain things are done such as putting up warning signs and placing mats at entrances. All stairways should have railings, and where feasible, be overlaid with non-skid material.

Trampoline Injury. A grade 6 student received spinal injuries during a physical education class when she attempted a "front drop" on a trampoline. The court held that trampolines are not "abnormally dangerous intrumentalities" under Illinois law and refused to hold the district "strictly liable." The court held that the trampoline is dangerous only when improperly used. The opinion provided no detail as to what constitutes improper use.[59]

> *Lesson:* Where schools elect to use trampolines, strict safety precautions should be set into place. Teachers should be expert in the dangers and proper use of trampolines and students should receive

adequate training before being allowed to use the trampoline. Schools might also consider restricting their use to students with proven athletic ability.

Students beaten by fellow students in the school. A student sued the board, principal, and teacher for damages arising from a beating by several students during lunch hour just outside the school cafeteria. The court found that *had* a supervisor been present nearby, he or she could have prevented the injury because the noise level was such as to be heard at a reasonable distance. The appeals court overturned the lower courts dismissal of the case and sent it back for trial.[60]

Lesson: Although, as the board argued in this case, there are insufficient supervisors to have one "everywhere all the time," schools should at least post supervisors within "hearing" distance of large groups of students. Supervisors need not be teachers, but could be aides (assistants), office personnel, or parents. If necessary the school may have to work out a system with teachers to alternate their lunch breaks so that the students can be properly supervised during lunch. Adequate supervision during lunch, between classes, and during other non-class time may be even more important than during class because of the structured nature of the activities which can lead to altercations between students.

Student injured in altercation with fellow student in locker room. In another "failure to supervise" case, a student was injured during an altercation with another student in the school locker room during a school-sponsored athletic event, when his finger was severed by a door closed on his hand by the other student. The case was dismissed because under state law the plaintiff must prove "willful and wanton" conduct.[61]

Lesson: Locker rooms should be supervised during sporting events or the rooms should be locked during games if supervisors are not available. Since parents are often active in extra curricular sporting events, schools may enlist their help in supervision.

Teacher injured in fall from bleachers with no guard rails. A teacher was injured during a pep rally in the school gym when a student jumped or fell from the bleachers, grabbing her as he went. The retractable bleachers were set up in the gym and because the guard rails, to be placed on the sides of the bleachers, were warped and time-consuming to set-up they were rarely used. Although finding that the failure to use guard rails was "arguably negligent," the court overturned the verdict against the school district because state law requires a showing of "willful, wanton and reckless" conduct.[62]

Lesson: When students are in an unstructured setting, like a rally, accidents are just waiting to happen. The school in this case took several steps to avoid accidents, including periodic structural inspections of the bleachers by a qualified expert. But structure is only one safety consideration. Schools should develop safety procedures to assure proper installation of all moveable equipment, including periodic inspections to assure the procedures are routinely followed. Multi-use facilities can give rise to multi-accident possibilities.

Schools should also develop procedures for reporting difficulties in complying with safety procedures. In this case it is likely no procedure existed for workers to report to the principal their difficulty in setting up the guard rails in the short time allotted between events. An alternative might have been devised, such as obtaining new guard rails or giving the workers more time for set-up.

Sample Cases

Collins v. Bossier Parish School Board, 480 So. 2d 846 (La. App. 1985).
During a noon kindergarten recess, Eugene Collins was playing on the horizontal "monkey" bars when Christopher Maleby wrapped his legs around Eugene, causing them both to fall. Eugene suffered a broken femur bone in his left leg. Eugene's parents sued the school board, claiming that its employees were negligent in their supervision of the recess period, which led directly to Eugene's injury.

The children had been instructed that only one child is to cross the horizontal bars at a time. A duty teacher is assigned to supervise the approximately 100 children during their recess in a fenced off area of the playground approximately the size of half a football field. At the time of Eugene's injury the duty teacher was preventing several children from throwing dirt.

How do you think the court decided?

Barth ex rel. Barth v. Board of Education of the City of Chicago, 490 N.E.2d 77 (Ill. App. 1986).
During morning recess on 30 October 1978, Daniel Barth and his grade 6 classmates were playing "kickball' at the McKay Elementary School in Chicago. At 10:35 a.m., Daniel collided head on with another boy. Both boys fell to the ground. The physical education instructor helped them to their feet and assisted them off the playground.

Crying, Daniel held his stomach and head. A teacher's aide walked the boys to the principal's office, where they arrived at approximately 10:40 a.m. Daniel's mother was reached at 11:00 a.m. and she instructed Meredith Kelley, the principal's secretary, to take Daniel to the hospital.

Daniel lost color and began vomiting. Kelley telephoned the city of Chicago's "911" emergency number and stated that an injured boy needed to be taken to the hospital. An ambulance did not reach the school until 11:50 a.m., after three calls to "911". It arrived at Holy Cross Hospital, which is directly across the street from the school, at noon. Doctors removed a subdural hematoma, about the size of an orange, from atop Daniel's brain.

Daniel sued the school district and the city, claiming willful and wanton conduct. At the time of the trial, six years later, Daniel's left side was severely weak, he required a cane, his intellectual functioning was impaired, and he experienced severe headaches.

What is your decision and supporting reasons?

White v. Moreno Valley Unified School District, 226 Cal. Rptr. 742 (Cal. App. 1986).

Yvonne White ordinarily rode the school bus both to and from high school. On 27 September 1978, the high school was let out early without any notification to parents. The students were released at 11:30 a.m. and urged to attend a school-sponsored parade scheduled to take place one and one half miles from the high school. No school transportation or student supervision was provided to the site of the parade.

Yvonne accepted a ride to the parade site from a fellow student. She was seriously injured when the car was involved in an accident.

A jury found the school district to have been negligent and 10 percent at fault for Yvonne's injuries. The verdict against the school district was $54,000.

Yvonne appealed, contending that the trial court erred in excluding evidence of medical expenses incurred to the time of the trial that had been paid by her mother through her medical insurance policy.

What is your decision and its rationale?

Lowe v. Patterson, 492 So. 2d 110 (La. App. 1986).

On 7 September 1979, Brett Lowe attended a school-sponsored dance at Covington High School, Louisiana, following a football game. Despite rules forbidding students to consume alcohol during school-sponsored events, Brett did so and became intoxicated. Toward the end of the evening, Brett was in the school's parking lot when he became sick and began to vomit. He then sat on a car belonging to George Patterson. George was some distance away talking with friends when he became aware that Brett was on his car. George approached Brett and told him to get off his car. When George returned to his car to leave, he checked over the hood and saw that Brett was no longer there. George was unaware that Brett was lying under the right side of the car. George drove over the left side of Brett's body, severely injuring him.

A jury found no liability on the part of George, and found that Brett was guilty of contributory negligence. However, the jury found that insurers for the school board and the Sheriff who was on duty at the dance should be held liable because they had the last clear chance to avoid the accident. The judge found no liability on the part of the school board, and ruled in its favor and against the Sheriff.

Your comments?

Kruchten v. Reichert Bus Service, Inc., 392 N. W. 2d 50 (Minn. App. 1986).

On 1 May 1981, Robert Kruchten, age fifteen, was riding on a school bus driven by Mary Tautges. Following Tautges's bus was a bus drive by Lonnie Goble. Robert was seated at the rear of the bus. He turned to face the bus behind him and began mouthing obscenities and making obscene gestures.

Robert claimed that he was gesturing towards his cousin, who was seated near the front of Goble's bus.

While the buses stopped to allow some passengers to exit, Goble exited his bus, entered the Tautges bus, and asked Robert to come forward. Robert refused, so Goble grabbed him and forcibly removed him from the bus. Robert claimed that once they were outside, Goble slammed his head into the side of the bus. Goble claimed that the two only talked and that he did not injure Robert. Goble then allowed Robert to return to the bus. Robert stumbled back onto the bus fracturing his finger in the process.

Witnesses who observed Robert when he got back on the bus testified that he appeared to be shaken and angry, but not injured. No one witnessed Goble battering Robert.

The next day Robert's finger was treated and his head and jaw were also x-rayed. Robert was diagnosed as having a bruise on his jaw. No other injuries were diagnosed.

In July, 1981, Robert began seeing a neurologist, Dr Resch, because of headaches. Dr Resch diagnosed Robert as suffering from "post-concussion syndrome" and related it to the 1 May accident. Testing indicated that Robert suffered from a depressive disorder, that he had some memory loss, and that his IQ had decreased from the time he was first tested while in the second grade. Robert claimed that all these symptoms stem from the 1 May incident.

What would you decide?

Griffith v. City of New York, 507 N.Y.S. 2nd 445 (App. Div. 1986).
On 18 August 1976, while Eugenia Griffith was attending Abraham Lincoln High School in New York City, she complained to the school nurse that she was feeling ill. Eugenia was then fourteen years old and asthmatic. The nurse provided no treatment and sent Eugenia back to her class. Eugenia instead chose to leave the school, apparently without permission. Shortly after she returned home, Eugenia met her mother, who determined that it was necessary to call for an ambulance. While her mother was in the kitchen using the telephone, Eugenia, unable to breathe, opened her bedroom window, apparently lost consciousness, and fell to the ground. She was seriously injured.

Eugenia's mother sued, claiming that the school had negligently failed to supervise and care for Eugenia while she was at school on the day of the accident.

What is your "judgement"?

Fallon v. Indian Trail School, 500 N.E. 2d 101 (Ill. App. 1986).
Mary Jane Fallon was a sixth-grader at the Indian Trail School in Addison, Illinois, when she sustained spinal injuries in an attempt to do a "front drop" manoeuvre on the trampoline during her physical education class. She sued the school district, claiming that the trampoline was an abnor-

mally dangerous instrumentality, and that the district should, therefore, be held accountable under strict tort liability for any injuries due to its use.

If you were the judge, how would you decide?

Notes

1. See Arneson v. City of Fargo, 303 N.W. 2d 515 (N.D. 1981) and Lloyd v. S. S. Kresge Co., 270 N.W. 2d 423 (Wis. App. 1978).
2. Johnson v. Municipal University of Omaha, 187 N.W. 2d 102 (1978).
3. 96 A.D. (2d) 708 (1983).
4. 2d at 705.
5. Leahy v. School Board of Hernando Co., 450 So. 2d 883 (Fla. App.) 1984.
6. See, for example, Brackman v. Adrian, 472 S.W. 2d 735 (1971).
7. Ehlinger v. Bd. of Educ. of New Hartford Cent. School Dist., 96 A.D. (2d) at 709.
8. Williams v. Eady. (1893), 10 T.L.R. 41 (C.A.)
9. [1981] 2 S.C.R. 21 (S.C.C.).
10. [1976], 5 W.W.R. 240 (B.C.C.A.).
11. 253 So. 2d 558 (La. C.A. 1971).
12. 259 A. 2d 794 (Md. C.A. 1969).
13. 289 N.W. 2d 112 (Minn. 1979).
14. 2d at 119.
15. 2d at 116.
16. 2d at 116-118.
17. 2d at 117.
18. 376 P. 2d 406 (1962).
19. 2d at 413.
20. No. 851224 (King Co. Wash.) 1982.
21. Lynch v. Bd. of Educ. of Collinsville Community Sidt. No. 10, 412 N.E. 2d 447, 459 Unit (1980).
22. 450 So. 2d 883 (Fla. App. 1984).
23. 2d at 886.
24. 2d at 886.
25. See Rutter v. Northeastern Beaver Co. School Dist., 437 A. 2d 1198 (1981).
26. See, for example, Meschella v. Archdiocese of New York, 52 A.D. 2d 873 (1976).
27. See Mattinson v. Wonnacott (1976), 8 O.R. (2d) 654 (Ont. H.C.).
28. (1961), 29 D.L.R. (2d) 290 (Ont. H.C.) affirmed (1963), 36 D.L.R. (2d) 244 (S.C.C.)
29. [1972] 2 O.R. 437 (H.C.).
30. 239 So. 2d 456 (La. App.) 1970.
31. 2d at 457.
32. 2d at 461.
33. Pirkle v. Oakdale Union Grammar School Dist., 253 P. 2d 1 (1953).
34. See Stineman v. Fontbonne College, 664 F. 2d 1082 (8th Cir.) 1981.
35. [1976], 9 N.R. 368 (S.C.C.).
36. [1963] 1 O.R.1 (C.A.).
37. See Re Stewart and Lincoln County Board of Education (1976), 8 O.R. (2d) 168 and Levine v. Board of Education of the City of Toronto [1933] O.W.N. 152 (H.C.).

38. [1973] 1 O.R. 35 (C.A.).

39. (1981), 30 O.R. (2d) 300 (Ont. H.C.), affirmed (1981), 127 D.L.R. (3d) 768 (C.A.).

40. [1979] 1 S.C.R. 275.

41. [1952] 2 S.C.R. 274, 2 D.L.R. 161.

42. Urzi v. Board of Educ. for the Borough of North York (1980), 30 O.R. (2d) 300, affirmed (1981), 127 D.L.R. (3d) 768 (C.A.).

43. See Collier v. Lake Superior Board of Education (1986), 10 C.P.C. (2d) 141 (Ont. Dist. Ct.).

44. Danis v. Nipissing Roman Catholic Separate School Board (1985), 49 O.R. (2d) 786 (Ont. H.C.).

45. (1986), 56 O.R. (2d) 403 (D.C.).

46. [1959] S.C.R. 465.

47. (1972), 8 O.R. (2d) 168 (H.C.).

48. (1977), 16 O.R. (2d) 828 (H.C.).

49. See Riddle v. University of Victoria (1978), 84 D.L.R. (3d) 164 (B.C.S.C.), affirmed (1979), 95 D.L.R. (3d) 193; Goodwin v. Oxford County Board of Education (1980), 30 O.R. (2d) 359 (H.C.); and Re Gallant and Roman Catholic Separate School Board of District of Sudbury (1985), 56 O.R. (2d) 160 (Ont. C.A.).

50. (1975), 7 O.R. (2d) 65 (Ont. Co. Ct.).

51. Jones v. City of Albany, 513 N.Y.S. 2d 554.

52. See Hanley v. Hornbeck, 512 N.Y.S. 2d.

53. See Fazzolari v. Portland School District No. 1J, 734 p. 2d 1326 (1987).

54. See Hopkins v. Spring I.S.D. No. C.-5209 (Texas, Feb. 25, 1987).

55. See Massie v. Persson, No. 85-CA-282-MR (Ky. App. March 6, 1987).

56. 506 So. 2d 888 (La. App.) 1987.

57. 403 N.W. 2d 171 (Mich. App.) 1987.

58. See Ausmus v. Board of Education of City of Chicago, 508 N.E. 2d 298 (see App.) 1987.

59. See Fallon v. Indian Trail School, 500 N.E. 2d 101 (Ill. App. 2d. Dist.) 1986.

60. See Comuntzis v. Pinellas County School Board, 508 So. 2d, 750 (Fla. 2d Dist.) 1987.

61. See Holsapple v. Casey Comm. Unit Sch. D., 510 N.E. 2d 499 (Ill. App. 4th Dist.) 1987.

62. See Miller v. Gibson, 355 S.E. 2d 28 (W. Va.) 1987.

5

Students and the Law

It is debatable whether there is in fact an inherent right to a public education in our country. Once, however, we have established an educational system such opportunities must and should be made available to all students on equal terms.

This chapter focuses on the various legal mandates pertaining to various requirements and rights associated with school attendance, the right to attend school, and, of course, student records.

Since student misconduct is one of the most difficult problems confronting educators, the various strategies employed to deal with disciplinary problems are examined from a legal perspective. Focus is on conduct regulations and the imposition of pupil punishment for failure to comply.

Reference is also made to search and seizure cases within the school context. Finally, as will be seen, courts have been called upon to balance the interests of students in selecting their attire and hair length against the authority of schools to prevent disruptions to the school environment. This is reviewed in some detail.

Compulsory Attendance: An Overview

The concept of compulsory attendance in educational institutions has long been viewed as a valid governmental interest.

The Education Act requires children between the ages of six and sixteen to attend school, unless they fall within one of the listed exclusions. Parents and guardians have a corresponding duty to ensure that their children attend school, and breach of this duty constitutes a provincial offence. Similarly, a child may be prosecuted under the Act for failing to attend school. The Act also authorizes attendance counsellors to take custody of truants in some situations and return them to their parents or the school. In addition, principals are authorized to suspend a child for persistent truancy.

These provisions may be used to require students to account for their absence and, coupled with attendance records and other information, might assist schools in identifying students with problems.

The most frequent attack in compulsory education cases has not involved a challenge to the validity of compulsory education legislation but rather the application of certain provisions of the laws to a given set of facts. The United States Supreme Court has ruled directly in three cases on the application of a state's compulsory education law to certain parties and in each case has resolved the matter against the state. In **Pierce v. Society of Sisters,**[1] the Court struck down an Oregon compulsory education statute that required attendance only at public schools. In **Meyer v. Nebraska,**[2] the Court invalidated a Nebraska law requiring teaching only in English and prohibiting instruction in modern foreign languages. Finally, in **Wisconsin v. Yoder,**[3] the Court refused to permit Wisconsin to require attendance of Amish children at a recognized school past the eighth grade. The Yoder decision reflects the current nature of attacks against compulsory education statutes. In contrast to Pierce and Meyer, which involved the validity of the compulsory education law itself, Yoder assumes the legitimacy of the governmental interest underlying the statute but challenges the applications of that statute to the case at issue.

The importance of formal education has been clearly recognized. In Yoder, Justice Douglas, in his dissenting opinion, observed that imposition of the parent's view of the child's need for formal education may limit educational opportunity and may be harmful, because "if his (the child's) education is truncated, his entire life may be stunted and deformed."[4]

In Wisconsin v. Yoder the U.S. Supreme Court marshalled an elaborate rationale to justify the Amish parents' exemption from the state's compulsory education law. Separation from the world is mandated for the Amish by the bible; existence of the Amish religious community depends on the right of parents to send their children to schools where the Amish ideals are taught; eight years of academic instruction in the basic skills of reading, mathematics, and English, followed by several years of practical training on farms, not only prepares young people to operate the farms but also makes them responsible citizens; Amish manner of education represents "almost 300 years of consistent practice with strong evidence of a sustained faith pervading and regulating respondents' entire mode of life."[5] The Supreme Court's concern about "a very real threat of undermining the Amish community and religious practice as they exist today"[6] generated confusion among state courts about whether the absence of a clear religious community gives a state greater latitude in enforcing its compulsory education laws. Where an identifiable religious community is not involved, and a court is dealing instead with individual parents, the focus of the court's attention appears to be more on the reasonableness or number of state regulations rather than on the burden placed on religious beliefs.[7]

Most of the recent problems concerning the definition of a school have involved home instruction, although religious schools have faced litigation over the application of state statutory or administrative requirements. Controversy arises when parents wanting to teach their children at home give their instruction program the name of a school[8] and then claim protection in the name of compulsory education.

A common question is whether the forum or forms of instruction meets the definition of a school. The problem for courts is one of judicial interpretation of legislative intent in enacting a compulsory attendance legislation. In **Delconte v. State**, a North Carolina appeals court was called on to determine whether that state's compulsory educational scheme was intended to include home instruction. North Carolina defined "schools" to include all public schools and such non-public schools as have teachers and curricula that are approved by the State Board of Education.[9] Non-public schools were dealt with separately and were required only to "maintain attendance and immunization records, operate at least nine months a year, and conform to fire, health and safety standards." To qualify for the less restrictive regulatory control as a non-public school, the school had to meet at least open of four characteristics:

(1) It is accredited by the State Board of Educators.
(2) It is accredited by the Southern Association of Colleges and Schools.
(3) It is an active member of the North Carolina Association of Independent Schools.
(4) It receives no funding from the state of North Carolina.

The appeals court rejected the parents' contention that their home instruction was a non-public school because the parents received no state funds with the result that home instruction should be subject to all of the standards from which non-public schools had been exempted. In reversing the appeals court, the North Carolina Supreme Court[10] observed:

> nothing in the evolution of our compulsory attendance laws supports a conclusion that the word "school" when used by the legislature in statutes bearing on compulsory attendance, evidences a legislative purpose to refer to a particular kind of instructional setting.

In addition the court suggested that placing home instruction outside the state's compulsory education statute raised state and federal constitutional problems.

Some compulsory attendance legislation provides only that students not attending public schools, or in some cases public or private schools, receive equivalent instruction. Several different kinds of legal questions have arisen regarding an interpretation of "equivalent instruction." In **Bangor Baptist Church v. State**,[11] children were excused from Maine public schools if the child "obtains equivalent instruction in a private school or in any other manner arranged for by the school committee or the board of directors and if the equivalent instruction is approved by the commissioner."[12] The federal district court in Bangor refused to find the word "equivalent" so vague "that persons of common intelligence would necessarily have to 'guess at its meaning and differ as to its application.'" The court determined that equivalent instruction was "capable of objective measurement" and most likely "would be interpreted as requiring private school instruction equal to that mandated by Maine law for public schools generally." Presumably "equivalent instruction" has a reference point in existing standards for public schools, whereas the term "school" without statutory or administrative definition must rely instead on courts to supply the definition.

A final interpretive problem involves the issue of burden of proof. Most courts have held that the burden of proof is on parents to prove that students are being provided an equivalent education. The allocation of burden of proof to parents or non-public schools apparently derives from two assumptions. Compulsory education requirements are a valid exercise of state policy power and, therefore, any exceptions requested are the responsibility of the parents or organization requesting them. Further, the information needed to prove equivalency is within the control of the parent or organization, and therefore the burden of proof should rest with the party having control over the information.

Jones v. The Queen (see Chapter 9) is a recent Supreme Court of Canada decision which dealt with freedom of religion and the right to liberty.

Jones, the appellant, a pastor of a fundamentalist church, was educating his three children and others in a program operating in a church basement. He had refused to send his children to public school as required by s.142(1) of the Alberta School Act, and had also refused to seek an exemption under ss143(1)(a) and (e), which excused a pupil from attending a school over which a board had control if a Department of Education inspector or a superintendent of schools certified that he was receiving efficient instruction at home or elsewhere or he was attending a private school approved by the Department of Education. He had been charged with three counts of truancy under s.180(1) of the Act.

He had invoked ss.2(2) and 7 of the Charter, maintaining that the requirement in s.142(1) of the Act and the requirement that he apply for an exemption pursuant to s.143(1) contravened his religious beliefs that God, rather than the government, had final authority over education of his children, and deprived him of his liberty to educate his children as he pleased, contrary to the principles of fundamental justice.

A provincial court judge had concluded that s.2(a) did not apply, but had upheld the defence based on s.7. He had held that since proof of efficient instruction was solely by means of a certificate issued by school authorities, this would prevent Jones from making a full answer and the defence from bringing all evidence relevant to the issue before the court. The Court of Appeal reversed, entering convictions on all three counts.

His appeal to the Supreme Court of Canada was dismissed. Although the effect of the School Act constituted some interference with his freedom of religion, impugned provisions did not offend s.2(a) of the Charter. The Act did not give the government absolute control over education. Considering the compelling interest of the province in the efficient instruction of the young, a requirement that a person giving instruction at home or elsewhere have that instruction certified was demonstrably justified in a free and democratic society as a reasonable limit on a parent's religious convictions concerning his children's upbringing. Even assuming that liberty as used in s.7 of the Charter included the right of parents to educate their children as they saw fit, impugned provisions did not deprive them of that right in a manner not in accordance with the principles of fundamental justice. The Act created a system which ensured compliance with the requirements that the province considered necessary to advance its interest in the quality of education by providing for certain standards and by delegating to the school authorities the power to particularize the requirements within the general confines of the Act. Such an administrative structure was not so manifestly unfair as to violate principles of fundamental justice.

The Obligation to Provide an Education

1. General

Section 149 of the Education Act lists a number of mandatory duties of boards, including the duties to:

- "provide instruction and adequate accommodation during each school year for the pupils who have a right to attend a school under the jurisdiction of the board" (s. 149(6))
- provide special education (s. 149(7), and see s. 8(2))
- keep school buildings and equipment fit for the intended purpose (s. 149(8). See also 236(j)
- "ensure that every school under its charge is conducted in accordance with this Act and the regulations" (s. 149(10)
- keep its schools open during the entire school year (s. 149(11)
- "appoint for each school that it operates a principal and an adequate number of teachers" (s. 149(12)
- provide textbooks to the pupils without charge (s. 149(13)

In addition, s. 150 lists powers that boards may choose to exercise, including powers to:

- "determine the number and kind of schools to be established and maintained and the attendance area for each school, and close schools in accordance with policies established by the board from guidelines issued by the Minister" (s. 150(1)(6)
- "provide instruction in courses of study that are prescribed or approved by the Minister" (s. 150(1)(7)
- provide school supplies, other than textbooks (s. 150(1)(12)
- "establish kindergartens and junior kindergartens" (s. 150(1)(14)
- "establish, subject to the regulations, special education programs to provide special education services for children who require such services" (s. 150(1).40)

Section 152 permits a secondary school board to provide vocational courses of study in one or more of its schools.

These provisions apply to Roman Catholic separate school boards and to Protestant separate school boards (of which there is one in the province) by virtue of their inclusion in the definition of "boards" (s. 1(1).3). Further, s. 104(e) obliges Roman Catholic separate school boards to "exercise all other such powers and perform all other such duties of boards as are applicable to public school boards except as otherwise expressly provided in this Act." Apart from the Act, numerous other duties are imposed on boards in the regulations.

2. Specific Schools

Cases considering the authority of a board to close schools have established that:

> "The Board is not under any obligation to maintain, in the sense of 'to perpetuate' any particular school it establishes. 'Maintain' in the Ontario Acts is not a direction to keep forever. It encompasses only authority and obligation to expend money upon the school and keep it in operation so long as the Board feels that it is desirable to do so for the provision of the educational needs of the pupils for whom it is responsible. 'Maintain' in my view means the duty from year to year to keep up the operation of the school so long as the Board is of the opinion that such school should be operated as an appropriate means of discharging its duty to provide accommodation for its pupils. The direction to maintain is not inconsistent to discontinue the operation of any particular school or class when it deems it can otherwise discharge the obligation imposed upon it to provide educational facilities for its pupils."[13]

Transportation

A board may choose to provide transportation to resident pupils of the board, and others who attend board schools (s. 166). The board may operate its own transportation facility, contract for transportation, or provide pupils with funds to purchase transportation. The grant regulations provide an elaborate calculation to determine the extent to which the province will reimburse transportation costs.

Where the board does not provide transportation, and a pupil resides beyond a certain distance from his local school, he or she is excused from attendance. (s. 20(2)).

The Right of Pupils to Attend School

1. General

The basic right of pupils to attend school is set out in s. 31(1) which provides:

> "31(1) A person has the right, without payment of a fee, to attend a school in a school section, separate school zone or secondary school district, as the case may be, in which he is qualified to be a resident pupil."

The right belongs to any person between the ages of six years and twenty-one years (s. 32(1) and s. 32(2)). Where the board chooses to operate a kindergarten, junior kindergarten, or beginners classes for those who are younger than six years of age, younger pupils who are resident pupils are also entitled to attend (s. 33).

It is the responsibility of the parent or guardian to submit evidence that a child has the right to attend an elementary school, including proof of age (s. 32(3)).

2. The Right to Attend a Specific School

(i) *General*

A board has no obligation to continue to operate any particular school. Similarly, pupils have no right to attend a particular school operated by a board.

On the other hand, proximity to a school is normally the basis upon which a pupil is admitted, subject to board policies. The importance of proximity is reflected in ss.32(1)(2) and 39. See also s.32 (4) and s.39(2) as well as special rules in sections 45 and 46.

The Obligation to Attend School

A child between the ages of six and sixteen years must attend school (s. 20(1)). This obligation is extended to younger children if they are enrolled in school (s. 20(4)). There is a positive obligation on the parent or guardian of a child of compulsory school age to cause the child to attend school (s. 20(5)) (s. 17). Failure to do so may result in a charge under s. 29 (1).

A child of compulsory school age who refuses to attend or is habitually absent from school can be charged with an offence under s. 29(5) of the Education Act, which is commonly known as truancy. However, this provision must be read together with s. 91b of the Provincial Offences Act, R.S.O. 1980, c. 400, as amended, which prevents a person under twelve years of age from being convicted of an offence.

While persons other than parents and guardians have no positive obligation to cause a child of compulsory school age to attend school, they are subject to prosecution if they employ children during school hours (s. 29(3)). This obligation extends to the directors and officers of a corporation who authorize, permit, or acquiesce in the employment of school age children (s. 29(4)).

The obligation to attend school is not absolute. Section 20(1) (2) lists a number of circumstances under which a child of compulsory school age may be excused from attending school. The most frequent defence to a prosecution is that the child was unable to attend school by reason of sickness or other unavoidable cause. Less frequently it will be alleged that the child is receiving satisfactory instruction at home or elsewhere.

A child is excused from attendance at school if her absence is authorized under the regulations (s. 20(2) (h)). The Supervised Alternative Learning for Excused Pupils program (SALEP) was enacted by O. Reg. 523/83 and came into force on 1 September 1983. It replaced the Early School Leaving program. Under s.3 of this regulation, a parent or guardian of a child aged fourteen years or older can apply to have the child excused from regular school attendance to participate in various programs.

Enforcing School Attendance

1. The Education Act creates an elaborate system for enforcing school attendance. There are various levels of responsibility:

(i)   the principal at the child's school (s. 27, s. 30(2));

(ii)   the school attendance counsellor (s. 24, s. 25, s. 30);

(iii) the Provincial School Attendance Counsellor (s. 23, s. 24(4), s. 25(3), s. 28, s. 29(7))); and

(iv) the Provincial Court Judge ultimately hearing prosecutions (s. 29(5).

(v)   suspension for e.g. non-attendance (s.22(1)(2)(3)).

In the prosecution of parents and guardians, ss. 29(1) and (2) authorize the Court to impose a fine of not more than $100 and, in addition to or instead of imposing the fine, require the parent or guardian to submit a personal bond in the sum of $200 with or without sureties, with the condition that the person shall cause the child to attend school. Under s. 72(a) of the Provincial Offences Act, the Court may suspend the passing of sentence and direct that the defendant comply with the conditions prescribed in a probation order.

Where a child is convicted of refusing to attend, or of habitual absence, the sentencing alternatives are not as clear.

Section 29(5) states that the child "is liable to the penalties provided for children adjudged to be juvenile delinquents under the Juvenile Delinquent Act (Canada)." On 2 April 1984, the Juvenile Delinquents Act, R.S.C. 1970, C.J-3, was repealed and replaced by the Young Offenders Act (Canada). Unlike the Juvenile Delinquents Act, the Young Offenders Act contains no provisions allowing it to be invoked where there has been a breach of a provincial statute.

If a child is under the age of twelve years, he or she may not be charged because of the prohibition in the Provincial Offences Act. Only the parent or guardian can be charged with failing to cause the child to attend school. If the child is twelve or more years of age then the child may be prosecuted as well. On one occasion, Ontario Provincial Court Judge James Felstiner found in 1984 that the dispositional powers of the Juvenile Delinquent Act had been incorporated by reference into the Education Act, even though the former Act had been repealed.

The choice of whom to prosecute is a matter of judgment for the school attendance counsellor in conjunction with the principal and the social worker. Parents often have less control over older pupils. The child may be refusing to attend despite everyone's best efforts. Where such is the case, it does not make sense to prosecute the parents. Where it is not clear who is really responsible for the absence, then prosecution of both the parents and the child may be justified.

Blindness, deafness, or mental handicap is not in itself an unavoidable cause (s. 20(3)). Normally, this defence is proven through medical evidence. In order to establish the defence, however, the evidence should cover all of the absences unless there are other excuses for them.

Student Records

Questions of who should have access to school records and the purpose of school records have long been a concern. Parents want to know how their children are doing and what school boards may well think of them. Teachers want to know what they can expect from particular students or ascertain whether or not a particular student had particular problems and how those problems were dealt with. Educators, particularly in special education programs, want as complete a set of records as possible in order to make their assessments. Courts may want to know the content of records for child welfare and custody hearings. Employers might like to know about the content of records in order to understand questions of discipline and learning capacity. In light of this, students want to know what is in their records so that they are able to understand the impression others have of them, and why. Can all these goals be met, particularly when the rights of children and the right to privacy are becoming important issues?

The present Ontario law with respect to student records is referred to in the Education Act and regulations. The *Education Act*, section 236(d), requires a principal to maintain a record for each student enrolled in the school. There are complicated regulations concerning what the record may and may not contain. A principal may place in the record any information he or she believes will be "beneficial to the teachers in the instruction of the pupil." However, Ontario Regulation 380, 1986, section 30(1), provides that a student record cannot contain any information that discloses a contravention or alleged contravention of federal or provincial penal legislation. It is hard to reconcile section 30(1) with section 237(13), which states "nothing in this section prevents the use of a record . . . for the purposes of a disciplinary proceeding." Although the issue is far from settled, presumably a principal can include in the record information on school infractions and disciplinary actions, even if the student's conduct also constitutes an offence. The Education Act, section 237(10), provides that school officials must preserve the secrecy of the contents of student records that come to their knowledge in the course of their employment. Unless otherwise provided for by the Act, this provision precludes the voluntary disclosure of the contents of the record without the written consent of the student, or the parents or guardians if the student is a minor. Section 237(3) gives all students the right to examine their records. Parents or guardians are only entitled to examine their child's record if the child is a minor. Students and their parents or guardians may request that the principal correct any inaccuracies in the record, and remove any information which is not conducive to improving the student's instruction.

Unless the appropriate written consent is provided, school officials must refuse any request for information from a student record. Even a police request must be denied. Similarly, a teacher could not disclose to the parent of an adult student any information contained in the student's record without the student's written consent. The Act's confidentiality provisions only apply to information that properly belongs in the record. The Education Act severely limits how any information contained in the record may be used. It provides that the record is inadmissable in any trial, inquest, inquiry, examination, hearing, or other proceeding except for the purpose of establishing the record's existence. It should be noted that in Section

237 (6) of the Education Act, records are only to be provided to employers where there is a written request by the former pupil, where the pupil is an adult, or the parent or guardian of the pupil, where the pupil is a minor.

In addition to the statutory provisions, Ontario Regulation 271 deals with the contents, preparation, maintenance, disposal, transfer, and other administrative matters with respect to student records. Although this regulation appears to be only administrative in nature, a child or parents may well be within their rights when expecting student records to expunge those matters which do not comply with Regulation 271.

Family law problems, such as who has access and what name should be on a student record, are ones which affect many boards and teachers. Ministry guidelines with respect to the change of a name indicates that:

> Where a pupil is known by a surname other than the pupil's legal name, and where the principal is satisfied that such name is obtained by repute and that its use is in the best interest of the pupil, the principal shall, at the written request of the parent or guardian, ensure that the pupil be identified by that surname, record the requested surname . . . the legal surname shall be enclosed in brackets in this case.

Provision has also been made when the name of the child is legally changed, such as by marriage, adoption, or other legal provisions, which would govern the status of the name of the child. In those cases the principal shall change the name completely, making no reference to the former name and enclose within the file a notorized copy of any legal documents supporting the change of name. This guideline is a restatement of the provisions of R.R.O., 1980, reg. 271, s.7.

The Ministry of Education, on 13 June 1983, issued Policy Memorandum No. 76 entitled "Custody and Guardianship of Minors." The Ministry's position is summed up on page 2 of that memorandum, which states:

> In general, this means that a non-custodial parent of a child is entitled to examine the child's pupil record under subsection 237 (3) of the Education Act unless a Court Order or Separation Agreement states that such parent is not entitled to access to the child; but that only a parent or other person having custody can claim for the child the right to attend school without payment of a fee.

Problems may rise with respect to Court Orders and Separation Agreements. If the wording of any order or agreement does not make it clear whether the person claiming the right to enroll a child or to examine a pupil record has custody or is entitled to access, the matter should be referred to the board solicitor.

One example of instruction given to staff from a Board is:

> A separated or divorced parent who does not have custody of his/her child . . . may have access to . . . child or children's school records . . . unless a court order or a separation agreement prohibits such access and the school has been supplied with a certified copy of the court order or the separation agreement as the case might be.

The onus must rest with the parent who has custody of the child to provide the school with a certified copy of any order, judgment, or separation agreement. Boards extend this policy to cover situations where a non-custodial parent without access rights attempts to enforce his or her right to access children's records. Unless ordered otherwise both natural parents or adoptive parents would have the right to access their children's records and to enforce any other rights with respect to their children's schooling.

Although the courts are specifically excluded from using school records in proceedings, other provincial statutes provide for paramount rights allowing access to records in limited circumstances. In cases where there is suspicion of child abuse, a court may, for example, pursuant to Section 70 of the **Child and Family Services Act** direct the holder of any record to deliver such records to court. Section 79 (6) provides that "this Section applies despite any other Act." This would include the Education Act.

There may also be a claim by a court of criminal jurisdiction with respect to the records. In other words, where there is a direct conflict between the Canada Evidence Act, which may authorize the admission of a school record, and the Education Act, which may prohibit admission, the federal legislation or Criminal Code takes precedence.

Child Abuse

Children have the right to be protected from abuse. Although this right is not specifically directed at abuse by educators, but rather abuse by relatives or friends of relatives, there is a duty on providers of education to report any abuse. Relating to "Duty to Report" child abuse, Section 68 of the Child and Family Services Act of Ontario, s.o. 1984, provides in part:

> 68. (3) Despite the provisions of any act (including the Education Act), a person referred to in subsection (4) who, in the course of his or her professional or official duties, has reasonable grounds to suspect that a child is or may be suffering or may have suffered abuse shall forthwith report the suspicion and the information on which it is based to a society.

> 68. (4) Section (3) applies to every person who performs professional or official duties with respect to a child, including, (b) a teacher, school principal . . .

With respect to School Records under section 68 (7):

> 68. (7) This section applies although the information reported may be confidential or privileged and no action for making the report shall be instituted against a person who acts in accordance with subsection (2) or (3) unless a person acts maliciously or without reasonable grounds for the belief of suspicion, as the case may be.

Section 81 (1)(b) specifies sanctions for non-reporting. It should also be noted that re section 37(2) the term abuse is broadly defined.

The statutory duty to report suspected child abuse creates a duty that must not be ignored or intentionally avoided. Boards must develop policies and procedures to comply with the requirements for reporting suspected child abuse. Building on specific requirements, these should include identifying who must report and who must receive reports; specifying what should be included in a report; establishing procedures and appropriate personnel for interviewing the child victim (for example, policy, social services agency staff); and establishing procedures for the retention and handling of evidence.

Merely having these policies and procedures on the books may not be enough. The reluctance of school personnel to report suspected child abuse, even when required to do so by law cannot be tolerated. In some schools teachers are made aware that the administration, wanting to avoid possible conflicts with parents, frowns on reporting. In other situations school personnel are simply unaware of the proper procedure. These practices could be viewed as amounting to intentional failure or deliberate indifference if a board accomplished no more than putting the policy and procedure on the books.

An argument might be made that an obligation exists to ensure that board policy and procedures are actually implemented. This obligation requires, at the very least, that some effort be made to be sure that those responsible for reporting are aware of their responsibility and of the procedure for meeting it. In particular, school personnel must be aware that they will not be held liable for making a report that turns out to be unsubstantiated. Boards should monitor reporting of suspected child abuse. If a teacher works with a principal who has indicated that reporting suspected child abuse creates more problems than it is worth, the teacher needs to know that the principal's view is unacceptable. Without some such indication of support, teachers may fear reprisals in their evaluations or other aspects of their working conditions.

Even knowing that reporting is required, what the procedure is, and that the board supports them in meeting these legal obligations, some school personnel will still have difficulty in reporting. Lack of knowledge regarding child abuse prevents many from knowing when they are staring abuse in the face. Recent developments regarding the identification of abuse allows this lack of knowledge to be overcome, and suggests that the failure to do so borders on unacceptable professional practice.

As knowledge regarding child abuse has grown, the implications of failure to meet reporting requirements are changing. The ease with which boards can meet their obligations, and the benefit to abused children from doing so, should be strong enough incentives for changes in practices. The development and implementation of workable policies and procedures, coupled with the provision of training, should provide better protection for school boards and abused children alike. In August 1984 the "Badgley Report" heightened public awareness of the problems of reporting. More children are feeling that it is safe to tell their story and that action will be taken.

Care Service Providers

The Child and Family Services Act grants children certain rights when they are in the care of various service providers, for example, Children's Aid, Halfway Houses, or other similar state agencies. Students may be in a position to assert a right not to be treated more harshly by the educational system than they would be if they were in the care of another state agency. These provisions include the following:

97. No service provider or foster parent shall inflict corporal punishment on a child or permit corporal punishment to be inflicted on a child in the course of the provision of a service to the child.

The Education Act provides that a child is to "accept such discipline as would be exercised by a kind, firm and judicious parent." If a service provider is a "parent substitute," there is specific direction to those in the place of a parent not to inflict corporal punishment upon a child.

Section 100 of the Child and Family Services Act provides that a child has a right to have reasonable privacy and possession of his or her own personal property; and Section 103 provides that a child in care has a right to be consulted and to express his or her views, to the extent that it is practical given the child's level of understanding, whenever significant decisions concerning the child are made, including decisions with respect to medical treatment, education and religion.

Student Responsibilities

Section 23 of Regulation 262 imposes upon a student the following obligations if not responsibilities:

23.　(1) A pupil shall,

(a) be diligent in attempting to master such studies as are part of the program in which the pupil has enrolled;
(b) exercise self-discipline;
(c) accept such discipline as would be exercised by a kind, firm, and judicious parent;
(d) attend classes punctually and regularly;
(e) be courteous to fellow pupils and obedient and courteous to teachers;
(f) be clean in person and habits;
(g) take such tests and examinations as are required by or under this Act or as may be directed by the Minister; and
(h) show respect for school property . . .

(4) Every pupil is responsible for his or her conduct to the principal of the school the pupil attends,

(a) on the school premises;
(b) out of school activities that are part of the school program; and
(c) while travelling on a school bus that is owned by a board or on a bus or school bus that is under contract to the board.

Student Discipline

"There is no discipline in our schools today." "Teachers are helpless; students are out of control." These assertions are components of the mythology that surrounds the issue of student discipline in schools. Such myths have led many teachers and school officials to believe, incorrectly, that they lack sufficient authority to impose discipline and order.

Few teachers seem to receive as part of their formal training very much information about the laws that affect their teaching. When teachers are confronted by the articulate assertion of student rights, many are over-whelmed. They had taken their own power for granted without knowing the legal basis of their power. Many teachers feel helpless to deal with students who misbehave or who defy reasonable requests. Often, school administrators, similarly hampered by ignorance and feelings of helplessness, fail to back teachers' discipline efforts.

What are the rights and responsibilities of teachers when students misbehave, violate legitimate school rules, or refuse to obey reasonable requests?

Teachers may exercise significant disciplinary authority over students, and they can legitimately insist that school officials support them in exercising their authority. The legal basis of school disciplinary authority is located in both common and statutory law. There is no question that students have significant rights. Nevertheless, these rights are balanced against the need of a school to maintain an orderly learning environment. The courts have consistently asserted their support for the efforts of school officials to maintain order. School authorities may write and enforce rules for student behavior, and they may punish students who violate rules. Furthermore, teachers and school administrators may respond immediately when students threaten to harm themselves, others, or school property. The common law is the primary source of teacher authority. Teachers have authority to act *in loco parentis* (in place of the parent) to enforce discipline in the school.

Once upon a time, when schooling was a voluntary arrangement, it was understood that the parent gave the teacher the right to discipline the child. This assumption changed when education became compulsory. Today, courts recognize that it is the state which gives a teacher the implicit right to discipline a child at school as a parent would at home. The parent is powerless to restrict the common-law disciplinary authority of the teacher over the pupil except as provided by statute. Our own provincial legislation buttresses the common-law disciplinary authority of schools officials.

How do courts interpret the laws? Many school personnel feel that the courts are looking over their shoulders, eagerly awaiting opportunities to reverse disciplinary decisions and undermine the school's authority. This is not the case. When it comes to discipline, the schools have received a great deal of support from the courts.

Generally, the courts prefer to stay out of school disputes. In 1968 the Supreme Court of the United States noted, in **Epperson v. Arkansas:**

> Judicial interposition in the operation of the public school system of the nation raises problems requiring care and restraint. . . . By and large, public education in our nation is committed to the control of state and local authorities. Courts do not and cannot intervene in the resolution of conflicts which arise in the daily operation of school systems and which did not directly and sharply implicate basic constitutional values.[14]

Our laws have been written to support the authority of the teacher and the school. Common law *in loco parentis* status gives teachers broad ranges of power. Nevertheless, all grants of authority have limits. The legitimate need of the school to maintain order must be balanced against various students' rights.

Schools receive a broad grant of disciplinary power which is often couched in very general language. Laws cite such terms as *disobedience, misconduct, disruption, discipline, order,* and *conduct.* It is essential that school authorities develop codes of conduct which specify the meanings of such terms, elaborating the conditions and contexts. It is not sufficient for a school system simply to adopt these terms and invoke them against students in an *ad hoc* fashion. Rather, disobedience must be explicitly defined as "refusal to comply with a reasonable request of the classroom teacher" and misconduct as "intentional destruction of school property" or "fighting on school grounds."

For rules to be legitimate, they must emanate from a legitimate authority. The school board is the legitimate authority and it should be the source of codes of student conduct. In practice, it is often common for boards to pass on some rule-making authority to school administrators.

Schools should give students advance notice of the rules and specify the punishments that may be assigned for various infractions. It is usually considered sufficient notice to publish the rules in a handbook and distribute it to students.

While it is preferable to have specific rules, school codes need not anticipate all eventualities and types of misconduct. Some behavior may be grossly out of line by any standard. In many cases, students are expected to have been able to anticipate that their conduct would be unacceptable.

The Education Act imposes a variety of obligations on teachers and principals. It also regulates the method and content of instruction, the conduct of principals and teachers, the conduct of students, and the learning environment in the school.

Both principals and teachers are charged with responsibility for maintaining order and discipline. Principals are ultimately accountable for ensuring order and discipline in the school, and they are expected to establish guidelines in this regard. Teachers, under the direction of their principal, are required to maintain order and discipline in the classroom and on the school grounds.

The Education Act and various Regulations grant school boards and principals extensive powers to deal with, protect, and inspect school property. Some of these powers are custodial in nature, focusing on the repair and maintenance of school property. However, there are other provisions which grant boards and principals virtually all of the powers of other property owners. These provisions are broad enough to empower boards, principals, and teachers to search student lockers, particularly if parents and students have been informed in advance of the school's policy in this area.

The duties of teachers in respect of discipline are prescribed by s. 235 (1)(e):

> "235 (1) It is the duty of a teacher and a temporary teacher,
>   ....
>> (e) to maintain, under the direction of the principal, proper order and discipline in his classroom and while on duty in the school and on the school ground."

This is expanded by s. 21 of RRO 262/80 which provides:

"21. In addition to the duties assigned to the teacher under the Act and by the board, a teacher shall,

....

(f) co-operate with the principal and other teachers to establish and maintain consistent disciplinary practices in the school."

Principals have the duties of teachers, and, in addition, the duties set forth in s. 236.

"s. 236. it is the duty of a principal of a school, in addition to his duties as a teacher;
(a) to maintain proper order and discipline in the school;

....

(j) to give assiduous attention to the health and comfort of the pupils, to the cleanliness, temperature and ventilation of the school, to the care of all teaching materials and other school property, and to the condition and appearance of the school buildings and grounds;

....

(m) subject to an appeal to the board, to refuse to admit to the school or classroom a person whose presence in the school or classroom would in his judgment be detrimental to the physical or mental well-being of the pupils; . . ."

These duties are qualified by s. 12 of RRO 262/80.

"12(1) The principal of a school, subject to the authority of the appropriate supervisory officer, is in charge of,

(a) the instruction and the discipline of pupils in the school;

....

(3) In addition to the duties under the Act and those assigned by the board, the principal of a school shall,

(g) provide for instruction of pupils in the care of school premises,
(j) report promptly any serious neglect of duty or infraction of the school rules by a pupil to the parent or guardian of the pupil."

Boards have no direct responsibility for administering actual discipline in a school. Board policy has an impact through s. 12 of RRO 262/80 set out above. The circumstances in which the Board is required to administer discipline are in a suspension appeal under s. 22 (3), or in respect of a recommendation for expulsion under s. 22(4).

The issue occasionally arises as to whether the authority to discipline exists off the school site. S. 23(4) of RRO 262/80 set out above suggests that the authority is limited to the school premises, except when the pupil is engaged in an out-of-school activity that is part of the school program.

On the other hand, and keeping in mind that the regulation is subordinate legislation, the definition of "school" is significantly more expansive than merely the building and lands. Section 1(1) para. 49 provides:

"1(1) 49 "school" means,

(i) the body of public school pupils or separate school pupils or secondary school pupils that is organized as a unit for educational purposes under the jurisdiction of the appropriate board,

...

and includes the teachers and other staff members associated with such unit or institution and the lands and premises used in connection therewith; . . ."

Further, s. 22(3) provides that a suspension may occur for "conduct injurious to the moral tone of the school." There is nothing to suggest that the conduct must occur on school property.

The authority of teachers and principals to discipline pupils may well extend off the school property, particularly where the incident leading to discipline occurs just off the school property, on the way to or from school, or at a recess.

The intent of the statutory and the regulatory provisions is that order and discipline should be maintained in the schools to permit instruction to occur in the optimal environment.

The Content of Discipline

Disciplinary responses form a continuum from least severe to most severe. Some samples are:

- private reprimand;
- public reprimand;
- removal from class for a short period;
- denial of privileges, for example, participation in sports, or field trips, and so on;
- extra work;
- detentions;
- corporal punishment;
- suspension;
- expulsion.

The selection of the appropriate disciplinary response to misconduct is a matter of judgment. With the exception of the last two responses, the only inherent limitation on the power to discipline is that the punishment should not impair the education of the child. Of course, suspension and expulsion must impair the education of the child to a point.

In an important Charter decision, of **Regina v. J.M.G.,**[15] the Ontario Court of Appeal said a principal had acted in a manner that was both "eminently reasonable" and "not excessively intrusive" when he inspected the pantlegs and socks of a fourteen-year-old boy for narcotics the youth had allegedly concealed in his clothing.

Since the search had been "reasonably related to the desirable objective of maintaining proper order and discipline" in the school, the Court of Appeal said the principal had not infringed the grade 7 student's s.8 Charter of Rights guarantee against unreasonable search and seizure.

Moreover, the court decided, the student had not been detained for Charter purposes because he had been subject to school discipline at the time of his search and had been required by the nature of his attendance in school to undergo any reasonable disciplinary or investigative procedure.

Accordingly, the principal had not been obliged to advise the boy of his s. 10(b) Charter right to consult counsel before asking him to remove his socks for the search.

The unanimous ruling marked the first time a provincial appellate court had considered how the Charter rights in question applied in the public school setting, where educators are obliged by provincial legislation to maintain proper order and discipline.

The case seems to suggest that once a student enters a school, he or she falls under "a form of consensual restraint . . . that extends through all the things that happen during the course of a student's day at the school, including a visit to the principal's office."

The decision was significant for its remarks about the Charter guarantee against unreasonable search and seizure within the school setting. This is a circumstance in which the court was prepared to lower the threshold as to the basis for a reasonable search, the reasonableness of the belief of the searching person. It also was significant the court "read a search power into the barest words of a statute," the Education Act, "by a kind of implication."

The judgment of Mr Justice Samuel Grange also was notable since it closely followed the United States Supreme Court decision which said "the legality of a search of a student should depend simply on the reasonableness, under all the circumstances, of the search."

In fact, Justice Grange actually applied the two-part reasonableness test the U.S. Supreme Court recommended using to judge the lawfulness of a student's search.

The incident which gave rise to the Charter challenge occurred in April 1984, when a teacher at James Michael G.'s elementary school told the principal another student had seen James place drugs in his socks.

After phoning a policeman and a high school principal he knew for advice, the principal called James into his office and said he had reason to suspect the youth was hiding drugs in his clothing. While a school vice-principal looked on, he asked James to remove his shoes and socks.

James subsequently pulled a cigarette from his pant cuff and quickly swallowed it, but the principal later found a tinfoil packet containing three cigarette butts in the boy's right sock or pantleg, and called the police.

An officer who arrived soon afterwards gave James the standard police caution, advised him of his Charter rights, and arrested the youth on a charge of possessing a narcotic. (It was later determined the butts contained marijuana.)

James was subsequently convicted of his charge and fined $25. However, he successfully appealed both the conviction and sentence in District Court. The Crown subsequently appealed the ruling to the Court of Appeal, where it contended the Charter of Rights did not apply to the situation at hand.

For the purposes of implementing discipline, of course, at common law, a schoolmaster stood in place of the student's parents.

Since parents have a common law right and duty to discipline their children for purposes of correction, they may delegate their parental authority to the school master.

But if the Charter did apply here there still had been no detention because, under the Education Act, principals have a responsibility to maintain discipline and order in the schools and students have a corresponding duty to be amenable to discipline.

The principal's search had been found to be reasonable and justified "because of the nature of the school environment, and the need not only to protect the student who is a youthful person who needed to be corrected if he was stepping out of line, and to protect society and the other children so there would be a proper environment for learning."

Counsel for the defence contended that the search in the principal's office had infringed his client's ss.8 and 10(b) Charter rights. They claimed the Charter did apply to his client since the public school system could be viewed as an extension of government. And under s.32 of the Charter, it was pointed out, the constitutional rights provisions specifically apply to provincial legislatures and government.

But Mr Justice Grange said the court did not have to decide whether or not the Charter even applied to the principal's actions. Rather, he said, the court could approach the constitutional questions simply by *assuming* that school boards, principals, and teachers are all subject to the Charter's provisions.

Turning to the search and seizure dispute, the judge noted that while there were no Canadian authorities to consider for guidance, the United States Supreme Court decision in **New Jersey v. T.L.O.,** was directly on point.[16]

What were the facts in the Supreme Court's decision in New Jersey v. T.L.O.?

T.L.O. and another girl were found in a restroom holding lighted cigarettes. Ms Chen, the teacher, took the girls to the assistant vice-principal, Mr Choplick. While the other girl admitted her guilt, T.L.O. claimed she was not smoking then and never smoked at all.

At this point Mr Choplick told T.L.O. to go into a private office where he asked to see her purse because he wanted to see whether she had any cigarettes which he believed would constitute proof that she had been smoking. T.L.O. complied, and when the purse was opened, Mr. Choplick observed that a package of Marlboro cigarettes was sitting right on top there. He then held up the cigarettes and said, "You lied to me." As he removed the cigarettes he observed a package of rolling papers and removed them too. Upon being confronted with the rolling papers, T.L.O. denied that they were hers.

Based on his experience that rolling papers meant that marijuana was possibly involved, he looked further in the purse and found the following items: (1) a metal pipe used to smoke loose marijuana; (2) a plastic bag containing marijuana; (3) $40 in one-dollar bills and $.98 in change; (4) an index card titled People who owe me money, followed by a list of names and amounts of $1.00 or $1.50 by each name; (5) two letters, one from T.L.O. to a friend and a return letter, both containing language indicating the sale of marijuana at school. The money was found in a wallet inside the purse, and the index card and letters in a separate compartment of the purse. Mr. Choplick testified that the purse was closed when T.L.O. gave it to him and that he could not see inside until he opened it. He also testified that at the time Ms. Chen initially accused T.L.O. of smoking, he had sufficient basis to impose a sanction without need for further evidence.

Subsequently, T.L.O. was suspended from school and delinquency proceedings led to the imposition of a one-year probation.

The U.S. Supreme Court recommended using a test of reasonableness to determine whether or not the search of a student was lawful.

> The test required the court to decide two crucial points:
>
> whether the search was justified at its inception; and
>
> whether the search, as conducted, was reasonably related in scope to the circumstances which justified the interference in the first place.

According to the U.S. Supreme Court, "Under ordinary circumstances, a search of a student by a teacher or other school official will be 'justified at its inception' when there are reasonable grounds for suspecting that the search will turn up evidence that the student has violated or is violating either the law or the rules of the school. Such a search will be permissible in its scope when the measures adopted are reasonably related to the objectives of the search and not excessively intrusive in light of the age and sex of the student and the nature of the infraction."

Applying those criteria, Mr Justice Grange concluded that the Thunder Bay boy's s.8 Charter rights were clearly not violated by the search.

The principal's action had been justified, the judge explained, because he had received word James had illegal drugs in his possession.

Furthermore, s.236(a) of the Education Act expressly directs the principal to "maintain proper order and discipline in the school."

Given this obligation, it was not unreasonable for the principal to require James to remove his socks in order to either prove or refute the allegation he was hiding drugs.

In other words the search here was reasonably related to the desirable objective of maintaining proper order and discipline. Moreover, the search was not excessively intrusive.

The judge went on to disagree with suggestions the principal should have called in the police as soon as he learned James G. might be carrying drugs.

Moving on to the right to counsel issue, Mr Justice Grange said James's case seemed to fit squarely within the detention criteria outlined by the Supreme Court of Canada in **R. v. Therens**[17] since, "There was an assumption of control over the movement of the accused by a demand which might have significant legal consequences and which impeded access to counsel."

James had not been detained within the meaning of the Charter. Therefore, the principal did not have to tell him he could contact a lawyer for advice before submitting to a search.

"The accused was already under detention of a kind throughout his school attendance," the judge explained. "He was subject to the discipline of the school and required by the nature of his attendance to undergo any reasonable discipline or investigative procedure. The search here was but an extension of normal discipline such as, for example, the requirements to stay after school or to do extra asssignments or the denial of privileges."

Mr Justice Grange went on to say he agreed with the decision in **R. v. Guberman**[18] where the Manitoba Court of Appeal distinguished Therens (a case involving breathalyzer testing) from drug search situations.

In Guberman, the Manitoba court said "The Charter right to retain and instruct counsel must be constructed in a manner consistent with its purpose, to enable an accused person to obtain advice as to his rights in the circumstances in which he finds himself and assistance in exercising those rights. This cannot extend to matters such as a physical search for narcotics to which the accused is obliged to submit and which no amount of advice or legal assistance would deter."

In breathlyzer cases, on the other hand, "an accused has an option as to whether or not he should blow and is entitled to advice as to the grounds on which he might refuse and the consequences of doing so," the Manitoba court explained.

In James's case, Mr Justice Grange noted, "no legal advice could possibly preclude the search."

Accordingly, he decided, there had been no violation of the student's s. 10(b) right either, and the conviction and sentence both had to be restored.

Even if the boy's rights had been infringed, however, Mr Justice Grange said he would have upheld the search and seizure under s. 1 of the Charter.

Corporal Punishment

There is nothing in the Education Act which specifically permits teachers or principals to administer corporal punishment. However, the right to do so has never been seriously questioned. It is based on the theory that parents delegate their disciplinary authority over their children when they send them to school. Support for this can be seen in the admonition in s. 23 of RRO 262/80 to the pupil, to "accept such discipline as would be exercised by a kind, firm and judicious parent."

Another theory is that "disciplinary authority arises from the need to maintain order and to act for the welfare of students." Support for this theory is found in the descriptions of the duties of both teachers and principals to maintain order.

A limitation on the administration of corporal punishment is found in s. 43 of the Criminal Code:

> 43. Every schoolteacher, parent or person standing in the place of a parent is justified in using force by way of correction toward a pupil or child, as the case may be, who is under his care, if the force does not exceed what is reasonable under the circumstances.

Canadian courts have interpreted this provision as authorizing physical punishment for violation of school discplinary rules. Attitudes, however, have changed as reflected by the increasing number of school boards that have prohibited or restricted the use of force.

Judicial attitudes also appear to be changing. In a recent case involving the use of force to discipline a mentally retarded adult, the Supreme Court of Canada stated that section 43 had to be strictly interpreted and applied. In affirming the residential counsellor's conviction for assault, the Court emphasized that force can only be used to benefit the student's education. Quoting earlier authority, the Court stated that the power of correction can only be used "in the interests of instruction" and that "any punishment . . . motivated by arbitrariness, caprice, anger or bad humour constitutes an offence punishable like ordinary offences." See Ogg-Moss v. The Queen (1984), 11 D.L.R. (4th) 549 (S.C.C.).

Hair and Dress Codes

It is not unusual to see all kinds of student dress styles.

In terms of time, money, and other resources spent on hair and dress code controversy and litigation, it is hard to imagine that there are so many cases over such an issue.

With few exceptions, student hair codes considered by the various courts are very similar. Most required boys' hair to be clean and neat, trimmed around the ears and back of the neck, and no longer at the back than the top of the shirt collar. Eyebrows could not be covered and little or no part of the ear covered. Boys had to be clean-shaven and sideburns were not to extend below the bottom of the ear lobe.

One of the most interesting aspects of court decisions regarding this issue is the variety of rationale offered by school officials to justify hair codes rejected by the courts. A list of reasons rejected by courts includes: Boys' long hair takes too long to dry after physical education showers. Boys with long hair tended to be rowdy and disruptive. Boys with long hair have a poor attitude toward school. The local community objects to long hair on boys. Long hair on boys makes it difficult to distinguish boys from girls in the supervision of restrooms and locker rooms. Boys with long hair perform lower academically, and dress codes teach discipline.

Some arguments for justification were found not to be well-based on the facts. Others were considered illogical and, for others, courts determined that the school's objective could be served by less onerous alternatives. The underlying view is a doubt that student hair codes are really reasonable.

In **Bishop v. Colaw**[19] Judge Lay stated his opposition to hair codes and expressly laid the issue at the doorstep of school officials. Judge Lay stated:

> The question confronting us is whether there exists any real educational purpose or societal interest to be served in the discipline the school had adopted. After due consideration I fail to find any rational connection between the health, discipline or achievement of a particular child wearing a hair style which touches his ears or curls around his neck, and the child who does not. The gamut of rationalizations for justifying this restriction fails in light of reasoned analysis. When school authorities complain variously that such hair styles are inspired by a communist conspiracy, that they make boys look like girls, that they promote confusion as to the use of restrooms and that they destroy the students' moral fiber, then it is little wonder even moderate students complain of "getting up tight." In final analysis, I am satisfied a comprehensive school restriction on male student hair styles accomplishes little more than to project the prejudices and personal distastes of certain adults in authority on to the impressionable young student . . .[20]

> . . . We believe that, among those rights retained by the people under our constitutional form of government, is the freedom to govern one's personal appearance. As a freedom which ranks high on the spectrum of our societal values, it commands the protection of the fourteenth Amendment Due Process Clause.[21]

Some have referred to the right as "fundamental," others as "substantial," others as "basic," and still others as simply a "right." The source of this right has been found within the Ninth Amendment and the Due Process Clause of the Fourteenth Amendment. A close reading of these cases reveals that the differences in approach are more semantic than real. The common theme underlying decisions striking down hair-style regulations is that the Constitution guarantees rights other than those specifically enumerated and that the right to govern one's personal appearance is one of those guaranteed rights.

The case of **Sims v. Colfax Community School District**[22] involved a girl's haircut. In Sims, the court was faced with a non-sexist rule that required both boys and girls to keep their hair length to no longer than one finger width above the eyebrow. Apparently the female student involved in Sims preferred another hair style and was suspended from school for violating the grooming rule.

In weighing the girl's rights against the school's justification for the rule, the court found school officials' arguments lacking and ruled the grooming rule unconstitutional.

The court noted that the case was the first student haircut case in the United States involving a female and could not resist a little humor:

> The Court well knows that the field of female coiffure is one of shifting sand trodden only by the most resolute of men. The Court thus undertakes this journey with some trepidation. Since time immemorial attempts to impose standards of appearance upon the fairer sex have been fraught with peril. Arbiters of hirsute fashion, perhaps understanding the chameleon nature of the subject matter, have approached the problem with more innovation than insight. Against this delicate social milieu and ever mindful of the equal protection clause, this Court undertakes to comb the tangled roots of this hairy issue.[23]

Several courts, faced with the legal issue of student hair codes in the context of extra-curricular activities, have found that such codes are not enforceable. In its decision in **Long v. Zopp**,[24] the court reviewed a haircut rule imposed by a football coach. The coach's rule prescribed a "hair code" during the football season and throughout the year. The student involved in the case observed the coach's rule during the football season but allowed his hair to grow longer than the prescribed length after the season ended. Because of his off-season non-compliance, the boy was denied an earned football letter at year's end. The coach's actions were later supported by higher school officials. The court in Long found that any valid reason for a haircut rule during football season, such as cleanliness, ended when the football season ended and determined that the boy was entitled to receive his letter. An earlier decision in Vermont went a little farther than the court in Long, ruling that school officials were not able to justify a hair-length code during the athletic season.[25]

In decisions that have upheld the legality of student hair codes, the courts have often considered health and safety issues in determining whether school officials were justified in their actions. This was obvious in **Gere v. Stanley**,[26] where students refused to sit by a student with dirty hair that was occasionally dipped in the student's cafeteria food. The student had the habit of throwing his hair back over his shoulders sending food particles flying. It was also present in **Gfell v. Rickelman**, where school officials merely alleged safety problems around bunsen burners in science classes and near power machinery in industrial arts classes. But even many of the courts that have ruled that student hair codes are illegal have expressed or implied that health and safety reasons would justify limitations on student appearance. Distraction resulting from extreme hair styles also has been used to justify the legality of hair codes.

Few court decisions have dealt with the application of school dress codes to clothing.

In **Fowler v. Williamson**,[28] a principal told students preparing for graduation exercises not to wear jeans to the ceremony. While waiting in line for the ceremony to begin, one boy wearing jeans was pulled out of the line by the principal and told he could not participate in the ceremony. He hurried home and changed but returned to school too late to participate. The boy brought suit alleging $500,000 damages for violation of his fourteenth amendment rights. The court found no "property" or "liberty" right involved in participation in graduation ceremonies, and since he was not deprived of any rights under the fourteenth amendment, he could not recover damages. Neither was the student or his parents allowed damages in state court.[29]

Another decision on the issue of wearing jeans had a different result. In **Bannister v. Paradis**,[30] the federal district court in New Hampshire overturned a school rule that prohibited wearing jeans to school. The court concluded that no disturbance, safety, or health factor was involved and school officials had been unable to justify the rule.

School officials that may wish to have a code of student attire should be aware that courts will generally recognize the special needs of maintaining a good academic environment. A problem arises when school officials allow their personal fashion prejudices to enter in the consideration. A dress code prohibiting student attire which disrupts the academic environment will stand much greater likelihood of success from legal challenge than one which prohibits all "punk" styles and fashion regardless of effect on the environment of the school.

The law clearly recognizes the right of students to express themselves in school in a non-disruptive manner.[31] A school dress code policy which prohibits all tee-shirts with writing or slogans is less likely to survive a legal challenge intact than one which prohibits clothings which disrupts the academic environment.

One can readily see that current law enables educators to respond to discipline problems in the schools. The challenge for educators is to use their legal authority judiciously and maintain the type of positive educational which is essential to a school's overall success.

The Young Offenders Act

Historically children were not recognized as being autonomous with their own individual rights. Instead they were considered simply property, like furniture, of their parents and eventually dependent on both their parents and the state for protection. The very doctrine of *parens patriae* whereby the state assumes the obligation of defining a child's best interests suggests a paternalistic framework where children presumably are incapable of exercising rights in their own best interests.

However, a number of forces over the past two decades have eroded this paternalism — the children's rights movement; a re-examination of the efficacy of treatment modalities within a criminal justice framework; demands for due process; a call for increased accountability of offenders for their actions; the need for protection of society from the criminal acts of youth; and most recently, the Canadian Charter of Rights and Freedoms. These forces served as the major impetus for reform and culminated in the **Young Offenders Act** which is significantly different from its predecessor, The Juvenile Delinquents Act, in terms of philosophy and procedures.

The policy and philosophy which are to govern where young persons come into conflict with the criminal law are set out in a Declaration of Principle, found in subsection 3(1) of the Young Offenders Act. It should be noted that the Declaration of Principle forms part of the text of the Act and is, therefore, to be relied upon and applied in interpreting the provisions of the Act.

While the Declaration contains a number of elements or principles which may initially appear to be contradictory, it is suggested that the Declaration as a whole provides a framework within which, at times, competing elements must be balanced and applied to a particular fact situation. While the elements of the Declaration of Principle will be elaborated upon below, a synopsis is provided to assist in defining the new parameters of juvenile law in Canada:

• first, young persons who commit offences should bear responsibility for their actions although they need not always be held accountable in the same manner as adults (para. 3(1)(a));
• second, society must be protected from the illegal behavior of young people but must also take reasonable measures to prevent criminal conduct by young persons (para. 3(1)(b));
• third, young persons have rights and freedoms in their own right, and young persons should have special guarantees of their rights and freedoms (paras. 3(1)(e), (f), and (g));
• fourth, a young persons who commit offences require supervision, discipline, and control, but they also have special needs and require guidance and assistance (para. 3(1)(c));
• fifth, alternative measures to the court process should be considered where not inconsistent with the protection of society (para. 3(1)(d));
• sixth, parents have responsibility for the care and supervision of their children, and thus, young persons should be dealt with within the family setting wherever appropriate (para. 3(1)(h)).

A. Responsibility for One's Actions

The first element states that:

While young persons should not in all instances be held accountable in the same manner or suffer the same consequences for their behavior as adults, young persons should, nonetheless, bear responsibility for their contraventions.

This element of responsibility must be viewed in its fullest sense.

Underlying it is the assumption that an adolescent is capable of independent thought and responsibility. Accordingly, any young person who has been found guilty should be accountable to society generally, to the victim where possible, and to himself by participating in his own reformation and self-improvement. Several examples illustrate these points:

- Whether by an alternative measure (diversion) program (s.4) or by a court-ordered disposition (s.20), a young person may assume responsibility through a wide variety of community-based measures, including compensation in kind or by personal service, restitution, community service, remedial education. The reparative dispositions also provide for a victim to be compensated.
- It is now open to a judge at the dispositional stage to order treatment for a young person suffering from a condition such as a "physical or mental illness or disorder, a psychological disorder, an emotional disturbance, a learning disability, . . ." where such treatment is recommended by a "qualified person" and the young person consents (ss. 20(1) and 22).

Responsibility is, however, tempered under the Act by the principle of reduced accountability which holds that young persons should not, generally speaking, be held accountable in "the same manner or suffer the same consequences for their behaviour as adults" (para. 3(1)(a). For example, the dispositions available under the Act are generally less severe, particularly with respect to duration: no disposition is to exceed two years except where the sentence for an adult could be life, or the young person is being sentenced for more than one offence committed at the same time, in which case the maximum period is three years.

B. Protection of Society

The second major principle is that society must be afforded protection from the illegal behavior of young persons. Protection should not be viewed in a narrow sense. Rather, protection encompasses the accountability of the juvenile justice system to the public and the long-term interests of society in the rehabilitation of young offenders as well as the more immediate needs of society for protection from the criminal acts of youth. Protection has been referred to as the community change model (s. 3(1)(d). Society may well have the responsibility to take reasonable measures to prevent criminal conduct by young persons. A number of provisions in this federal legislation reflect the increased onus on the juvenile system to afford the public such protection.

As a general rule, court proceedings are open to the public and subject only to a ban on the publication of the name or any other information which would serve to identify the accused young person, and a child or young person who is a victim of or a witness to the offence (section 38); and a number of factors, including judicial control over dispositions and review thereof, and open court, will make judges and the public increasingly aware of both the effectiveness and the ineffectiveness of much of what is being done to and on behalf of young offenders. It may well be that the open court concept is unique to juvenile justice in Canada. It was certainly not provided for in the previous legislation.

Notwithstanding the scope within the juvenile justice system to deal with young persons charged with or convicted of serious offences, the Act provides for transfer of a young person to adult court under specified circumstances (section 16). Where a transfer is ordered, a young person is to be tried in adult court and, if convicted, subject to the same sentences as an adult. A young person will serve an "adult" sentence in a youth facility until the age of eighteen.

C. Rights of Accused Young Person

The third element in the Declaration of principle gives recognition to the rights of young persons. The Act provides that

> young persons have rights and freedoms in their own right, including those stated in the Canadian Charter of Rights and Freedoms and the Canadian Bill of Rights.

As a result of the Young Offenders Act and the Charter a young person has rights which include the following:

- The right to retain and instruct a lawyer at any stage of the proceedings (s. 11(1));
- the right to the least possible interference with freedom that is consistent with the protection of society having regard to the needs of young persons and the interests of their families (para. 3(1)(f);
- the same rights to appeal as adults (s. 27);
- the right to initiate reviews of a disposition (ss. 28-32);
- the right to be heard and to participate in proceedings (para. 3(1)(e)); and,
- the right to the destruction of fingerprints and photographs where this destruction has been earned by the young offender (s.45). Earned here in the sense of (s.40-46) following a crime-free period of two to five years after the completion of a disposition.

In addition, "young persons should have special guarantees of their rights and freedoms (para. 3(1)(e)). By way of example, subs. 11(4) and (5) provide for the appointment of counsel where the young person is unable to do so.

These special rights of course are not dissimilar to adults having regard to ss. 7, 8, 10, and 11. Family participation may take place in all stages of the proceedings. There are also provisions for separate detention facilities from adults and anonymity of young persons in the media.

Thus far, the elements discussed concern responsibility for one's criminal behavior, the right of society to be protected from such behavior, and the rights of an accused young person. While these elements are integral to the Young Offenders Act and while this Act is basically criminal legislation, it does have a broader social objective. The remaining elements in the Declaration of principle speak to this broader objective.

D. Special Needs of Young Persons

The most notable element to be discussed in terms of the broader social objective of the Young Offenders Act concerns the needs of young persons. Paragraph 3(1)(c) of the Act states that

> Young persons who commit offences require supervision, discipline, and control, but, because of their state of dependency and level of development and maturity, they also have special needs and require guidance and assistance.

Thus, while the new law differs fundamentally from the Juvenile Delinquent Act by emphasizing the elements of responsibility, protection of society, and the rights of young persons, it retains in common with its predecessor the belief that young persons should be dealt with differently from adults.

The clear acknowledgement that young persons have special needs bears closer examination. The new juvenile justice system is premised on a fundamental assumption that young persons, collectively, have needs arising from the state of adolescence. The needs, whether they be to form positive peer relationships, to develop appropriate self-esteem, or to establish an independent identity, understandably vary in degree and nature from one young person to another at any given point in time. Over and above these and other needs which are characteristic of youth generally, the Act recognizes the particular needs of a subgroup of youth who may be suffering from such problems as a physical or mental illness or disorder, a psychological disorder, or a learning disability.

The emphasis on special needs of the offender remains unique to the juvenile system. Numerous provisions in the new law give effect to this recognition of needs:

- The less frequent use of medical and psychological assessments and more frequent pre-disposition reports enhance the information (here particularly common with custodial dispositions) available to the court, thereby making it more aware of the special needs of the young person (ss. 13 & 14);
- The involvement of parents throughout the process through the notice provisions to increase the court's understanding of the young person's needs, to help safeguard the rights of the young person, and to elicit the family's support. The judge can even order parents to be present;
- Limitations on the duration of dispositions;
- A review process to ensure continual monitoring of dispositions in order that they remain relevant and geared to the changing needs and circumstances of young persons (ss. 28-32); and,
- The ban on publication of the identity of the accused/convicted young person to limit the unintended and negative consequences that could flow from publicity (s. 38).

Another aspect in the Declaration which speaks directly to the issue of special needs of youth is found in paragraph 3(1)(h):

> Parents have responsibility for the care and supervision of their children, and, for that reason, young persons should be removed from parental supervision either partly or entirely only when measures that provide from continuing parental supervision are inappropriate.

This element goes beyond a mere affirmation that parents, not the state, have responsibility for the care and supervision of their children and speaks directly to the parent–child relationship and the needs of adolescents which can ordinarily best be met in this setting.

Implications for Educators

A brief overview of the philosophy of the Young Offenders Act may leave one with the sense that the Act is philosophically ambivalent. Some have argued that the various elements in the declaration should have been priorized to lend greater certainty and uniformity of application. These and other commentaries are perhaps best dealt with by way of application of the principles to three main stages which are of direct relevance to educators: preventive education; pre-arrest through adjudication; and meaningful intervention following sentence.

A. Preventive Education

While many factors inhibit any kind of empirically based conclusions to be drawn from the impact of education on the prevention of crime, the potential for positive influence, however, is clear.

Within the past decade, there has been increased attention on the role of educators in law. Such focus has not only included a proliferation of legal courses offered in post-secondary institutions but also includes community youth agencies, law enforcement officials, and public legal education associations who have prepared considerable age-specific, legal education materials for dissemination in schools. It is believed that educators, by virtue of their training and opportunities for formal and informal access to youth, are best able to make optimum use of these materials.

While there may be a tendency to consider youth at risk and youthful offenders as the principal beneficiaries of instruction, the broader audience affected by the Young Offenders Act and the Criminal Code are equally worthy of attention. If the law is presented and understood from the perspective of an accused, or a witness to an offence, or the victim — whether as an individual or as a broader community such as a school — the relevance of the law for all will be much better understood. In any event, when one considers self-report studies which conservatively indicate that over 70 percent of youth are, at one time in their adolescence, involved in behavior which could constitute an offence, little more need be said to justify the relevancy of legal education for youth.

B. Pre-Arrest through to Adjudication

Several situations may give rise to the question of how the Young Offenders Act impacts on educators, beginning prior to any involvement by police and carrying through to a finding of guilty or not guilty.

The Young Offenders Act should not necessarily be a factor for day-to-day discipline in the schools. Where, however, school authorities suspect a young person of a criminal offence and charges are a possible outcome, a number of provisions in the Young Offenders Act will become relevant. In such circumstances, it may be appropriate for the police to be called and for the investigation of the offence to await their arrival. This is particularly important with respect to statements made by the youth to school officials which may not be admissible as evidence unless certain safeguards contained in the Young Offenders Act and the general law of evidence have been met.

It has long been recognized that children and youth are vulnerable to influence by persons in authority such as a school principal, guidance counsellor or teacher, or a uniformed police officer. To protect young persons from being open to suggestion and from adopting a statement suggested by such an individual which may not in fact be true. The Young Offenders Act provides that statements made to persons in authority will be inadmissible in evidence unless the following safeguards are met:

— the statement was "voluntary"
— before any statement was made, it was clearly explained to the young person that:
  • there is no obligation to make a statement;
  • the statement could be used in evidence in proceedings against the young person;
  • the young person has a right to consult counsel, a parent, a relative or appropriate adult; and
  • any statement to be made must be made in the presence of the person consulted unless the young person desires otherwise;
— before any statement was made, a reasonable opportunity was given to consult counsel, a parent, a relative, or another appropriate adult person; and
— where a person is consulted, the young person was given a reasonable opportunity to make the statement in the presence of such person.

Where a school official receives a statement but is not found to be a "person in authority," a court may still rule the statement inadmissible if the young person is able to satisfy the court that his or her admission was given under duress.

Alternative Measures

Alternative measures to the court process may be used to deal with a young person who is alleged to have committed an offence upon certain conditions being satisfied, including the following: the measure is part of an authorized program; the young person has accepted responsibility for the act; the young person has consented to the program; and there is sufficient evidence to proceed.

Provinces have provided a range of such programs which enable a young person to assume responsibility for his/her alleged act in the community through community service, restitution, compensation. Some schools have participated allowing youth to fulfill their commitment through any number of initiatives within the school.

Certainly there is a fundamental difference between accepting responsibility and pleading guilty. If a youth does not fulfill the obligations of the alternative measures program he or she can be brought to court and dealt with by way of judicial proceedings. Such programs where implemented in a school must be taken seriously so as not to label or stigmatize a youth by proceeding through the court process.

Identification of a Learning Disability

Where a student has been accused of committing an offence and police have been notified, the presence of a learning disability may be relevant and should be brought to the attention of the police at this stage and possibly to other juvenile justice personnel. These youth may be more vulnerable, depending on the nature of their learning disability, and may require greater assistance to ensure protection of their rights and interests. In fact, the presence of a learning disability raises issues of procedural fairness from the time of arrest through trial. There is, of course, the feelings of some that youth with a learning disability are disproportionately represented in juvenile justice because they not only get picked up much easier but they are simply not as articulate as their peers at sometimes talking their way out of an offence.

Assessments and Pre-Disposition Reports

As indicated the Act promotes the use of medical and psychological reports to ensure that the needs of a young person are brought to the attention of the court. It specifically identifies learning disability, along with physical or mental illness or disorder, psychological disorder, emotional disturbance, and mental retardation (section 13(a)). These reports may be ordered where a young person's fitness to stand trial is at issue, where there may be a defence of insanity raised, where a transfer to adult court is being considered, or for making or reviewing a disposition. Where a report is ordered for the purposes of assisting the court to determine the most appropriate sentence, the assessment would only be ordered following a finding of guilt.

Where an assessment report is ordered, it is to be prepared by a "qualified person," which is defined in subsection 13((11) as

> one who is duly qualified by provincial law to practice medicine or psychiatry or to carry out psychological assessments, as the circumstances require, or, where no such law exists, a person who is, in the opinion of the youth court, so qualified, and includes a person or a person within a class of persons designated by the Lieutenant-Governor in Council of a province or his delegate.

The last clause was added to provide a province/territory the flexibility to have those who were traditionally performing, and qualified to perform, assessments continue that practice. Under this clause, an educator who had been designated by his/her respective province to perform a particular kind of assessment could fall within the definition of qualified person. The more likely situation, however, is that such an individual would work as part of a multidisciplinary team.

Teachers should be aware how information they may present to a probation officer doing a predisposition report can be used for a youth for purposes of sentencing.

In some instances, such as where a custodial disposition may be ordered or a transfer is being considered, the court must order a predisposition report (ss. 24(11) and 16(3) respectively). The Act specifies that a predisposition report should include the results of an interview with the parents and the young person (ss. 14(2)(a) and, where applicable, his/her school attendance and performance record (ss. 14(2)(c)(vii)). These are being ordered not only in cases where open secure custody is being considered.

Where the "qualified person" considers the educational profile of the youth to be relevant, which is normally the case, release of information forms would be signed by the family of the youth to permit access to the personal records of the relevant educational facilities in accordance with provincial law. This inquiry would normally seek the following information: grade; attendance; any involvement with an attendance counsellor, guidance counsellor, or school psychologist; failure of any grade; involvement in any specialized classes; any difficulties with school and, if so, a description; and any difficulty in relationships with teachers and peers and, if so, a description.

C. Intervention Following Adjudication

Disposition

Where a young person has been convicted of an offence under the Young Offenders Act, the court has a broad range of dispositions from which to choose. These include a fine up to $1000; an order for compensation for loss of or damage to property, for a loss of income or support, or for special damages for personal injury; an order for restitution; an order for compensation in kind or by way of personal service; an order for community services; an order for treatment where specified conditions have been met; probation; or an order of open/secure custody.

The principles of the Act must be applied by the court at this sentencing phase. Four principles are paramount: protection of the public; assumption of responsibility by the youth, although not necessarily to the same degree as adults; the right to the least possible interference with freedom, consistent with the protection of society and the needs of the youth; and recognition of the special needs of youth, including their need for guidance and assistance. This last principle does not, on its own, justify lengthier or more intrusive interventions. Thus, for example, completion of a school term would not justify a longer custodial term than commensurate with the offence, notwithstanding that it is in the young person's interest to finish his/her year.

While youths are sentenced to open custody facilities, which are usually group homes in the community, they usually attend an in-house s.16 school. The goal of such programs is to reintegrate youth into the community. Many offenders from open custody facilities frequently attend community schools.

Educators will have a role during the sentencing phase. Where an assessment report and/or a pre-disposition report have been ordered, it will undoubtedly require input from the school. In addition, where the offence occurred at school and, for example, resulted in damage to its property, the principal could be approached by the youth worker to determine the school's willingness to allow the young person to redress his/her wrong through some form of activity at the school.

Alternatively, where a probation order is made, one of the conditions which a judge may impose is that "the young person attend school or such other place of learning . . . as is appropriate, if the court is satisfied that a suitable program is available for the young person at such place." If the youth does not comply with the conditions of the order to attend school, there is a breach of probation which may constitute another criminal charge and may lead to a more onerous disposition such as open custody. Sometimes, therefore, teachers frustrated with problem youth should temper their anger when reporting school behavior to the probation officer.

Finally, guidance counsellors, teachers, or principals could be called upon to act as character witnesses.

Review

The Act provides for review of a disposition to ascertain whether it remains appropriate. It also provides for enforcement in cases of wilful failure to comply with the disposition.

Where a school is involved in a disposition, there will undoubtedly be arrangements made to ensure proper monitoring. Without such supervision and commitment to ensure compliance, a young person may be "set up" for failure which might not become apparent to the system until he/she comes before the court on another offence. In such cases, a subsequent conviction will bring an escalated disposition on the basis that the lighter intervention did not succeed. What may not be apparent to the court is that the youth was not given any message which would indicate that the "system meant business." Where such a message is given and ignored, the court should be so informed.

Where it appears to a teacher or guidance counsellor that a student who is serving a disposition in the community is suffering academically as a result of the court order, a review of the disposition is in order and should be initiated. There is a right to a review of these dispositions six months after they are made and earlier with leave. In short, such a review would allow the court to alter a disposition by extending the time for its satisfaction, or otherwise altering it to allow a young person to take advantage of new programs or opportunities or simply to cope with his/her course load.

Re-Integration During or Following a Custodial Order

Where protection of the public is at issue and custody must be ordered, a number of provisions may contribute to the rehabilitative success of a custodial program. For example, intermittent custody (subs. 24(12)) may be ordered by a youth court judge. Temporary release may be arranged by the provincial director to allow a young person "to attend school or any other educational or training institution" ss. 35(1)(b)(i)), or to participate in a program that will enable the young person to carry out his employment or improve his education or training more successfully (ss. 35(1)(b)(iii)). These options may well call upon the flexibility, creativity, and motivation of teachers to coordinate between the education resources and programs within the institution and those in the regular curriculum.

Where a young person has completed a custodial order mid-term and returned to the community on probation, a concerted effort by the youth worker, parents, teachers, and counsellor will offer the most promise of success.

Notes

1. 268 U.S. 510 (1925).
2. 262 U.S. 390 (1923).
3. 406 U.S. 205 (1972).
4. Ibid. at 246.
5. Ibid. at 219.
6. Ibid. at 218.
7. See State v. Monhead, 308 N.W. 2d 60 (1981).
8. See Delconte v. State, 329 S.E. 2d 636 (1985).
9. 308 S.E. 2d 898 (1983).
10. 549 F. Supp 1208 (D. Me. 1982).
11. Ibid. at 1227.
12. (1986), 28 C.C.C. (3d) 513 (S.C.C.).
13. Crawford v. Ottawa Board of Education, [1971] 1 O.R. 267 (H.C.) at 272; [1971] 2 O.R. 179 (C.A.).
14. 393 U.S. 97 (1968).
15. (1987) 56 O.R. (2d) 705 (C.A.).
16. 105 S. Ct. 733 (1985), reversing State ex rel. T.L.O., 463 A. 2d 934 (1983).
17. (1985), 18 C.C.C. (3d) 431.
18. (1985), 23 C.C.C. (3d) 406.
19. 450 F. 2d 1069 (8th Cir.) 1971.
20. Ibid. at 1078.
21. Ibid. at 1075.
22. 307 F. Supp. 485 (S.D.Sa.) 1970.
23. Ibid. at 486.
24. 476 F. 2d 180 (4th Cir.) 1973.
25. Dunham v. Pulsifer, 312 F. supp. 411 (D. Vt.) 1970.
26. 453 F. 2d 205 (3d Cir.) 1971.
27. 441 F. 2d 444 (6th Cir.) 1971.
28. 448 F. Supp. 497 (W.D.N.C.) 1978.
29. 251 S.E. 2d 889 (1979).
30. 316 F. Supp. 185 (D.N.H.) 1970.
31. Tinker v. Des Moines 2nd. Comm. Sch. Dist. 393 U.S. 503 (1969).

6

The Impact of AIDS

The dissemination of communicable diseases has been a significant problem afflicting civilization throughout our history. Epidemic diseases such as cholera, yellow fever, typhus, scarlet fever, and swine flu have decimated communities. Between 1918 and 1919, a total of twenty-one million people world-wide lost their lives to swine flu.

More recently, epidemics of rabies, cholera, measles, and malaria are occurring with increasing frequency throughout the world. Each day, epidemiologists and scientists are confronted with new strains of virus and bacteria that could change the course of human existence. Presently, medical researchers are grappling with a disease that threatens to fracture our society: namely, acquired immune deficiency syndrome (AIDS).

Since its recognition in 1981, acquired immune deficiency syndrome, or AIDS, has grown from relative obscurity to almost epidemic proportions. As with the spread of any fatal disease, public fear and misconception concerning this disease and the general welfare of society soon emerge bringing about significant changes in societal behavioral patterns. The rapidity of those societal changes quickly demonstrated the gravity of the AIDS phenomenon as the fear of infection began to permeate all levels of society.

Nowhere else is the problem of AIDS more compelling than in our schools. On any single day, large numbers of students and teachers interact within the confines of a relatively close environment. It is against this background that educators now find themselves caught in a vortex of emotion and fear that may well submerge public education in a sea of ignorance.

The magnitude of the morality associated with acquired immune deficiency syndrome obliges all educators to respond in a well organized and decisive manner. Educators must align their actions with members of the medical, public health, and legal community if they are logically to address the challenges of protecting the rights of the individual against the compelling desire to protect society as a whole from the consequences of AIDS.

Acquired immune deficiency syndrome (AIDS) is characterized by a severe breakdown in the human body's natural immune system brought upon by a transmittable agent known as the human T-lymphotropic virus type III (HTLV-III).

If you are interested in further facts about AIDS, the Ontario Ministry of Health in March 1987 published "Information about AIDS" and "Detecting AIDS," prepared by the Ontario Public Education Panel on AIDS. Similarly, the April 1986 Report of the Canadian Bar Association–Ontario, Committee to Study the Legal Implications of AIDS is very informative.

Despite continuous medical attempts at formulating a cure for AIDS, there is yet no real known treatment available to restore full immune function to individuals already infected. The indiscriminate nature of the HTLV-III virus has generated considerable concern about child and adolescent transmission of the virus within the school environment. There appears to be no danger of HTLV-III virus transmission through normal classroom contact. The greatest risk of transmission appears to be with preschool-age and neurologically handicapped children who may lack control of their bodily secretions. Those involved in the educational placement of HTLV-III positive children must consider the child's emotional, physical, and neurological condition. This should be decided cooperatively by groups consisting of parents or guardians, physicians, public health officials, and school personnel.

In the midst of some of the worst epidemics in history people still believed that the power of a state to regulate matters pertaining to something as personal as health represented an unconstitutional infringement on individual liberty. This premise was tested as early as 1905 in **Jacobson v. Massachusetts**[1] when the Supreme Court reviewed a state compulsory immunization statute enacted to avert a possible smallpox epidemic. The Court upheld the action as a valid exercise of state police power. It found that public interest must take precedence over individual liberty in circumstances involving public health, safety, and welfare. The Court stated:

> We are not prepared to hold that a minority, residing or remaining in any city or town where smallpox is prevalent and enjoying the general protection afforded by an organized local government, may thus defy the will of its constituted authorities, acting in good faith for all, under the legislative sanction of the State. If such be the privilege of a minority then a like privilege would belong to each individual of the community and the spectacle would be presented of the welfare and safety of an entire population being subordinated to the notions of a single individual who chooses to remain part of that population.[2]

Actions, therefore, are presumed valid unless proven to be arbitrary, capricious, or exhibit no reasonable relationship to a legitimate state interest. If a fundamental interest is involved, the state must demonstrate that a compelling interest exists and that no less restrictive alternative is available. To accomplish this task, one must determine whether (the) public health should be based upon the number of people actually or potentially affected, the severity of the disease, or the possible economic consequences to society. Regardless of what criteria are chosen, the mortality often associated with contagious diseases may well remain the most compelling state interest.

In some cases, state prescribed immunization programs for school children have been considered inconsistent with state compulsory education laws. It is suggested that the imposition of health-related admission requirements deprive children of their basic right to obtain a public education. The courts have rejected both of these arguments under the shadow of state police power and the necessity of promoting public safety.[3] The importance of public health was clarified in an early case, **Freeman v. Zimmerman**, where the court held:

> The welfare of the many is superior to that of the few, and, as the regulations compelling vaccination are intended to and enforced solely for the public good, the rights conferred thereby are primary and superior to the rights of any pupil to attend the public schools.[4]

As has been discussed earlier, parents who justifiably remove their children from the classroom may be prosecuted pursuant to s.29(1) of the Education Act. See the **Toronto Board of Education v. Tanya P. and Michael P.**, an unreported decision of Provincial Court (Family Division) Judge David Main.

While it may appear to some that the exercise of police power in circumstances pertaining to public health is now settled, there remains some additional legal considerations that provide arguments against state intervention that could have significant impact upon the control of AIDS.

Some attacks against state imposed health regulations, such as the immunization of school children, have centred upon the infringement of religious expression. The individual right to a free exercise of religion is preferentially protected under the provisions of the U.S. First Amendment. The concept of free exercise of religion was originally considered to extend only to religious beliefs.

In **Wisconsin v. Yoder**[5] the U.S. Supreme Court considered the constitutionality of a compulsory attendance law involving a group of Amish children. The Amish challenge of religious infringement was upheld by the Court in its balancing analysis. It found that the state could not demonstrate a compelling interest in requiring the Amish children to stay in school beyond the eighth grade.

The contentions raised by the Amish against compulsory education statutes might be utilized by individuals objecting to state prescribed AIDS regulations. Religious groups could raise deeply held religious objections to any prescriptive province-wide action requiring either medical screening or treatment for AIDS. In light of Yoder, state legislators shifted away from rigid precedent to provide religious exemptions to individuals in non-epidemic circumstances. By applying the strict scrutiny test to these cases, courts have expanded their considerations to include more of the circumstances surrounding the state regulation looking for the least restrictive alternative.

Issues surrounding the regulation of public health in circumstances involving communicable diseases are certainly compelling. Especially important has been our overwhelming interest to protect our citizens from the threats of potentially fatal diseases. Throughout judicial history, courts have been sensitive to the needs of children and the importance of safeguarding their safety, health, and welfare. Faced with this conclusion, a balance must be struck between the needs of children in obtaining an unobstructed education and the necessity of protecting them and society from epidemic diseases. Obviously, this balance is not struck easily. To arrive at an equitable balance within the public school setting, administrators must consider the most recent medical information available concerning AIDS.

School nurses and other school employees attempting to care for children infected with AIDS should be adequately appraised about a child's health and the specific modes of possible disease transmission. Parents of children infected with AIDS should be made aware of the possible social and medical consequences of sending their children to public school.

Public fear and misconception about AIDS is still very common within the general population. The fact that present medical evidence suggests that AIDS cannot be transmitted through casual contact has not ameliorated public fears concerning this disease. The emotional nature of the AIDS dilemma often thwarts school officials' attempts to reach an equitable decision for all concerned. This may be particularly true in cases involving HTLV-III positive employees.

U.S. Surgeon General E. Everett Koop has described the risk of transmission according to the generally accepted standard as follows:

> There is no known risk of non-sexual infection in most of the situations which we encounter in our daily lives. We know that family members living with individuals who have the AIDS virus do not become infected except through sexual contact. There is no evidence of transmission (spread) of AIDS virus by everyday contact even though these family members shared food, towels, cups, razors, even toothbrushes and kissed each other . . .

> Everyday living does not present any risk of infection. You cannot get AIDS from casual social contact. Casual social contact should not be confused with casual sexual contact which is a major cause of the spread of the AIDS virus. Casual social contacts such as shaking hand, hugging, social kissing, crying, coughing or sneezing will not transmit the AIDS virus. Nor has AIDS been contracted from swimming in pools or hot tubs or from eating in restaurants (even if a restaurant worker has AIDS or carries the AIDS virus). AIDS is not contracted from sharing bed linens, towels, cups, straws, dishes or any other eating utensils. You cannot get AIDS from toilets, doorknobs, telephones, office machinery, or household furniture. You cannot get AIDS from body massages, masturbation, or non-sexual body contact.

Those identified as the high risk population for contracting AIDS are homosexual and bisexual males who have had sexual contact with other homosexual or bisexual males as well as those who "shoot" street drugs. Sexual partners of these high risk individuals are at risk, as well as any children born to women who carried the virus.

School Boards

School boards' risks in dealing with AIDS victims as students and employees extend to many different levels. The first and most obvious level of concern is the contagion to students and employees. In most cases medical experts conclude that the risk of transmission through casual contact such as would be found in a school setting is minimal. The uniformed conclusion of the general public is that no medical risk is acceptable where the impact is almost always guaranteed to result in death. But the risk to school boards as employers involves several legal issues.

Each legal risk in one area carries with it a risk in another area. The risk of depriving an employee or a student of his or her rights is balanced against the public's increasing demand to know of those conditions within the schools and the workplace which present health hazards. The apparent legal trend to protect AIDS victims from handicap discrimination is countered with the growing demand that all cases of AIDS be treated as contagious diseases for public reporting purposes. The evolving right to privacy in blood screening and testing may, for example, conflict with the insurance company's right to exclude pre-existing conditions from health and life insurance coverage. The prohibition against insurance companies from excluding AIDS patients from coverage under their policies is contrasted with the limitations on employers to declare asymptomatic AIDS carriers permanently disabled. A similar trend appears to be evolving in the context of protecting student AIDS victims from discriminatory exclusion from schools.

Boards should be aware of Part IV of the Ontario Health Protection Act, s.o. 1983, c.10 as amended relating to both communicable and reportable diseases. Regulation 161/84 and 162/84 should also be reviewed.

The American precedent, as we shall see, is relevant in view of the Ontario Human Rights Code, s.o. 1981, c.53. In particular, ss.9(b), 4(1) and 10(1).

There have been several legal developments in the United States indicating that AIDS victims would be accorded handicap protection under the applicable deferral laws. First, there was a large settlement of a 1985 case which had been filed before the Florida commission on Human Relations.[7] Todd Shuttleworth was discharged as an administrative and management intern when diagnosed with AIDS. In court, Shuttleworth sought $15 million in damages. The eleventh hour settlement included two years' back pay, the County's assumption of all outstanding medical bills, reinstatement of health and life insurance and attorney's fees. In addition, Shuttleworth was rehired in a new job developing a policy to deal with the County's 400 AIDS cases.

The U.S. Supreme Court ruled in March 1987 that a Florida teacher with contagious tuberculosis was covered under the federal law that prohibits discrimination against the handicapped.

The Supreme Court decided 7 to 2 in **School Board of Nassau County, Fla. v. Arline**[8] that a public employee cannot be fired solely on the basis of having a contagious disease. But the high court remanded the case back to the district court to determine whether the teacher in question was "otherwise qualified."

The decision had been eagerly awaited because of its potential implications for school policies on teachers and students with AIDS. The Supreme Court, however, did not decide on whether a carrier of a contagious disease such as AIDS who is not impaired by the disease could be considered handicapped on the basis of contagiousness alone.

The case originally began in 1978 when the Nassau County school board discharged grade 3 teacher Gene Arline because public health officials had confirmed that her infectious tuberculosis posed a danger to young children.

A federal district court ruled in favor of the school board, holding that

Section 504 of the U.S. Rehabilitation Act does not apply to persons with communicable diseases. Section 504 prohibits discrimination by recipients of federal funds against "otherwise qualified" handicapped persons.

That decision was overturned by a federal appeals court.[9] The Supreme Court was generally in support of the appeals court ruling.

The Supreme Court rejected the position taken by the U.S. Justice Department which argued that an employer does not discriminate on the basis of "handicap" when it takes action against an employee because of fear of "communicability."

Justice Brennan, writing for the majority, indicated that Arline's contagiousness and her physical impairment each resulted from the same underlying condition, tuberculosis.[10] He said that it would be unfair to allow an employer to seize upon the distinction between the effects of a disease on others and the effects of a disease on a patient and then use that distinction to justify discriminatory treatment.

In a footnote, the judgement noted the Justice Department's contention that, in some cases persons may be carriers of a disease, such as AIDS, but not suffer any symptoms or impairment from the disease. However, because the employee in this case had a history of impairment from tuberculosis, the court refused to answer the question of whether non-symptomatic carriers are protected by Section 504.

Chief Justice Rehnquist, joined by Justice Scalia, wrote a dissenting opinion that chastized the majority for resting its holding on its own sense of fairness and implied support from the act. The dissenters, noting the long-standing history of state regulation of persons with contagious diseases,[11] would exempt from coverage discrimination based on contagiousness, unless there was explicit language in the statute which evidenced congressional intent to cover such discrimination.

The Supreme Court sent the case back to the district court to answer two questions: (1) whether Arline is "otherwise qualified" for the job of elementary school teacher and (2) if she is not qualified to teach, whether the district could have "reasonably accommodated" her?

The Supreme Court adopted a set of criteria put forth by the American Medical Association for deciding whether Arline posed a risk to the health and safety of others. The criteria included an examination of how the disease is transmitted, how long the carrier is infectious, the potential harm to third parties, and the probabilities as to whether the disease would be transmitted and would cause varying degrees of harm.

The judgement suggests that lower courts should normally defer to the reasonable judgements of public health officials. The Supreme Court did not decide whether courts should defer to the reasonable judgements of private physicians.

It noted that the district court made no findings with respect to the duration or severity of Arline's condition and whether she was contagious at the time she was discharged.

Regarding the question of "reasonable accommodation," the court held that employers are not required to find another job for an employee who is not qualified for the job he or she was doing, but they cannot deny an employee alternatives reasonably available under the employer's existing policies.

In light of this decision, Boards perhaps should follow the lead of the

Center for Disease Control and other public health agencies, which have generally held that AIDS is not transmitted by casual contact, and therefore there is normally no reason to exclude persons with the disease from the classroom.

The Arline decision has apparently affected the handicap protections of students. In **Thomas v. Atascandero Unified School District**,[12] a federal district court ruled that a child with AIDS could not be barred from kindergarten. In ordering the school board to readmit Thomas Ryan to class, the judge stated that Ryan's condition amounted to a protected handicap under Section 504 of the Rehabilitation Act. The school district had not shown that Ryan presented a risk of transmission of the virus by being in the classroom. As such, the burden of proof was transferred from the AIDS victim to the Board to demonstrate why the exclusion was necessary.

Ryan Thomas, age five, was infected with the AIDS virus. He became infected as an infant as the result of a contaminated blood transfusion. He suffered from significant impairment of his major life activities.

On his fifth day in kindergarten, Ryan was involved in an incident with another child. Ryan bit the other child, but no skin was broken. After the incident, school officials told Ryan's parents to keep him at home until a school placement committee could determine whether or not Ryan's potential for biting another student again posed any danger to the health of others in the class. A week later, the Committee recommended that Ryan be evaluated by a psychologist. The board accepted this recommendation.

On 30 September 1986, Dr Marcus Shira, a psychologist, concluded that Ryan would behave "aggressively" in a kindergarten setting because his level of social and language skills and maturity was below that of his classmates. Based on Dr Shira's study, the Committee recommended that Ryan be kept out of class in "home tutoring" for the rest of the academic year. The board voted to exclude Ryan until January 1987 and to have him evaluated before the decision to exclude him further would be reconsidered.

The federal district court ordered the board to admit Ryan and awarded $40,000 in attorney's fees and $2,387 in costs to his parents. The court concluded that Ryan is a "handicapped person" within the meaning of Section 504 of the Rehabilitation Act of 1973. The court said that the district had failed to meet its burden of demonstrating that Ryan is not "otherwise qualified" to attend kindergarten.

In the case of **Ray v. School District of DeSoto**,[13] parents of three hemophiliac school children who were identified as carriers of antibodies for AIDS sought a court order to compel a Florida school board to admit their children to school.

Richard, Robert, and Randy Ray were all hemophiliacs of moderate severity. Because of their hemophilia, all three required injections of blood products to promote coagulation and clotting of their blood. Before 1985, blood products were not regularly screened for AIDS.

In August 1986, Randy Ray was hospitalized for minor surgery. During the course of routine blood work, it was discovered that Randy tested positive for the HIV virus, meaning that Randy was a carrier of AIDS antibodies. Further testing revealed that Richard and Robert were also carriers while the parents and their daughter, Candy, tested negative for the HIV virus.

The Rays decided to disclose voluntarily to school officials that the boys had tested seropositive. The boys were removed from school and placed on home instruction.

The Rays filed a lay suit in federal district court. They claimed that the school's denial of regular classroom instruction to their boys violated various portions of Florida statutes, the United States Constitution, and Section 504 of the Rehabilitation Act of 1973.

The Court noted that it would be guided in its decision by the present medical evidence about AIDS rather than on public policies that were pursued during earlier public health crises. The medical evidence that the court found most persuasive and relevant included the following:

1. The U.S. Public Health Service has estimated that 20 to 30 percent of individuals testing seropositive, as the Rays had in this case, may develop AIDS by 1991. Other medical experts, however, project a much higher figure.
2. An individual is not considered to have AIDS by testing seropositive. Rather, an essential element of the definition of AIDS used for reporting purposes by the Center for Disease Control is affliction with one or more of the opportunistic diseases which take advantage of the suppressed immune system.
3. The AIDS virus has been found in a wide range of body fluids, including blood, semen, saliva, tears, breast milk, and urine.
4. The risks of communication are known to have occurred in the following ways: (1) intimate sexual contact with an infected person; this is the most frequent method of transmission; (2) invasive exposure to contaminated blood or blood products, that is, intraveneous drug use or blood-transfusion; or (3) perinatal exposure, from infected mother to infant.
5. The Surgeon General of the United States, C. Everett Koop, in a 31 July 1987 interview, recommended that we regard the presence of the AIDS virus in body fluids other than blood, semen, and breast milk as if it were not there.
6. Researchers have found no apparent risk of AIDS infliction by individuals exposed through close, non-sexual contact with AIDS patients. These studies demonstrated that the sharing of household items, such as toothbrushes, eating utensils, baths, and toilets, do not lead to AIDS infection.

The court concluded therefore that present medical evidence established that the Ray's interest in a normal edcuation outweighed any potential harm to others. The court stated:

> The reality is that the Ray boys have already been dealt a hand not to be envied by anyone. The boys at their young ages are having to face two potentially life-threatening diseases. This is more than most people face in their entire adult lives. Denial of the opportunity to lead as normal an educational and social life as possible is adding insult to injury. *Unless and until* it can be established that these boys pose a real and valid threat to the school population of Desoto County, they shall be admitted to the normal and regular classroom settings, to which they are respectively educationally entitled.

In an earlier 1987 decision a federal district court judge refused to order the Orange County, California Department of Education, to allow a man with AIDS to return to his duties as a teacher of the hearing-impaired. The court said that it could not be assured with certainty that the teacher did not pose a risk to the students.[14] The Ninth Circuit Court of Appeals reversed and ordered the Orange County Department of Education to restore Chalk, the teacher concerned, to his original position. Casual contact incident to the performance of his teaching duties in the classroom presented no significant risk of harm to others, and that although handicapped because of AIDS, he was otherwise qualified to perform his job within the meaning of section 504 of the Rehabilitation Act of 1973.[15] Chalk was the first case relating to school employees.

It is obvious that the full impact that the AIDS epidemic will have upon the public schools is only beginning to be comprehended. It seems clear that for a variety of legal reasons children with AIDS will not be automatically excluded without a demonstration by boards that the risk of transmission of AIDS by such children is an unreasonable or significant one. Boards must take a leadership role in educating the public and its students with respect to the risk of AIDS transmission. Concurrently, the school boards must respect the privacy rights of infected individuals and adopt a policy which will treat all AIDS victims in a manner that accords them the maximum legal and medical protections required in each individual case.

Notes

1. 197 U.S. 11 (1905).
2. Ibid, at page 37-38.
3. See, for example, Hartman v. May, 151 So. 737 (1934).
4. 90 N.W. 783 at 786 (1902).
5. 406 U.S. 205, 92 S. Ct. 1526 (1972).
6. From the Surgeon General, JAMA, 11/28/86, Vol. 256, No. 20 at pp. 2785-86.
7. Shuttleworth v. Broward County, 649 F. Supp. 35 (S.D. Fla.) 1986.
8. 107 S. Ct. 1123 (1987).
9. 772 F. 2d 759 (11th Cir. 1985).
10. See Southeastern Community College v. Davis 442 U.S. 397, 406 (1979).
11. See Pennhurst State School and Hospital v. Halderman, 451 U.S.1 (1981).
12. 662 F. Supp. 376 (C.D.Cal. 1987).
13. 666 F. Supp. 1524 (M.D.Fla. 1987).
14. Chalk v. United States District Court, Central District of California, 832 F.2d 1158 (1987).
15. 840 F.2d 701 (9th Cir. 1988).

7

Special Education in Ontario and the United States

On Friday, 23 May 1980, the Honorable Betty Stephenson, Minister of Education, introduced Bill 82 in the legislature of Ontario.

The Bill did two things:

> First, the basis of universal access contained within the Bill guarantees the right of all children, condition notwithstanding, to be enrolled in a school. Second, school boards must assume responsibility for providing suitable programming for all children. This will include the provision of special education programs and special education services for exceptional pupils in the language of instruction of such pupils.[1]

In December 1980, as a result of Bill 82, Section 8 of the Education Act was amended, and special education was mandated as a "right," at public expense, for all exceptional pupils in Ontario, as follows:

> The Minister shall ensure that all exceptional children in Ontario have available to them, in accordance with this Act, and the regulations, appropriate special education programs and special education services without payment of fees by parents or guardians resident in Ontario, and shall provide for the parents or guardians to appeal the appropriateness of the special education placement.

This amendment also included the right to an appeal procedure for parents when they disagreed with the identification or placement of their child as an exceptional pupil and gave them the right to request a review on behalf of their exceptional child. The Education Amendment Act, known as Bill 82, included the right to ongoing identification, continuous assessment, and review of the pupil's placement. It stipulated that the exceptional pupil had the right to a special education program that included a plan which outlined specific objectives for the pupil and outlined the services that would be made available to meet the needs of the exceptional pupil. One in fact must start by determining whether a child is *exceptional* or not.

These programs and services, phased in on 1 September 1985, target two areas: these areas provide special education programs and services (school boards), and exceptional pupils (their parents or guardians) to whom such programs and services must be provided.

> Every Board shall,
> 7. Before the 1st day of September, 1985, provide or enter into an agreement with another board to provide in accordance with the regulations special education programs and special education services for its exceptional pupils in the English language or, whether the pupil is enrolled in a school or class established under Part XI, the French language, as the case may be (paragraph 7 of subsection 149(1)).

Provision is also made requiring each school board to establish a special education advisory committee(s) (Section 182) according to one of the following options:

> (i) one advisory committee, which is to be either:
> (a) special education advisory committee (SEAC); or
> (b) an expanded advisory committee on schools for trainable retarded pupils (TRAC) to form the SEAC.
> (ii) two separate advisory committees:
> (a) an advisory committee on schools for trainable retarded pupils (TRAC);
> (b) a special education advisory committee (SEAC). This Act defines an exceptional pupil as follows: "exceptional pupil" means a pupil whose behavioral, communicational, intellectual, physical, or multiple exceptionalities are such that he or she is considered to need a placement in a special education program. If a child is not determined to be an exceptional pupil in need of a placement, he or she is not entitled to special education programs or services.

The Ministry of Education and school boards are empowered or required to carry out the mandate for special education under the following sections of the Education Act:

- Definition "exceptional pupil" (paragraph 21 of subsection 1(1))
- Definition "special education program" (paragraph 63 of subsection 1(1))
- Definition "special education services" (paragraph 64 of subsection 1(1))
- Definition "trainable retarded child" or "trainable retarded pupil" (paragraph 68 of subsection 1(1))
- Minister ensuring appropriate special education programs and services (subsection 8(2))
- Regulations (subsection 10(1))
  - (a) special education programs and services (paragraph 5);
  - (b) procedures with respect to parents (paragraph 6);
  - (c) payment of cost of education (paragraph 15); and
  - (d) schools for trainable retarded children (paragraph 26).
- Qualification of resident pupils (public school) (subsections (1), (5), and (6) of section 32)
- Hard-to-service pupils (section 34)
- Special Education Tribunals (section 35)

- Appeal procedures (section 36)
- Qualification of resident pupils (secondary school) (subsections (1), (3), and (4) of section 39)
- Admission of wards of children's aid societies or training schools to an elementary or secondary school (subsections (1) and (2) of section 45)
- Roman Catholic pupils enrolled in public boards (subsection (1) of section 47)
- Trustees of schools for trainable retarded children (subsection (5) of section 55)
- Schools for trainable retarded children (sections 71, 72, 73, 74, 75, 76, 77, and 78)
- duties and powers of boards:
  - (a) special education programs and services (paragraph 7 of subsection 149(1));
  - (b) Ministry requirements (paragraph 18 of subsection 149(1));
  - (c) education of children in charitable organizations (paragraphs 47 of subsection 150(1));
  - (d) programs in detention homes (paragraph 38 of subsection 150(1)); and
  - (e) assumption of treatment centres schools (paragraph 41 of subsection 150(1));
- Transportation of pupils (section 166)
- Special Education Advisory Committee (section 182)
- Estimates to include costs of schools for trainable retarded pupils (subsection (3) of section 209)
- Transitional provisions (section 278)

Ontario Regulations made under the Education Act contain specific references pertaining to the education of exceptional pupils:
- R.R.O. 262, section 35 (Elementary and Secondary Schools and Schools for Trainable Retarded Pupils — General), outlines provisions with respect to maximum class size for exceptional pupils. This regulation has been amended. See 416/81, 617/81, 785/81, 761/82, 465/85, 195/87, and 233/88
- Regulation 269 (Ontario Teacher's Qualifications)
- Regulation 268 (Ontario Schools for the Blind and the Deaf)
- R.R.O. 274 (Special Education programs and Services) amended by Ref. 553/81
- Ontario Regulation 554/81 (Special Education Identification, Placement and Review Committees and Appeals), Reg. 62/82 and 77/86

Funding for Special Education programs and services is made available to school boards by the Province through:
- general special educational funding: funding of services in lieu of provincial services; funding of programs for children in government-approved care and treatment facilities; funding of transportation; capital grant allowances. Section 1.1.(63) (64) defines special education program and special education services as:

  "special education program" means, in respect of an exceptional pupil, an educational program that is based on and modified by the results of continuous assessment and evaluation and that includes a plan containing specific objectives and an outline of educational services that meets the needs of the exceptional pupil;

"special education services" means facilities and resources, including support personnel and equipment, necessary for developing and implementing a special education program;

Prior to 1 September 1985, during the phase-in period for special education, boards were required to submit to the Minister what are referred to as "special education plans." These plans were the subject of a decision in the Supreme Court of Ontario case of **Re Dolmage et al. and Muskoka Board of Education et al.**[2]

The Dolmage case involved an application for judicial review to quash the decisions of certain boards and tribunals made with respect to the placement of an exceptional pupil of the Muskoka Board of Education. The parents had argued that their son needed a "total communication" special education program. The plan which the Muskoka Board had prepared and had approved by the Minister for 1982-83 did not provide for that particular program. It was not called for in the plan until 1984/85. The applications were dismissed. Mr Justice Eberle stated at page 553:

> The priorities of the board in the process of phasing in special education programmes was a matter for the Minister, not the court. The ministerial approval is the means by which the Minister can be assured that government policies are followed. Since the Muskoka plan was satisfactory to the Minister, it is not for the Court to meddle with the details of implementation of government policies nor with the rate of progress of their implementation. Those are administrative, financial and policy matters primarily. Equally, I do not think it is for the court to attempt to take over the control of such matters even though our American brothers have done so in some instances. I am not at all tempted by their example. It is my firm view that matters of that kind are for elected officials and not for judges and I readily confess to possessing no aptitude for such a role.

> In sum, the Minister's approval of the Muskoka Board's plans from time to time spells the end of any justifiable complaint about the content of the plans in each year of the phase-in period.

School boards across the Province are still, in fact, phasing-in special education programs and services.

The Education Amendment Act, states that only an Identification, Placement and Review Committee can deem a pupil exceptional and prescribe placement. Regulation 554/81 (1981) defines an "Identification, Placement and Review Committee" (IPRC) as follows:

> 3. (1) A committee shall consist of such number of members, not fewer than three, as the board that establishes the committee may determine, all of whom, subject to subsection (2), shall be appointed by the board and one of whom shall be a supervisory officer or a principal employed by the board, except that where the board does not employ a supervisory officer and employs only one principal, one of such members shall . . .

One must start by determining whether a child is *exceptional* or not. Exceptional as defined in paragraph 21 of subsection 1(1) of the Education Act: "A child whose behavioural, communication, intellectual, physical or multiple exceptionalities are such that he or she is considered to need a placement in a special education program." If a child is *not* determined to be an exceptional pupil in need of a placement, he or she is not entitled to special education programs or services.

If a child is determined to be exceptional, there are two further classifications. First, the *trainable retarded child*. That is a child whose intellectual functioning is below the level at which he or she could profit from a special education program for educable retarded pupils. Second, the *hard-to-serve pupil*. That is a pupil who is determined (by a specially constituted committee under subsection 34(2) of the Education Act) to be unable to profit by instruction offered by a board due to a mental handicap or a mental and one or more additional handicaps.

The provisions dealing with the hard-to-serve pupil are contained in section 34 of the Education Act.

There are certain differences in the identification and placement process between hard-to-serve pupils and other exceptional pupils. In making the hard-to-serve pupil determination, any costs of the original assessment or of any examination or of the review are to be paid by the board of whom the hard-to-serve pupil is a resident pupil. The costs of the parents for any expenses incurred by the parent in locating a placement suited to the needs of the hard-to-serve pupil may also be reimbursed by the Board. S. 34(17) of the Education Act states that Ontario shall pay the costs of hard-to-serve placement. Without an "exceptional" designation, a child cannot be placed in special education. To be identified a child must be a "pupil." A child must be enrolled in a school under the jurisdiction of a board before the child can be a pupil to be identified. For the first time, the Act defines trainable retarded children as "pupils," hence bringing them within the education provisions. That issue was addressed in the case of **Re Maw et al. and Board of Education for the Borough of Scarborough.**[3]

Parents of three children who were not enrolled in their borough schools sought to obtain "hard-to-serve pupil" hearings. It was conceded none were "resident pupils" since they were not enrolled in a school. Because of that it was also concluded that the three children were not entitled to an IPRC hearing. The court, however, determined that they were not entitled to a hard-to-serve pupil hearing for the same reason they were not entitled to an IPRC hearing. They were not enrolled in a board school. It is the entitlement to a hearing that starts the process of access to special education programs and services. Without a right to the initial hearing, nothing else can flow to the exceptional child. Mr Justice Osborne stated at page 697:

> Is a 'hard to serve pupil' hearing available to a student, exceptional or otherwise, if that student is not enrolled in a school in the relevant board area?

> The dominant consideration in s.34(2) is what is meant by the word "pupil". In our view, "pupil" must be given its plain ordinary, English meaning. There is no reason, consistent with our view of this statutory scheme, to do otherwise. A "pupil" is one who is taught by another within the context of our education system. In s.34(2) "pupil" does not

refer to a student at large. It means a student enrolled in a particular board school. The use of the words "the principal" in the middle part of s.34(2) suggests the statutory identification of the principal of the school at which the pupil is enrolled. It cannot mean any principal.

Pupils are referred to through the Education Act. In each case "pupil" is given its ordinary meaning. Section 31 illustrates the manner in which the word "pupil" is consistently used in the Education Act. That section provides:

> 31(1) A **person** has the right, without payment of a fee, to attend a school in a school section, separate school zone or secondary school district, as the case may be, in which he is qualified to be a **resident pupil**.

> (2) Notwithstanding the other provisions of this Part, except subsection 48(6), where it appears to be a board that a person who resides in the area of jurisdiction of the board is denied the right to attend school without the payment of a fee, the board, at its discretion, may admit the person from year to year without the payment of a fee.

The right to an education is given to "a person". The person possessing that statutory right may only exercise it as a resident pupil in accordance with the Education Act.

Section 8(2) of the Education Act, a section which does not refer to a "pupil", provides another relevant illustration. That section provides, in part

> 8(2) The Minister shall ensure that all exceptional **children** in Ontario have available to them, in accordance with this Act and the regulations, appropriate special education programs . . .

The reference to "exceptional children" is a general reference as distinct from a reference to "pupils" in sections such as s.34(2). "Exceptional pupils" are "exceptional children" who have enrolled in a board school, and who are otherwise eligible as pupils.

There was also a finding by the court that the denial of such a hearing because the children were not enrolled in a school did not infringe the right to liberty referred to in s.7 of the Canadian Charter of Rights and Freedoms since such a condition does not interfere with the right to choose any particular school system.

The steps in the admission of a student to Special Education (O.Reg. 554/81.s.2) set out in Anne Wilson's *A Consumer's Guide to Bill 82*[4] are as follows:

Steps	Parent's Rights and Options
1. Principal refers student IPRC	(Interpretations of the Act) Parent has option of requesting in writing to principal that child be referred to IPRC.

2. Principal notifies parent that student is referred.	Parent must receive written notification. Parent may be requested to give written permission for psychological and health assessments.

3. IPRC meets:

(a)	interviews pupil if practicable	
(b)	interviews parent	parent must be interviewed unless he/she waives this right.
(c)	considers reports of assessments: (i) educational	Educational assessment is required and does not need parental consent.
	(ii) psychological (iii) health	Psychological and health assessment are only reviewed if the IPRC requests them, and provided parent permission was given in 2.
(d)	recommends and the board decides (i) whether student is/is not exceptional (ii) what category of exceptionality (intellectual, communicational, behavioral, physical, multiple) (iii) appropriate program placement for student	IPRC must send written statement of its decision to parents and include date on which School Board will be notified of its decisions.
(e)		Prior to date in 3(d), parent may write to principal requesting a meeting with the IPRC to discuss decisions.

4. IPRC may change its recommendations following discussion in 3(e)	Parent received written notification of IPRC final decisions including changes.

5. Student is placed in special education or is returned to regular class as in 3(d)(iii):
  (i) if parent consents
  (ii) if within 30 days of 4. parent chooses not to respond, or fails to consent but does not commence an appeal.
	Within 15 days of 3(e), parent must provide consent in writing for student to be placed.
	
	Parent is notified in writing that child has been placed.

---

1. "Parent" is intended to include mother and/or father and/or legal guardian of child.

Regulation 554/81 states that a parent handbook must be developed which describes for parents their right to appeal and the process involved:

2. (7) Each board that has established one or more committees shall prepare a guide for the use and information of parents that,

(c) explains the function of and the right to appeal determinations of a committee to the Appeal Board; the IPRC, according to Regulation 554/81, shall indicate whether a pupil is exceptional or not and when the committee finds the pupil to be exceptional it shall recommend a placement. According to the Regulation, the committee shall interview the parent, unless the parent waives that right or refuses to take part in the interview, and may interview the pupil, where applicable. A parent, through a written request, has the right to meet with the IPRC to discuss the committee's findings, particularly if they disagree with the identification and/or placement of their child.

The Special Education Appeal Board is required to invite persons whom it believes may be able to contribute.

1. *The Exceptional Pupil*

21. "exceptional pupil" means a pupil whose behavioral, communication, intellectual, physical, or multiple exceptionalities are such that he is considered to need placement in a special education program by a committee, established under subparagraph iii of paragraph 5 of subsection 10(1) (an IPRC), of the board,

(i) of which he is a resident pupil,

(ii) that admits or enrols the pupil other than pursuant to an agreement with another board for the provision of education, or

(iii) to which the cost of education in respect of the pupil is payable by the Minister.

(a) *When?*
- after enrolment in a school
- after referral to an IPRC by a principal upon (I) written notification to a parent or (II) at the written request of a parent

- after the IPRC has obtained and considered an educational assessment, health and psychological assessment where required, interviewed, with consent and participation, the pupil and a parent. In practice no IPRC is convened only once. It considers the assessment is part of the decisions.

(b) *By Whom?*
- Special Education Identification, Placement and Review Committee (IPRC) established by the board
- IPRC to consist of not less than three members appointed by the board (trustees not eligible), one of whom shall be a supervisory officer (or designate) or principal
- French- or English-speaking IPRC depending on language of instruction.

(c) *How?*
- by procedures established by a board and included in a guide for the use and information of parents prepared and made available by the board.
- written statement (to parent and principal) of identification.

(d) *What?*
- consider exceptionality groupings, specific exceptionality identification and specific exceptionality definition (see s.8(2)(b)).
- Groupings: I. Behavioral; II. Communication; III. Intellectual; IV. Physical; V. Multiple
- Identifications:

I. Behavioral: Emotional Disturbance and/or Social Maladjustment

II. Communication:
1. Autism
2. Hearing impairment
3. Language impairment
4. Speech impairment
5. Learning disability

III. Intellectual:
1. Giftedness
2. Educable retardation
3. Trainable retardation

IV. Physical:
1. Orthopaedic and/or physical handicap
2. Visual impairment

2. The Needs of the Pupil

The written statement of the IPRC is to contain the identification it has made of the needs of the pupil. (See O.Reg.554/81.) Those needs should be determined from the assessment data and all relevant opinions, views, and information, but in some cases only achievement test scores are considered.

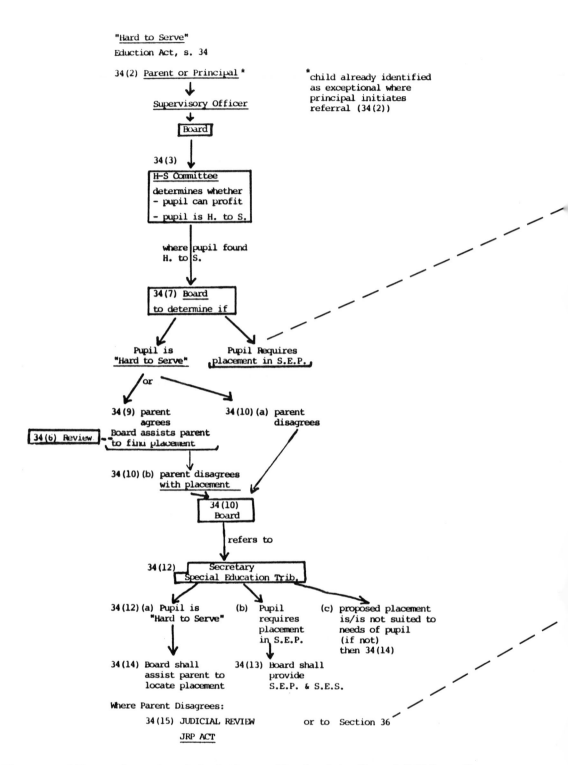

"Hard to Serve"
Eduction Act, s. 34

34(2) Parent or Principal *

*child already identified
as exceptional where
principal initiates
referral (34(2))

Supervisory Officer

Board

34(3)

H-S Committee

determines whether
- pupil can profit
- pupil is H. to S.

where pupil found
H. to S.

34(7) Board
to determine if

Pupil is
"Hard to Serve"

Pupil Requires
placement in S.E.P.

or

34(9) parent
agrees

34(10)(a) parent
disagrees

34(6) Review

Board assists parent
to find placement

34(10)(b) parent disagrees
with placement

34(10)
Board

refers to

34(12)

Secretary
Special Education Trib.

34(12)(a) Pupil is
"Hard to Serve"

(b) Pupil
requires
placement
in S.E.P.

(c) proposed placement
is/is not suited to
needs of pupil
(if not)
then 34(14)

34(14) Board shall
assist parent to
locate placement

34(13) Board shall
provide
S.E.P. & S.E.S.

Where Parent Disagrees:

34(15) JUDICIAL REVIEW
JRP ACT

or to   Section 36

Figure 1 / Procedure for Admitting a Student to Special Education

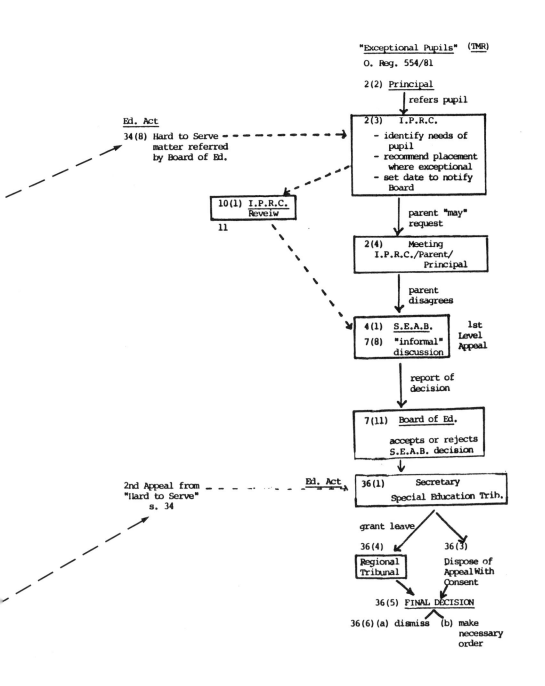

"Exceptional Pupils" (TMR)

O. Reg. 554/81

2(2) Principal
refers pupil

2(3) I.P.R.C.
- identify needs of pupil
- recommend placement where exceptional
- set date to notify Board

Ed. Act

34(8) Hard to Serve matter referred by Board of Ed.

10(1) I.P.R.C. Reveiw
11

parent "may" request

2(4) Meeting I.P.R.C./Parent/ Principal

parent disagrees

4(1) S.E.A.B.
7(8) "informal" discussion

1st Level Appeal

report of decision

7(11) Board of Ed.
accepts or rejects S.E.A.B. decision

2nd Appeal from "Hard to Serve" s. 34

Ed. Act

36(1) Secretary Special Education Trib.

grant leave

36(4) Regional Tribunal

36(3) Dispose of Appeal With Consent

36(5) FINAL DECISION

36(6)(a) dismiss (b) make necessary order

Source: Fasken & Calvin, Donna J. Gallant/82. Reprinted with permission.

109

Placement

Subsection 8(2) of the Education Act provides in part the following:

> The Minister shall ensure that all exceptional children in Ontario have available to them, in accordance with this Act and the regulations, appropriate special education programs and special education services without payment of fees by parents or guardians resident in Ontario
> . . .

Paragraph 63 of subsection 1(1) defines a "special education program" as follows:

> means, in respect of an exceptional pupil, an educational program that is based on and modified by the results of continuous assessment and evaluation and that includes a plan containing specific objectives and an outline of educational services that meets the needs of the exceptional pupil.

Paragraph 64 of subsection 1(1) defines "special education services" as follows:

> means facilities and resources, including support personnel and equipment necessary for developing and implementing a special education program.

If, in the opinion of the IPRC a pupil is an "exceptional pupil" (that is, one whose exceptionalities are such that he or she is in need of a placement), the IPRC must then recommend a placement in respect of that pupil. The placement must be *appropriate* to meet the needs of the exceptional pupil.

Does a placement include details of a program? This was considered in the **Re Dolmage and Muskoka Board of Education** case. The applicants in that case had strong ideas and very high standards for the type of setting, course program, and teacher qualifications for their child. The **Dolmage** tribunal refused the case on the basis that the parent alone had the right to appeal the placement and not the contents of the program with the placement. Mr Justice Eberle expressed an opinion, clearly in obiter, as to the concepts of what is involved in "placement." He stated:[5]

> As well, a great deal of the argument revolved around the notion of the "appropriate" placement of Matthew. This word is found in s.8(2) of the ACT, previously referred to, but it is to be observed that s.2 of O.Reg.554/81 which established the I.P.R.C., does not use the word "appropriate". Subsection (3) of that section provides for the I.P.R.C. to make an identification of the needs for the pupil; and a recommendation made in respect of the placement of the pupil.

> The argument was put in the context of asking the court to make a declaration, in conjunction with quashing the decision or decisions in question, as to the factors that the bodies in question and particularly the I.P.R.C. and the special education tribunal should consider in dealing with Matthew's placement.

As the decisions in question are not to be quashed, there is no necessity to make any declaration, nor is it essential in this case to deal with the argument presently under discussion. However, in the peculiar circumstances of this case there may be some merit in the court expressing an opinion, which it recognizes is clearly obiter and which must be taken as such. One of the circumstances that impels us in this direction is the fact that in the only two special education tribunal decisions made to date, there are differing views and concepts of what is involved in "placement." As well, we recognize that we are dealing only with the phase-in period which will end on September 1, 1985, and it is unlikely that there will be many more matters that will come before such tribunals from the phase-in period. Accordingly, it is clear that nothing in these reasons can affect the period after September 1, 1985. The applicants argue that in making a placement, the I.P.R.C. should look only at the needs of the pupil and disregard the availability of programmes, facilities and services. In looking at the needs of the pupil, they say, regard should be had to such things as pupil-teacher ratio, specific methodology, teaching philosophy, particular teaching qualifications, especially fluency in sign language, and other detailed requirements.

I cannot help but think that the language of s.8(2) should not be read in any more absolute sense than the words reasonably require. To do so would ignore the practicalities previously adverted to. The idea of an "appropriate" special education programme, and the "appropriateness" of the placement of the pupil, surely involves the idea of suitability, and is not to be confused with a placement which amounts to perfection.

The I.P.R.C. is required by O.Reg.554/81, s.2(3) to identify the "needs" of the pupil; and, disjunctively, to "recommend" a "placement" for him. Although these two functions are undoubtedly interrelated, the language used is a far cry from language which would, for example, require the I.P.R.C. to "recommend a placement which fulfills the needs of the pupil". Such language would directly conjoin the two functions with each other, but such language is lacking in the regulations and in the Act.

In considering the placement of a child in the phase-in period, the first step is to ascertain the needs of the child. This must include a consideration of such things as the nature and content of the programme and the services required to accomplish this purpose. When turning to placement, one must be sought which is suitable to the needs of the pupil. In doing so, however, it is essential to consider what programmes and services are available and perhaps even the degree of availability. The most appropriate placement during the phase-in period may not only be less than ideal, but may be far less than ideal. To recommend the placement of a child in a non-existent programme seems to me absurd.

The court in the **Dolmage** case found no ground for interference by way of judicial review and, based in part on the concept of the availability of ongoing review of placements by the IPRC, declined to exercise the court's discretion in favor of the applicants.

It would appear that what is appropriate and whether the needs of an exceptional pupil are met by a placement will be professionally and not legally determined.

There are two types of *review*. First, the ongoing review of a placement of a pupil after it has been made. The wording in 554/8/s 10(1) is "whether the placement of the pupil appears to meet the needs of the pupil." The Annual review under S.10 of 554/81 is appealable: (s11) a review by way of appeal from the determination of whether the pupil is or is not an exceptional pupil.

Where a placement has been made by an IPRC of a pupil which is consented or not objected to by a parent, there must still be an ongoing review of that placement. A parent or the principal of the school (defined in S 1.1(63) program) may, three months after the placement has been in effect, apply for a review by an IPRC. If none is requested, an IPRC *shall* (defined in 554/81 (10)) review such placement at least once every twelve months. If, as a result of such a review, the placement is to change, there must be notification to, discussion with, and consent by, a parent. The review process must, in addition to considering an educational assessment, consider written reports and evidence of a parent as to whether the placement of the pupil appears to meet the needs of the pupil.

Once a pupil is enrolled in a school, the next process is that of *identification*. It is twofold. First, is the pupil "exceptional"? That decision, however, may be subject to *review*. Under the legislation, parents who disagree with the decision of an IPRC have the right to appeal. It should be noted that the process for identification and placement through the IPRC and the subsequent appeal routes do not provide for reimbursement of any costs of the parent who participates in the process.

If such an appeal is lodged with a board, it is necessary for the board to establish a Special Education Appeal Board in order to deal with the appeal within thirty days of receipt of the parents' letter.

A Special Education Appeal Board consists of three members. One member of the Special Education Appeal Board shall hold qualifications as a supervisory officer. (See Figure 1 on pages 108-109.)

It is expected that an initial organizational meeting of members of the Special Education Appeal Board alone will be required in order to set guidelines for the appeal.

The Chairperson of the Appeal Board should arrange with the parents for a meeting with the Appeal Board "at a convenient time and place." The chairperson should make such arrangements forthwith after appointment to the full Special Education Appeal Board by the board of education. If the parent has retained a solicitor, arrangements should be made through him or her. No specific time limit is set within which discussions must take place. It is in the pupil's best interests if it takes place as quickly as possible while still allowing reasonable time for persons whom the Special Education Appeal Board wishes to hear from to arrange to attend. During the appeal the pupil remains in his/her original placement.

Parties before the Special Education Appeal Board should receive equal treatment and the individual presiding at the meeting should be impartial and independent. Moreover, the chairperson must be able to disregard all prejudicial influences and conduct an unbiased examination of the information presented during the discussion. The panel of three consists of two appointed by the Board and one by the parent or a parent's organization. Evidence by some authors suggests that equal treatment is not always achieved.

The Special Education Appeal Board has no powers other than those given to it by statute or regulation.

The Special Education Appeal Board is directed to adjourn the discussion after it is satisfied that it has before it all relevant information, views, and opinions. The Special Education Appeal Board is not required to complete the discussion in one session if it is of the view that additional information would be of assistance. It may adjourn and re-convene the discussion. Within three days after the final discussion, the Special Education Appeal Board must render its decision.

The Special Education Appeal Board can undertake the following options:

(a) it can agree with the IPRC determination and dismiss the appeal;
(b) it can disagree with the IPRC and refer the matter back to the IPRC, stating the reasons for its disagreement;
(c) it can determine that the pupil does not need a special education program or services and set aside the IPRC's determination that the pupil is exceptional.

The Special Education Appeal Board has no power to determine a placement for an exceptional pupil or to determine that a pupil is exceptional in the face of an IPRC decision to the contrary. It can only refer the matter back to the IPRC in such circumstances. The Special Education Appeal Board must report its decision in writing to the parent, the IPRC, and the secretary of the Board of Education. Reasons for the decision need only be provided where demanded. This demand may be made by the Board, the IPRC, or the parent or his/her solicitor.

The Board of Education, upon receipt of the written decision of the Special Education Appeal Board, may or may not accept this decision.

The parent also may or may not accept the decision of the Special Education Appeal Board. If the parent does not accept this decision, or if the board has rejected the Special Education Appeal Board's decision and the parent is still unwilling to accept the original IPRC decision, then the parent may appeal to a Special Education Tribunal for leave to appeal to the regional tribunal. All communication among the parties concerning decisions or requests for identification, placement, review of placement, or appeals must be in writing.

If the parent does not agree with the decision of the board, he or she may apply in writing to the secretary of the Special Education Tribunal. The Special Education Tribunal may (1) grant leave to appeal to a regional tribunal or (2) may hear an appeal. The Special Education Tribunal or a regional tribunal may (1) dismiss the appeal or (2) grant the appeal and issue an order to the board on identification or placement. The decision is final and binding. If the parent or board disagrees with the decision, other courses of action may be open, such as an application for judicial review. The recent trend of the Provincial Special Education Tribunal since it heard its first application in February 1984 (Re Dolmage) seems to be to grant leave in each case without giving reasons for that decision. The tribunal does not grant an appeal or deny same as we normally think of it. Rather it defines the placement best suited to meet the needs of the exceptional pupil. See, for example, Omerod and the Wentworth County Board of Education of 5 June 1987, and Lewis and the York Region Board of Education decision of 10 September 1985, both tribunal decisions.

In addition to proceeding to the courts, some parents have gone to the

Ontario Human Rights Commission. A recent case that has moved from a Board of Inquiry is Re Lanark, Leeds & Grenville County Roman Catholic Separate School Board and Ontario Human Rights Commission et al. (1987) 60 O.R. (2d) 441 (Div.Ct.). An appeal from the Divisional Court's dismissal of the Board of Inquiry at this writing is before the Ontario Court of Appeal.

Judicial review, which is often the final step, is a step that really one should never have to reach. The importance of maintaining open and frequent contact with parents of handicapped children cannot be overstated. Limiting school-home communications to brief telephone calls, notices of meetings, and formal meetings may not adequately convey the extent of the school's concern and its efforts on behalf of a handicapped child. Special educators most directly involved in providing services to handicapped children should make every effort to keep the parents informed not only of their child's progress but also of other special education programs and activities. Invitations to attend such informal special education functions as class parties and plays, opportunities to observe instruction in progress, and a chance to volunteer time for making instructional materials and assisting with clerical tasks, all represent constructive attempts to involve interested parents.

More substantively, the parents of handicapped children should contribute to the development stages of new special education programs. They should be encouraged to bring a friend, an advocate, or some other support person to special education meetings. They should be offered a selection of readings pertinent to handicapped children and their parents. Finally they should have the opportunity to meet with other parents of handicapped children to share mutual interests and concerns.

The key consideration is that the handicapped child, the parents, and the school all benefit from parental commitment and involvement. Inclusion at various levels of the special education process beyond the formality of meetings and conferences increases the likelihood that parents will feel satisfied with the programs and services being provided. Frequent opportunities to communicate concerns, complaints, or questions should help resolve potential conflicts before they grow and fester.

One strategy that enhances the effectiveness of communication between school personnel and the parents of handicapped children is the designation of a professional as a coordinator-monitor of a handicapped child's total educational program. Since the needs of a handicapped student are varied, several professionals are often involved in providing the instruction and services prescribed in an individualized education program. At the initiation of such a program, the multidisciplinary team should assign one professional to serve as liaison between home and school, thereby offering the parents consistent contact with one person who can provide direct, complete information. Such a monitor can eliminate or greatly reduce parental frustration while simultaneously ensuring the coordination of the total educational program.

Despite all efforts to maintain open channels of communication between school and home, disagreements that require the attention of the multidisciplinary team can develop. Intervention by a neutral third party to negotiate disagreements between a parent and a school district at this early stage may produce a resolution at the local school level without recourse to the courts. Such a result would presumably be preferable to both parties, particularly when it keeps the parties from adopting rigidly adversarial positions. Channels of communication and rapport can be more readily preserved through early intervention by an impartial negotiator.

Documentation, too, is crucial throughout the entire special education process. Hearing decisions are based on findings of fact, which in turn require documented proof.

Special educators have the responsibility of working not only among themselves but also with regular educators to foster an understanding of the spirit and intent of Ontario's special education legislation. A superficial grasp of the letter of the law inadequately informs one of the task of providing handicapped children with a meaningful education. In-service activities may include but not be limited to presentations by staff members, the parents of handicapped children, handicapped adults, experts, consultants, and other speakers. Expanding the scope of such activities to encompass the community at large is another step toward educating and involving citizens who may not otherwise be linked to special education. Their commitment and support can provide invaluable help in augmenting existing services and developing new programs.

The responsibility for meeting the learning needs of all children is a responsibility shared by all educators.

Special educators must not stand isolated from the rest of the profession. The responsibility is a collective one. Educators should take steps to keep special education from becoming so "special" that it is no longer viewed as part of the education profession. It is the hope that Bill 82 will result in schools where all children receive more precise instruction. Just because a person is less able does not mean that person is less worthy.

Special Education in the United States

Special education in the United States is defined in the Education of the Handicapped Act (EHA) as specially designed instruction, at no cost to parents or guardians, to meet the unique needs of a handicapped child, including classroom instruction in physical education, home instruction and instruction in hospitals and institutions. Known as Public Law 94-142, the EHA of 1975 provides federal funds to assist states and local agencies in providing children with specific learning disabilities with a "free appropriate public education" (FAPE) which includes "special education and related services."

No precedent had been established by the U.S. Supreme Court as to the constitutional rights of handicapped children's rights to a public education. An early case where handicapped plaintiffs sought relief under the equal protection clause of the U.S. fourteenth amendment was initiated in Pennsylvania, challenging the constitutionality of the state law that allowed school systems to exclude handicapped children from school.[7] The case resulted in a consent agreement stating that handicapped children could not be denied admission to public school programs or have their educational status changed without procedural due process. Each mentally retarded child had to be placed in a free public program of education and training appropriate to each child's capacity.

A District of Columbia case followed the principle established in the Pennsylvania agreement.[8] The Court in **Mills** held also on equal protection grounds that handicapped children could not be totally excluded from publicly supported education or be denied an education without due process.

The U.S. Supreme Court's 1973 decision in **Rodrigues**[9] gave support to the contention that the total exclusion of selected children, such as the handicapped, from public schools would not withstand constitutional scrutiny. Although stating that the right to an education is not an inherent fundamental right, the Court conceded that "some identifiable quantum of education" may be constitutionally protected.

Section 504 of the Rehabilitation Act of 1973 prohibits the recipients of any federal financial assistance from discriminating against an otherwise qualified handicapped person solely because of the handicap. It states that "an otherwise qualified handicapped individual in the United States . . . shall, solely by reason of his handicap, be excluded from the participation in, be denied the benefit of, or be subjected to discrimination under any program or activity receiving federal financial assistance. . . ."[10] Public Law 94-142, the Education for All Handicapped Children Act (EAHCA) of 1975, provides federal funds to assist state and local education agencies in offering appropriate educational programs for handicapped children.[11]

The basic statutory right is that of "free appropriate public education." How does one measure an "appropriate" education? Is it an optimum program to maximize a child's potential, or is it educational benefits appropriate to achieving passing marks and advancing from grade to grade.

In **Board of Education v. Rowley**,[12] it was requested that the school board provide a sign language interpreter for Amy Rowley in her academic classes. Amy's IEP ("individualized education program") included a regular first-grade placement with special instruction from a tutor for the deaf one hour per day, a speech therapist three hours per week, but not a sign language interpreter requested by her parents. Based on the advice of the IEP committee and others familiar with her program, school officials concluded that an interpreter was unnecessary since she was achieving at an above-average level.

In rejecting the lower courts' definition of "appropriate," the Supreme Court did not provide a specific substantive educational standard but rather noted that access should be meaningful. The Court reasoned that "the intent of the Act was more to open the door of public education to handicapped children on appropriate terms than to guarantee any particular level of education once inside.[13] The Supreme Court held that judicial review in these cases would be limited to whether the state has complied with the procedures set forth in the Act and whether an IEP is reasonably calculated to enable a child to receive educational benefits.

Extensive procedural safeguards are provided to ensure appropriate identification, evaluation, and placement of handicapped children. Prior to any evaluation, parents must be informed of their procedural rights, including a description of the process and procedures. This includes the opportunity to examine their child's records and to obtain an independent educational evaluation of the child. If parents are not satisfied with the classification or proposed IEP, they have the right to a hearing to present complaints

116

at local and state levels. After exhausting their administrative rights parents may apply for judicial review of the decision. Elaborate procedural safeguards are considered central to the goal of assuring free appropriate education by means of open communication between parents and school representatives.

"To the maximum extent appropriate, handicapped children, including children in public or private institutions or other care facilities, must be educated with children who are not handicapped."[14] The term "to the maximum extent appropriate" does suggest a preference for the concept of mainstreaming. Mainstreaming must be balanced with the primary objective of providing handicapped children with an "appropriate" education. The U.S. legislation requires that public school boards must place handicapped children in private facilities if an appropriate public placement is unavailable.

The United States Supreme Court addressed parental rights in connection with unilateral placement changes in **Burlington School Committee v. Department of Education.**[15] The parents disagreed with the assessment of their son's learning problems as emotional rather than neurological, and they rejected a proposed IEP to place their child in a highly structured public school class of six students. After diagnosis by specialists, the parents placed the child in a private school at their own expense. The Court rejected the board's argument that a change in placement without the board's consent waived all rights to reimbursement. In the Court's opinion, denying relief would defeat the major objective of providing a free appropriate education. The Court awarded reimbursement to the parents for the costs of the private school education. In rejecting the argument that reimbursement was "damages," the Court stated that an award of reimbursement of private tuition simply required the school belatedly to pay expenses that it should have paid all along and would have borne in the first instance had it developed a proper IEP.[16] However, the Court did not endorse indiscriminate unilateral placement of children by parents in a private school. Parents who unilaterally seek private placement do so at their own financial risk. Related services are defined as:

> transportation, and such developmental, corrective, and other supportive services (including speech pathology and audiology, psychological services, physical and occupational therapy, recreation, and medical services shall be for diagnostic and evaluation purposes only) as may be required to assist a handicapped child to benefit from special education . . .[17]

In 1984 the Supreme Court in **Irving Independent School District v. Tatro**[18] clarified a state's obligation to provide "related services." This case involved an eight-year-old with spina bifida and a neurogenic bladder requiring clean intermittent catheterization (CIC) every three or four hours. On appeal, the Supreme Court affirmed the order requiring the school to provide CIC.

In assessing whether CIC was a related service, the Supreme Court observed that a school need provide only these services which would allow a handicapped child to obtain and benefit from special education. It emphasized that such services are "no less related to the effort to education than are services that enable the child to reach, enter, or exit the school."[19] Basically, these were services routinely provided to the non-handicapped. In determining whether CIC was a medical service, the Court concluded that since CIC is a service that could be furnished by a nurse or readily taught to a layperson, it was not a medical service which the school was not required to provide. While this case indicated that the legislation does not apply to the services of a physician, it does apply to the services of other qualified people, but not to equipment.

Disciplinary practices form another area that may impair the rights guaranteed to handicapped children. Specifically, several courts have found expulsions of these children to be changes in placement and thus prohibited such disciplinary actions for behavior related to handicapping conditions.[20] What is critical is determining whether the misconduct is related to the handicap. Neither legislation nor the regulations expressly address the general question of discipline of handicapped students. The Supreme Court recognized in **Goss and Lopez**[21] in 1975 that a student's entitlement to public education was a property right of which he or she could not be deprived through long-term suspensions of expulsions without the formality of a due process hearing. Suspensions less than ten days in length required only informal hearing procedures. If misbehavior is not a manifestation of a child's handicap, is expulsion a disciplinary alternative? Few handicapped children seem to be expelled. They are simply moved from a less restrictive environment to a more restrictive one.

Most litigation involving discipline of handicapped students has focused on expulsion rather than suspension, or removal of students short of expulsion. Courts have noted that temporary suspensions do not require special safeguards. Brief suspensions may not be a change in placement necessitating procedural protection. You can't, of course, label something a suspension as opposed to an expulsion, for example, an "indefinite suspension," and assume that this will not be considered a change of placement.

If expulsion is an option for handicapped students, provision for continuation of educational services should be addressed. It is unlikely that complete termination of the educational program is legally defensible.

Finally, what is the effect of a transfer of a student to another school when the transfer results in a more restrictive environment or when the transfer is behavior related?

Recently, the U.S. Supreme Court held that the administrative procedures governing in this case a disruptive emotionally disabled child could not be overlooked but concluded that school authorities could bypass "stay put" provisions provided they could convince the court that maintaining the child in current placement until exhaustion of the administrative remedies is most likely to result in harm to self or to others.[22]

Notes

1. Speech of the Honourable Betty Stephenson, 23 May 1980 in *Hansard*, pp. 2135-2138, Volume 2, 1980 Debates.
2. (1985) 49 O.R. (2d) 546 (H.C.).
3. (1984) 43 O.R. (2d) 694 (H.C.).

4. See Anne Keeton Wilson, *A Consumer's Guide to Bill 82: Special Education in Ontario* (Toronto: OISE Press, 1983), p. 77.
5. Supra, note 2 at 553.
6. Wilson, *A Consumer's Guide,* p. 79.
7. Pennsylvania Ass'n for Retarded Children v. Commonwealth, 343 F. Supp. 279 (E.D.Pa. 1972).
8. Mills v. Board of Education of the District of Columbia, 348 F. supp. 866 (D.C.D.C.1972).
9. San Antonio Independent School Dist. v. Rodriquez, 411 U.S. 1, 36 (1973).
10. 29 U.S.C. #794.
11. 20 U.S.C. #1401.
12. 458 U.S. 176 (1982).
13. 458 U.S. 192 (1982).
14. 20 U.S.C. #1412 (5).
15. 105 S.Ct. 1996 (1985).
16. 105 S.Ct. 2003 (1985).
17. 20 U.S.C. #1401 (7).
18. 468 U.S. 883 (1984).
19. 468 U.S. 891 (1984).
20. Stuart v. Nappi, 443 F.Supp. 1235 (D.Conn. 1978).
21. Goss v. Lopez, 419 U.S. 565 (1975).
22. Honig v. Doe, 108 S.Ct. 592 (1988).

8

Teachers and the Law

This chapter presents an overview of provincial requirements relating to teachers' employment, contracts, tenure, and conditions of employment. Specific job requirements that implicate Charter rights or anti-discrimination mandates are also addressed. Rights as defined by the courts in connection with freedom of expression, academic freedom, freedom of association, and privacy rights. Some cases are highlighted in the following chapter on the Charter of Rights.

The rights of a board to determine the fitness of a teacher have been well-established. Courts have in fact declared that school boards have a duty as well as a right to make such determinations. Procedures must be followed in terminating a teacher's employment as well as in the grounds for dismissal.

As we are all aware, the employment of teachers has been dramatically affected by the advent of collective bargaining. Unless of course bargaining is mandated by statute, courts do not normally compel boards to negotiate.

Teaching is considered a restricted employment. Governmental approval of who may teach is prima facie assurance to the public of an acceptable standard of service at the time of contracting and, as with all professions, of the candidate's personal suitability to the profession.

Generally the burden to assess a candidate's suitability for licensing[1] and for certification devolves to the teacher training schools, particularly with the evolution of the teaching practicum or internship concomitant to the professional degree. Accordingly, possession of the degree tends to be a de facto licence since the Minister of Education is responsible for establishing teacher education.

The certification process is a provincial determination. A board has neither the means nor the expertise to make such a determination. Certificates are normally issued in accordance with the regulations made by the Minister of Education.[2] Because the certificate is the pivotal determinant of the teacher's salary, classification is critical to both collective and individual contracting. Placement on the salary grid is normally based on classification. Once hired and placed, the teacher is entitled to all benefits of the collective agreement.

Tribunals established to make such determinations primarily address issues of classification, embracing category placement and decisions on years of teaching experience for placement on salary grids. A determination is made on initial employment and additional study or experience. These decisions are authoritative for substantive matters relating to collective bargaining.

Changes in classification may, of course, be subject to grievance, where review is equally limited.[3] It may be anticipated that the agreement and documents will be regarded as authoritative and to be strictly construed. Such is consistent with a general governing principle of uniformity of application to all teachers under the agreement. Generally the teacher has a right (and the board has an obligation) to be paid in accordance with the experience and category attained. The onus, however, is on the teacher to establish his or her qualifications, and to place all information before the assessing body. The school board has the right to correct genuine errors it uncovers. A teacher takes his or her status from his or her licence — the basic certificate of qualification. Consistent with general legal principles regarding licensing, the licence is a privilege not an absolute right, and while normally not issued for a particular time may be subject to future conditions. Statutory definitions under collective bargaining legislation usually further include employment as a co-determinant of the definition of a teacher.

The exception to the requirement for proper professional qualifications is that of an emergency created by an insufficient supply of teachers. While essentially an historic condition, teacher shortages may occur in specialized subjects. Thus discretionary provisions allow, with Ministerial approval, temporary appointments where no teacher is available. Such "letters of permission" appointments are temporary in nature by express statutory or regulatory provision.

Statutory Background

Prior to 1975, teachers (save for "occasional teachers") in Ontario had no right to bargain collectively. It was specifically stated in The Labour Relations Act, R.S.O. 1970, Chapter 232, section 2 (f), that the said Act did not apply to teachers. The rights and duties of teachers were by and large dealt with under The Education Act 1974, S.O. 1974, Chapter 109, and the myriad of regulations passed thereunder.

In 1975 Ontario passed **The School Boards and Teachers Collective Negotiations Act**, R.S.O. 1980, c.228 (called "Bill 100"), which amongst other things permitted collective bargaining on behalf of permanent and probationary teachers and required the appropriate branch affiliate to represent in negotiations all teachers composing its membership.

Although the legislation gave teachers the right to bargain collectively, the Legislature nevertheless left in place legislation and regulations that had previously governed the rights and duties of teachers. The result today is that if one wishes to know what are the rights of teachers and boards with respect to hiring discipline and termination of teachers, one must look at the Education Act, R.S.O. 1980, Chapter 129 (as amended), the regulations, and any appropriate collective agreement.

Employment

The concept of probationary employment did not really exist at common law, primarily because there was no need for it since the employee was subject to the whim of the employer by means of proper notice. Rather, it seems to have now evolved as a quid pro quo to mitigate the impact of the administrative rigors of discipline being subject to just cause under collective agreements, with the remedy of reinstatement (over damages), and with other benefits established via seniority, which is usually acquired with the completion of a probationary period.

Labor arbitration has viewed probationary status as allowing the employer time to assess a new employee.[4] Simply put it has been stated:

> One cannot reasonably expect an employer to be able to assess the full capabilities and potentiality of a job applicant from a brief interview, an application form, references and the like. Rather he must be entitled to an opportunity to view the new hire in the particular context of his own work environment. That is the sole purpose of the probationary period. It is, as we have said, a legitimate purpose.[5]

The courts have been in accord with that purpose behind the creation of statutory probationary periods for teachers:

> The provision for the three-year probationary period is not for the benefit of the school board but for the protection of the public educational system and the benefit of the school children to ensure an adequate appraisal time as to the fitness of the teacher before he or she attains tenure and cannot be dismissed except for cause. Such statutory provisions cannot be varied by individual boards or trustees for such would be contrary to public policy as well as contrary to s.33 of the School Act which requires every trustee to comply with the Act and Regulations.[6]

Mr Justice Limerick construed the probationary period to effect the general public policy of promoting better education through the proper appraisal of teachers. Boards act here not only in the performance of a public authority, but in the performance of a public duty. It is then, not only consistent with the private sector presumption that the probationary period is a test, it more strongly focuses on the duty to afford appraisal based on standards.

Where a probationary period exists, the failure to meet the suitability standard must be regarded as cause for termination. Meeting it entitles the employee to additional benefits, in particular, entitlement to full "cause" however regulated by The Education Act or agreement. The phrase probationary "contract" when used is generally a misnomer for what is a status or designation, in the same way that a principalship, or other position of responsibility, bestows additional benefits under the contract of employment. Thus it is accepted that unilateral resignation,[7] or a dismissal from a position as a principal, does not permit one to retain a position as a teacher. Rather a demotion is the proper board response. Only one contract of employment is involved.[8]

The probationary period is one concept that is finding its way back into the common law after having been shaped by the common law of collective agreements. Because it is being written into individual contracts of employment our courts have had occasion to take judicial notice and explicate certain views.

The probationary/permanent contract is one contract, probation is but a trial or test. If the probationary period was truly a separate fixed term contract, rather than a fundamental and usual term of regular employment to demonstrate suitability satisfactorily, some rather harsh consequences would, in education, flow to the employer. A teacher's probationary period is usually two years which may be reduced to one for those with experience. Common law expectation would be that if a probationer were dismissed for other than just cause that individual would be entitled to damages measured against the period contracted for, that is, the full two years. What must be kept in focus is the concept inherent in probationary employment which requires that the employer,[9] and equally that the teacher's professional colleagues, direct their attention to the individual's suitability to the status as a teacher, as a career, and not merely temporary employment.

The employment of teachers (other than occasional teachers) is dealt with in section 230 of the Education Act, which provides as follows:

"(1) A full-time or part-time teacher who is employed by a board and who is not an occasional teacher shall be employed as a permanent or a probationary teacher.

(2) A memorandum of every contract of employment between a board and a permanent teacher or a probationary teacher shall be made in writing in the form of contract prescribed by the regulations, signed by the parties, sealed with the seal of the board and executed before the teacher enters upon his duties, but if for any reason such memorandum is not so made, or has not been amended to incorporate any change made in the form of contract so prescribed, every contract shall be deemed to include the terms and conditions contained in the form of contract prescribed for a permanent teacher."

The "form of contract" is prescribed by Regulation 277 under the Education Act, which prescribes both a Permanent Teacher's Contract and a Probationary Teacher's Contract. The length of the probationary period, which in a normal labor relations setting is negotiated between the employer and union, is in the case of teachers determined by the Education Act, which provides in section 232 that:

"A board shall not offer to a teacher, and no teacher shall accept, a contract as a probationary teacher for a period greater than,

(a) two years where the teacher has less than three years' experience; and
(b) one year where the teacher has three or more years' experience,

as a teacher in an elementary or secondary school in Ontario before the commencement of the contract."

The obverse of the coin of teacher classification is the casual teacher, one employed on a temporary, fixed term basis of less than one year.[10] Such a teacher is traditionally provided for under the Education Act and/or regulations as a supply or an occasional teacher. The Ontario definition is illustrative:

> 1 (1) 30 'occasional teacher' means a teacher employed to teach as a substitute for a permanent, probationary or temporary teacher one under a mere letter of permission who has died during the school year or who is absent from his regular duties for a temporary period that is less than a school year and that does not extend beyond the end of a school year.[11]

Such a definition clearly classifies the substitute teacher as a kind of "teacher," and proper qualifications are implied. The expectation and working relationship is that the substitute takes direction from the teacher who is sick, or on conference, if he or she has organized the learning or course for the time required.

Judicial notice has recognized the distinction and, as with the letter of permission, addressed the element of necessity that has through custom alleviated the normal requirement for a memorandum in writing. Further recognition that the temporary contract may be oral flows in Ontario from the "deeming" provision s. 224(2), which where a board fails to execute a written probationary contract deems the relationship a permanent one.

That deemed contract does not apply to occasional or temporary teachers. They may therefore be beyond the jurisdiction of an arbitrator under the collective agreement in regard to any oral provisions. The supply teacher's contract is usually then created by a telephone call from the board.

The usual supply teacher has been scrutinized by the board through a screening process via an invitation to treat in the capacity of an occasional teacher. The important element is the nature of the contract, or series of contracts which are for fixed terms, which are often called "short-term" contracts. As the contract is for a fixed term it is not capable of being determined or ended by either party until expiry, except through breach, or repudiation, or operation of law. Recovery in such a case is through damages calculated on the unexpired portion of that term, and as damages are not wages, the concept of mitigation applies.[12] Because termination is automatic there is no requirement for notice.[13]

There is an important distinction between such positions of added responsibility (the arbitration involved a principal's position and a Family Life Consultant position, both advertised for a fixed term appointment) and the contract *per se*. It was held that in such cases a permanent contract with the Board remains intact and the termination of the fixed term of office has no effect on the basic teaching contract, which remains subject to termination in accordance with the agreement and Education Act. The Board's power, then, is a function of its management's rights as governed by the Act and curtailed by the collective agreement. In **Wright v. Hamilton Board of Education**,[14] the plaintiff had been engaged as an occasional to replace a teacher on maternity leave for a full term, September to December. With the return of the teacher for the final term, as there was alternative employment, the plaintiff, in the interests of not "replacing" the student's "teacher" in mid-year, was offered what is best regarded as a second contract rather than an extension. In a subsequent action for wrongful dismissal the plaintiff argued that said contract was, once the teacher being replaced had been given alternative employment, no longer an occasional contract, rather she had become a career teacher.

The Court found for the Board on the basis of intent. The decision was made only with the teacher's return, not before, and the transfer and retention satisfied genuine educational concerns of all parties. Nonetheless once the Board and teacher recognized that it was in the best interest of the students to retain what was first the replacement it is clear that she was being conceived as "the teacher." Thus she was entitled to the rights, and subject to the duties as such.

A teacher is either on a permanent track, which embraces the test of probation, or is an occasional teacher. This is the extent of legislative, and collective agreement, contemplation. However, as the teaching relationship is contractual, it is possible for the teacher, provided there is no conflict, to be operating under two or more separate contracts. Thus a teacher may be a part-time teacher (as an expression of the proportion of a position that the teacher holds), and an occasional or supply teacher at the same time, or on educational leave and supplying by means of a second contract.[15]

To be eligible to be employed as a teacher in a school, one must, of course, hold the requisite qualifications in accordance with Regulation 262, section 20, and Regulation 269 under the Education Act.

Having met the qualifications required by the regulations, having been employed under the form of contract required by the Education Act and these regulations, a teacher will still find a good deal of the employment relationship governed by the Act and regulations. For example, section 235 of the Education Act and section 21 of Regulation 262 set out extensive duties to be complied with by teachers. At the same time the Act and regulations provide the teacher with a number of rights.

R.R.O. 1980, Regulation 269, has been amended since 1980 and reference should be made to O.Reg. 415/81, 567/82, 288/83, 27/84, 231/84, 451/84, 474/84, and most recently 157/87 and 703/87.

Teacher Evaluation

Discipline begins and ends with the employee's personal record. Its essence lies in the negative impact it may have on the employee's future. Discipline establishes or begins the record in the form of warnings, or in our context negative teacher evaluations. When discipline is applied in a severe form such as dismissal, courts may turn to an examination of that record to ascertain if it sustains the necessity of severing the relationship, or other chosen penalty.

As a first consideration, one must consider then, whether the teacher's conduct "in its totality, or in any particular, was incompatible with or inimical to the continuance of the employment relationship."[16] The tests or doctrines that would establish this are contained in the personal record.

The significance of the record is best seen in two doctrines: first, the doctrine of progressive discipline, and second, that of the culminating incident. The concept of "progressive discipline" may be illustrated by two citations from arbitrations concerning teachers, which also set the concepts limitations.

Accordingly, what must be stressed is that the graduated punishments convey the relative importance of the misconduct on which they are predicated, and thereby permit the employee to guide his future course of conduct.[17] Incremental discipline allows the parties to document and keep track of the relative harmony within the relationship.

The culminating incident is, in total, "the straw that broke the camel's back." The doctrine holds that once the employee has engaged in any act of misconduct, however slight (called the final incident), which exposes him to discipline, the quantum imposed by a way of a climax may be traced and justified via the employment record. On the employer's part the record is being brought forward on the premise that it is checkered and blameworthy such that it sustains the action.

Implied as a condition precedent to the evocation of the doctrine is that a final incident of misconduct exist. As the significance of that incident standing alone need only be slight, it is sufficient that it only merit a written warning to justify recourse to the record. Nonetheless it must first be shown to exist in fact. The doctrine applies to all discipline, not just to discharge, and is broad enough that the culminating incident itself need not be the same as that to be found in the record.

There is consensus that identifying valid criteria of "teaching success" is an imperfect process. For all the effort there is still a paucity of empirical research on the evaluation techniques which possess reliability (production of consistent results) and validity (measurement of what the instrument purports to measure, that is, adequate teaching). Research continues to reflect the importance of the evaluator's preference for a particular style of teaching and the influence on evaluators of oral comments that lead them to expect either excellent or poor performance.

Personnel evaluation or the periodic appraisal of teaching performance is partially interested to ensure a quality teaching staff. It must really be considered a positive process, not an excuse to punish. Results of evaluations may be used in a variety of employment decisions, including dismissal, promotion, sometimes salary, reassignment, and possibly retention.

The most pervasive method employed to demonstrate that the teacher has been apprised of the contents of any report is to have it signed by the teacher who is its subject. Caution, however, should be taken in making much of this procedural technicality. On the teacher's part signing the report is usually meant to attest to the fact that the teacher has "read" the report, not that he attests to its veracity. Unless the collective agreement states otherwise, if the teacher regards the report as incorrect in any substantial way, the wiser approach is not to sign it until it is corrected. Nor is any annotated or written appendix a wise course, even where the report allows for, or solicits, comments.

Where a collective agreement establishes evaluation procedures these must be strictly adhered to. This may be as simple as insistence of notification to the teacher of the filing of an adverse report, or any holding to the letter of the agreement in the name of procedural fairness.

It should be noted that at the root of procedural fairness in employment is the provision for correction, for the opportunity to improve. Where boards have been attestive to evaluation requirements, challenged employment decisions have been upheld by the courts.[18]

Allowances must be made for the subject being taught, its intrinsic motivation to students in the class, the construction of that class, and, in short, those elements of classroom composition that are so critical to the creation of proper order and learning environment.

A common objection is inaccuracies made as to the length of the supervisory visit or inspection. This is particularly objectionable where remarks are made on the basis of classroom visitations commenced after the period is in progress, and assumptions being either erroneously projected, or potentially such, without the supervisor being in a position to properly so ascertain. On the other hand the fact that the visitation is brief does not disqualify its being relied on. The consistent general principle is that the reports must be prepared from the personal observations of their author. The gravity or seriousness and relevancy of the incidents cited in an evaluation report have been scrutinized, and struck from the record were remarks as to simple errors in language, and whether the teacher made use of the chalkboard, as well as a misunderstanding surrounding certain administrative forms.

An evaluation report must be as objectively permeated as possible. Failure to meet such tests will normally allow the report to be corrected or amended to reflect a more accurate picture. It is, of course, recognized that reports are part of an on-going process.

The primary objective of teacher evaluation is to improve teachers' performance. If the evaluation does not produce this positive result the teacher may be replaced, by resignation or termination.

Depending upon the nature of a teacher's contract, various degrees of procedural due process must be observed in relieving a person of the job. Due process does not shield them from termination. Incapable or insubordinate teachers can be terminated. Due process requirements simply prescribe procedures which must be followed in effectuating those terminations. Of course, the allowable grounds for termination will usually be enunciated in the teacher's contract and/or a collective bargaining agreement.

In termination hearings, principals are often met with the claim that there is too little documentation or evidence of help being given to the teacher. In other cases the claim is made that the principal has developed so much documentation that the teacher has been harassed. At other hearings complaints are made that the process is unfair and that the teacher did not know what was expected in the performance of his or her duties. As a result of these attacks, there has been an unwillingness to recommend termination to boards. Often the principal, not the teacher, is on trial.

Proper documentation is founded on the concept of communication. Its goal is to humanize the evaluation and documentation process with the ultimate objective of improving a teacher's performance to an acceptable level. If a teacher's performance does not improve, the system is designed to provide an incentive for voluntary resignation or provide the necessary documentation for the principal recommending termination to the Board.

Courts are reluctant to substitute their judgement into the teacher evaluation process. The main concern is that criteria must be applied uniformly and consistently. An opportunity and direction for improvement must be provided and procedures specified must be followed.

The Documentation System

The documentation contemplated in a teacher evaluation system involves the use of several types of written memoranda.

(1) First, *memoranda to the principal's file* should be used sparingly to record less significant infractions or deviations by a teacher.

(2) Second, *specific incident memoranda* should be used to record conferences with a teacher concerning a more significant event.

(3) Third, *summary memoranda* should be used to record conferences with a teacher in which several incidents, problems, or deficiencies are discussed.

(4) Fourth, *visitation memoranda* should record observations made of a teacher's on-the-job performance.

(5) Fifth, an *assessment instrument* should be used to evaluate the teacher's overall performance.

The documentation concerning a teacher can and should be used for several purposes. First, it enables the principal to follow a teacher's actions and performance, thus enabling the principal to pinpoint weaknesses and problem areas. Second, it enables the teacher to understand what problems he or she may have and take what corrective steps are necessary. Third, if a teacher's performance does not improve, it serves as concrete evidence to support a recommendation for termination.

1. Memoranda to the File

File memoranda can be used for the following:

(1) Conference with the teacher concerning the incident or incidents; (2) Assessment of the teacher's performance; (3) Refreshing the memory of the principal for testimony at any proceeding or hearing relative to the teacher's performance if the memos have not been incorporated into summary memoranda or the evaluation documents.

These file memoranda should be used sparingly and only for minor matters. If an incident is in any way serious the specific incident memorandum should be used.

2. Specific Incidents Memoranda

If the principal observes an incident or behavior, or receives a complaint from a third party, it may be appropriate to send the teacher a memorandum concerning the incident. This memorandum should be sent only after the principal meets with the teacher at which the incident is discussed. The memo should summarize the third party's complaint, the principal's observation(s) of the action by the teacher, the teacher's response, the principal's determination, and any directives and/or reprimands to the teacher. If the incident is so serious that termination should be recommended immediately, the memorandum should say so.

It is wise to have the teacher acknowledge receipt of the specific incident memorandum by signing a copy. If the teacher does not agree with the facts stated in the memorandum or the action taken, he or she should be given the opportunity to respond in writing either on the memorandum itself or on a separate document.

It is important to establish on the face of the specific incident memorandum that the teacher received a copy of the document. In teacher termination hearings, a dispute will often arise over whether the teacher ever received a copy of some document.

3. Summary Memoranda

Summary memoranda are ideal ways to outline the results of conferences concerning several incidents, classroom visitations, or a conference regarding general teacher performance. A copy of each summary memorandum should be given to the teacher and the teacher should acknowledge receipt as with the specific incident memorandum. The teacher should again be invited and be given an opportunity to offer any differences in writing with the facts and conclusions stated in the memorandum.

4. The Assessment or Evaluation Document

The assessment or evaluation of performance document should be completed as prescribed by policies and procedures. A summary narrative or memorandum should be considered for each assessment document or on an attachment to the evaluation itself.

In order to avoid difficulties with any ratings on an evaluation, a teacher should not be rated highly or too positively when he or she is initially employed or assigned to a school. Rather, a straightforward and truthful evaluation should be made. It is much easier to raise evaluations in subsequent years than it is to lower high ones.

5. The Close Out Memorandum

Occasionally, a teacher will write a response to the memorandum if he or she disagrees with the facts or directives set out. When this occurs, it is incumbent on the principal to hold a conference with the teacher and work out any differences. At some point, however, the memorandum writing must be brought to a close, and, in normal circumstances, the sending of the follow-up memorandum to this conference may be an appropriate time.

Documentation in General

It is the quality of the memorandum and not the quantity of words or the number of pages that counts. Directives given in a memorandum should be direct and to the point. For example, when directing a sometimes tardy teacher to arrive at school on time, state: "You are required to be at school by (time) and you will be expected to have signed in by that time," rather than, "You are required to be at school on time." Instead of directing that: "Your lesson plans are due once a week," one might state, "Your lesson plans are due in my box by 4 p.m. on each Friday, and I expect you to have them there beginning this Friday." When written in a constructive atmosphere, precise directives like these tend to clear the air and avoid real or imagined confusion about what is expected.

The specific incident memorandum, the summary memorandum, the visitation memorandum, and the assessment document should be written in the first person and be personalized as much as possible. The use of "we" or "they" should be avoided unless two or more persons are involved and then the others should be identified by name. The key to the success of this documentation system is to provide an opportunity for the principal and the teacher to sit down and mutually work out the problem and determine the future actions of the teacher.

Evaluating Termination Options

Before a final recommendation is made to the board concerning a teacher's contractual status, the principal and his or her superintendent should hold a conference with the teacher. The teacher should be confronted with his or her inadequacies or problems and be given an opportunity to explain his or her position. This is a hedge against misunderstandings of the basic reasons for the proposed termination, and it offers the teacher a chance to present his or her side before a final recommendation for termination is made to the board. This will give an opportunity to consider any additional facts or viewpoints a teacher may present, examine the situation more closely, and determine whether termination is the proper alternative.

If there is actually a personality conflict between the principal and teacher, rather than a professional performance problem, a transfer to another school or department might be appropriate. In many cases, it will be appropriate to give the teacher specific directives and cite the teacher to specific policies which, if violated, could result in a recommendation for immediate termination in the future.

Discipline

Discipline, including the discharge of teachers, is dealt with today in collective agreements. Many collective agreements contain clauses similar to: "A teacher may be disciplined only for just cause."

Prior to Bill 100, in the case of discipline short of termination, there was very little restraint on the power of a board to discipline a teacher. If a potential termination was involved, a teacher, whether probationary or permanent, did have certain rights to be warned and to be given assistance. For example, section 12 (3) (f) of Regulation 262 states that the principal of a school shall:

> "(f) recommend to the board,
>
> (i) the appointment and promotion of teachers, and
>
> (ii) the demotion or dismissal of a teacher whose work or attitude is unsatisfactory, but only after warning the teacher in writing, giving the teacher assistance and allowing the teacher a reasonable time to improve."

In the case of actual dismissal or termination, permanent teachers are also given the right to apply to the Minister of Education for a Board of Reference.

The following are some examples of disciplinary action that might be taken against a teacher:
(i) written warning;
(ii) suspension; and
(iii) demotion (in the case of a teacher holding a position of responsibility).

There has been some question as to whether a board of education could impose a suspension without pay. That question has now been answered in the affirmative in the case of **Re Board of Education for the City of Hamilton and Ontario Public School Teachers' Federation.** Where there is a clause in the collective agreement to the effect that discipline may only be imposed for "just cause," any disciplinary actions may be challenged through the grievance procedure and by arbitration.

Termination

Perhaps the most important question to the employment relationship is what constitutes cause for the dismissal of a teacher? Is there cause for dismissal?

In Ontario, where in most cases a teacher may elect to remedy his dismissal either through grievance or board of reference, one arbitrator noted:

> In substance, the grievor was dismissed, and the real question before us is whether that dismissal was for just cause.
>
> In coming to our conclusion on that issue, of course, it is the arbitral jurisprudence on just cause which we should apply, not the common law jurisprudence; the parties having chosen arbitration as a mechanism for resolving cases of dismissal, they must be taken to have intended the carefully developed body of disciplinary awards.

Nothing takes us more swiftly to the heart of the current evaluation of the employment relationship than a consideration of insubordination as cause for dismissal. Generally the employee warrants that he will not harm his employer, and while the question of public criticism arises more from the employee's obligation to protect his employer's best interests, rather than the duty to obey a lawful order, it has been suggested that the implied duty to obey is better understood in modern times as an example of the contractual duty of co-operation.[19] Educators understanding of insubordination descends from statute where the common law language of an intentional "refusal or neglect to obey a lawful order of the board," or "insubordination" itself, was stated as statutory cause for dismissal.

Common law understanding may first be quickly sketched by reference to two Alberta Boards of References heard by McFayden J.[20] In **Bozynski v. St. Albert Protestant Separate School**, he stated:

> At common law an employer has the right to direct what work shall be done by his employees provided that the work directed is lawful and reasonable and within the terms of the contract of employment.[21]

Once again limitations are established, namely, "lawfulness," "reasonableness," and "within the scope of employment." On application of this standard, insubordination was found to justify the dismissal of the appellant in **Keegstra v. Board of Education**[22] as he wilfully and persistently ignored School Board directives ordering him to modify his teaching. McFayden J. found:

In continuing the teaching practices I outlined earlier (teaching his own highly prejudiced view of history) the respondent (*sic*) refused to comply with the lawful and reasonable direction of his employer. The appellant also refused to comply with the Alberta Social Studies curriculum.

. . . these constitute sufficient cause for summary dismissal at common law.[23]

At common law, therefore, the approach is one of treating disobedience as a breach of the implied duty to obey and then measuring the right to terminate for repudiation on the seriousness of the breach and the employee's intention.[24] The critical question becomes whether the act was a minor disobedience or a willful one of some substance.[25] Insubordination, as a direct affront to the employer's right to manage, is regarded as a serious offence,[26] for which discharge or at least a period of suspension[27] may be anticipated. Monnin J. A. established an appropriate tone relative to the seriousness of insubordination:

> It would not be tolerated in ordinary commercial enterprises, in government sectors, in public corporations and in non-profit or benevolent associations. I see no reason why school boards should have to accept that kind of insubordination from teachers. . . . What was exhibited was serious insubordination which warrants more discipline than a simple order of suspension, no matter how long that suspension be. The board was empowered to suspend, but I find it was absolutely correct and the evidence warranted a discharge for good, proper, and just cause.
>
> . . . [U]nqualified insubordination, such as is visible on this record, cannot with impunity be brushed aside and the blame placed on the shoulders of the principal and superintendent to whom respect and obedience was due. On the basis of so-called provocation on their part, the pair did not cause the eruption. The events were the act of the teacher alone.[28]

Emerging from his remarks is that the essence of insubordination lies in the contempt given the employer's directions.

That contempt is usually expressed in an intentional refusal to co-operate or carry out an order. First, it is essential that the employer prove that the order was not only given, but understood. A request, for example, is not an order, nor would be the passing on of expectations from district office, nor is it clear if the person in the position of responsibility takes a joking stance.[29] Second, the communication must not only be clear but must stem from someone with proper authority. Ostensibly, numerous individuals from chairpersons through to the Minister of Education may purport to exercise authority over the teacher. Usually, however, that person will be at the level of immediate supervision, and most clearly is the building principal.[30] What will be tested is whether the person has the actual authority, which includes those in acting positions, and whether the grievor is cognizant of that authority.

Third is the actual disobedience itself. As a starting point insubordination, while a refusal, is not to be confused with inability.

A distinction must be made between a failure to carry out orders and a failure to undertake to implement orders. Refusal to follow instructions may be defended on the basis that: (1) the request is an illegal act; (2) it jeopardizes health or safety; (3) the grievance is remedially incompetent; or (4) the order is an affront to reason. The onus is on the teacher to show that he or she properly communicated the reasons for their refusal to those in authority. There must have been a "reasonable order," an order that deserved obedience. One application of reasonableness is in any personal appearance or attire regulations adopted by the employer.

Off-Duty Conduct

One's obligations are then not totally severed while off-duty. It is anticipated that behavior will remain consistent with the continuity of particular employment. Under the just cause umbrella incompatibility with continued employment, or irreparable injury to the employer's interests, must be adduced. Therefore the employer's right to make rules concerning off-duty conduct is subject to the rule's legitimate connection with his or her business.

The essential rationale from which reasonable supervision of the teacher's off-duty conduct springs is his or her inescapable role model function. A bridge must be established between the board's complaint and the teaching relationship itself. Teachers share, in common with all employees, the natural response that would flow from somewhat obvious off-duty acts where the nexus is clear; acts such as assaulting supervisory staff, sexual assault, or trafficking in narcotics, for example. The crucial consideration, however, is the particular purpose for which the teacher has been hired.

Immorality and Crime

It is generally accepted that the employer may demand a reasonable moral standard among its employees.[31] Indeed, arising out of the "corruption" element in sexual-criminal jurisprudence is that it is usual where those employees are teachers to strike that expectation more emphatically.

Immorality committed while one is on duty is, then, clear grounds for dismissal.[32] The proper penalty for impropriety committed off duty is less clear. What must be considered is the effect the immoral behavior will have on the employment relationship, particularly how it is perceived by parents, students, and colleagues.

Sexual misconduct is connotated by the term immorality, and is grounds in any employment for at least discipline.[33] In schools even the appearance of sexual misconduct may be subject to discipline. Indeed, if boards suspect one's mental or emotional health is such that it might impose a sexual threat to students, it may have a proper case to require a psychiatric examination. Nor is the concern[34] simply a factor of a student's young age or of unlawfulness.

It cannot be claimed that a teacher's marital status or off-duty personal living relationships are beyond employer concern, or confined to separate schools and issues of denominational cause.[35] That is, a distinction may be made between a life-style embracing morality generally and the life-style or morality of a particular denomination.

As immoral behavior shades into or becomes criminal, it is easier to be certain of the permissible employer response. Should a teacher, or any employee, be convicted of a criminal act that touches on his or her employment such that it puts his or her employer's property or public image at risk, he or she may be dismissed.[36] It is the employer's legitimate interests that are important, thus it is not relevant that the teacher was off-duty.[37] However, if the facts demonstrate criminal acts to have taken place, but charges are not brought, dismissal may still be an appropriate response. If the teacher is dismissed because of the premise of a crime having been committed, or a criminal conviction *per se*, and is then found to be innocent, or is granted a discharge, then the dismissal cannot stand. However, the court's decision does not in itself dictate reinstatement. On acquittal, if there remains a reason for the employer to do so, he may require an explanation from the employee about the circumstances out of which the charge arose.

Alcohol and Drugs

There is not only a concern for a board's reputation, but also for the health and safety of the teacher and students, particularly in labs, gyms, or industrial shops. Discipline is rooted in more than just morality.

The alcoholic problem is not, however, apt to be one of reporting to work impaired (although this may be the culminating incident). It consists in a general deterioration of efficiency and escalating absenteeism. As the employee should be on duty, the focus moves from a concern with off-duty conduct to one of illness or disease, and the relationship between manifest conduct and continued employment. Whether a physical incapacity results in placing the alcoholic beyond the ability to meet the qualification of fitness for employment is the issue.

Conceptually, marijuana use by an employee may be treated like alcohol, except that it is immediately complicated by the fact that its possession is a crime.[38] However, first its use on the job has been held to be just cause for dismissal where its impairment properties would jeopardize safety, or where no mitigating factors interceded.[39] More importantly for teachers, and stemming directly from the criminal component, is that conviction for possession of cannabis has in itself been accepted as just cause for dismissal loosely akin to that levelled at the drinking teacher.[40]

Dismissal is a recognition that the teacher's conduct has been such that it has irretrievably damaged the employment relationship. A common law repudiation of a contract sufficient to justify dismissal is analysed in terms of the importance of the obligation breached, the intention to be found, and whether the incident is an isolated one.[41]

Attention should also be focused on the implied duty of co-operation. It may be that an employee is perpetually antagonistic toward his employer without good reason. This may lead first to discipline and ultimately to an employment breakdown. Co-operation is not merely with the employer, but, of necessity, extends to mutuality necessary to work with colleagues engaged in what is in reality teamwork. Moreover this would extend to a willingness and ability to work co-operatively within the total teaching environment, and would not be intended to alienate students, parents, or any organization or institution with which the school is coupled. When co-operation begins to fail it is clear that if it cannot be restored discharge is a response.

"Termination" means not only a termination because a teacher's work or attitude is unsatisfactory but also a termination because of redundancy.

Regardless of why someone is terminated, there are many technical requirements that a board must observe if it wishes to terminate a teacher. For example, in the case of both probationary and permanent teachers, the statutory forms of contract provide that termination can only take effect on certain dates, that written notice of termination must be given, and that such written notice must be given by a certain date. In addition, in the case of a permanent teacher, the reasons for the termination must be stated in the written notice of termination.[42]

The rights that a teacher has following the termination will depend on a number of factors such as

> (i) whether the teacher is probationary or permanent,
>
> (ii) whether the collective agreement has a clause which only permits a board of education to terminate for just cause, and if so, whether such clause distinguishes between probationary and permanent employees and
>
> (iii) whether, in the case of a Roman Catholic separate school board, denominational cause is involved.

A permanent teacher who is terminated has the right to apply for a Board of Reference. Section 239 (3) of the Education Act provides that:

> (3) Where a teacher (defined for this section to mean a permanent teacher) is dismissed or the contract of a teacher is terminated by the board or the teacher, the teacher or board if not in agreement with the dismissal or termination may at any time within twenty-one days after receiving the notice referred to in subsection (1) or (2), as the case may be, apply in writing by registered letter to the Minister for a Board of Reference, stating the disagreement."

If the Minister agrees to the request, a three-person Board is constituted with a District Court Judge as the Chair. The Board of Reference's mandate is then to "inquire into the matter in dispute" and ultimately it must either:

> ". . . direct the continuance of the contract or the discontinuance of the contract."[43]

Whether a probationary teacher will have any remedy in the case of termination will depend on whether he or she is covered by a clause in the collective agreement that requires that terminations be for just cause. If there is such a clause and it does not distinguish between probationary and permanent teachers, the probationary teacher may be allowed to grieve and arbitrate the termination of his or her contract. (See **Re Board of Education for the Borough of Scarborough and Ontario Secondary School Teachers' Federation, District 16.**)

In the case of a permanent teacher, who may be able to grieve and arbitrate a termination as well as apply for a Board of Reference, most collective agreements provide that the teacher must choose one route or the other. An example of such a provision is:

> "Any matter to which the Board (i.e., the board of education) or the Teacher may have a right to a Board of Reference shall not be subject to this grievance procedure, unless and until a Board of Reference has been refused, or until the application for the Board of Reference has failed or has been waived under the provisions of the Education Act . . ."

Special consideration may apply in the case of Roman Catholic separate school boards if the cause for the termination involves a denominational reason. This can be demonstrated from the case of **Re Essex County Roman Catholic Separate School Board and Porter et al.**[44] In that case two teachers were dismissed by a separate school board for contracting civil marriages. A Board of Reference ordered their contract to be continued and the school board applied for judicial review. The divisional Court set aside the decision of the Board of Reference and the teachers appealed to the Court of Appeal.

The Court of Appeal held that separate school trustees had a right to dismiss teachers on denominational grounds in 1867 and that this right was preserved by section 93(1) of the British North America Act, 1867 (now the Constitution Act, 1867), which provides as follows:

> "93. In and for each Province the legislature may exclusively make Laws in relation to Education, subject and according to the following Provisions:
>
> (1) Nothing in any such Law shall prejudicially affect any Right or Privilege with respect to Denominational Schools which any Class of Persons have by Law in the Province at the Union:"

Notwithstanding the Legislature may not require a separate school board to have a termination for denominational cause inquired into by a Board of Reference, a separate school board can agree in a collective agreement that a teacher may seek arbitration of a dismissal for denominational cause by agreeing to a clause that prohibits dismissal without just cause. (See **Re Essex County Roman Catholic Separate School Board and Tremblay — Webster et al.**) In order to avoid such a result, many separate school boards follow up a "just cause" clause with an additional sentence to the effect that the "just cause" clause does not apply in the case of a dismissal for denominational reasons.

Principals and Vice-Principals

For any principal the daily practical realities of the position's broad supervisory function over a school's operation confirms an incumbent as the first line of fire for parents, teachers, students, and the board. The role as captain, rather than manager of the team, has prevailed. That inclusion is consistent with the evolution of the position of the principal. The genesis of the principal's duties is that the principal is first of all a teacher. It is, of course, the principal's expertise as a teacher that is really relied upon to create an effective school.

The importance to the principal of such employment status is that it affords him full recourse to the employment security of the collective agreement. The principal's status flows from the fact that collective agreements usually refer to the position of principal as one held by a teacher.

The principal is *primus inter pares*. It is his additional duties that make him first among equals, and that characterizes the position as one added responsibility. In turn, this additional workload is appropriately measured and recognized within the collective agreement by a higher salary. In this way the collective agreement recognizes the principal's administrative duties.

The principal, in preparing records of attendance and in reporting to an attendance counsellor, may properly be said to be performing administrative duties. Where teachers make calls with respect to the daily attendance of pupils, however, they are performing tasks ancillary to their proper work, which includes the maintenance of discipline and the adequate reception of their teaching. This task is not considered within the scope of the "supervisory" duties properly required of a teacher. Again, the focus, as with all positions of responsibility, is on responsibility.

Principals and vice-principals in Ontario are in essentially the same position as ordinary teachers when it comes to ascertaining what are the rights of such persons and their employing boards with respect to hiring, discipline, and termination. Principals and vice-principals are covered by Bill 100. Reference must therefore be made to the collective agreement as well as the Education Act and regulations.

Principals and vice-principals also retain the legal status of teachers. As teachers, they will already be on the statutory form of contract. In the transition from ordinary teacher to principal or vice-principal, their terms and conditions of employment will, of course, change as reflected in the collective agreement and the applicable legislation.

To be employed as a principal or vice-principal of a school, a person, in addition to holding qualifications as a teacher, must hold principal's qualifications under Regulation 269 relating to the Education Act of Ontario.

As with teachers, the Education Act and regulations set out extensive duties to be complied with by principals and vice-principals. See, for example, Education Act, section 236 (Duties of principals), and Regulation 262, section 12 (Duties of principals), section 13 (vice-principals).

Most comments made in dealing with the discipline and termination of teachers apply also to principals and vice-principals. Since they are covered by Bill 100, as are teachers, principals and vice-principals should be afforded whatever protection is contained in the collective agreement with respect to the discipline of teachers. Principals and vice-principals might be disciplined by way of written warnings, suspensions, or demotions. Since they would presumably be on the form of permanent teacher contract, a principal or vice-principal would also have the right to apply for a Board of Reference.

Non-teaching staff might be disciplined by way of warnings, suspensions, demotions, and ultimately, discharge or termination. Assuming such employees are unionized, their rights to challenge the employer's actions will depend on whether the collective agreement contains a "just cause" clause. If it does, then, of course, disciplinary actions can be challenged through the grievance procedure and arbitration. Employees not covered by collective agreements who felt they had been unjustly discharged would have the common law right to sue for damages for wrongful dismissal.

Life-Style Choices

Recently, teachers have challenged boards' authority to restrict personal life-style choices. As we can see the courts have attempted to balance the privacy interests of a teacher with that of a board's legitimate interests in safeguarding the welfare of the student and the management of the school.

What is "proper"? What is "socially acceptable"? What is legal? The answers to such questions have changed dramatically. Alternative life styles have gained acceptance. People's hair styles, clothing, places of residence, and leisure-time activities have become recognized as extensions of their personalities. Individualism has led to concepts of individual rights being strengthened.

General tolerance for individual rights can be chronicled in terms of changes in laws restricting personal freedom.

Changes in attitudes and laws have had considerable impact on the lives of teachers. Communities have often taken an active interest in the public as well as private lives of teachers. A teacher's friends, visitors, socializing, dancing, drinking, worshipping, marrying, and parenting were all considered legitimate concerns of school authorities. Teachers were expected to consume inconspicuously and to refrain from offending local business interests. They were expected to be non-political and non-partisan.

Today, teachers have private lives. They can make significant choices in their life styles. Boards cannot justifiably regulate *every* phase of a teacher's existence.

This is not to say that there are no limits on a teacher's personal freedom. Some *legitimate demands* associated with the job have been recognized by the courts. Schools representing the public may require employees to conform to certain rules or regulations as a condition of employment. The public may reasonably expect teachers to conform to particular moral or socio-cultural standards as a condition for entrusting minor children to the care of the school.

What are the *limits to teachers' rights* to pursue their own life styles? Two issues are relevant: (1) How does a given behavior affect students, co-workers, or the school? (2) How important is the behavior or activity to the teacher's sense of self?

Is the harm so great that no interest of the teacher can justify the teacher's activity? Or is the teacher's interest in the activity so important to his or her sense of self that the school ought to adjust to it? Is a particular living arrangement such that it would offend community norms and have an adverse effect on students? Courts not only consider the conduct in question but also the notoriety surrounding the conduct and its impact on teaching effectiveness.

138

A teacher's private life is protected. A teacher's adherence to conventional behavior in public is expected. Deviations from the norm are noticed. Some curiosity about the sex lives of teachers is unavoidable. Sexual behavior is at the core of "morality" for many people. Parents and other citizens may be legitimately concerned about the moral standards of those who teach. Schools have been viewed as islands set apart from the real world. The island protected students from the harsh realities of life, work, and sex. School authorities and their most vociferous clientele groups have preferred to maintain the image of traditional family morality despite widespread evidence of divorce, teen pregnancies, and even promiscuity.

It does not follow that school authorities are free to fire any teacher who is involved in an unconventional sexual relationship. The courts have recognized changes in prevailing attitudes and behavior. They have conceded that sexual relations outside marriage do not compromise the moral integrity of the teacher. The standard recognized by the courts is that of harm to students or school.

There can be little evidence that the student or the school has been harmed as long as sexual behavior remains private and personal. However, any disclosure can diminish a teacher's right to privacy. Teachers who intentionally expose their private lives to public view may forfeit their right to privacy. The same is true if they expose their private behavior indirectly. If others expose a teacher's private behavior, their motives for doing so are relevant. Courts have supported teachers whose isolated incidents of misconduct were exposed for malicious motives.

Conduct Required Today

Two married teachers were recently found guilty of misconduct under the B.C. School Act when a husband's photograph of his semi-nude wife was published in a sex magazine. The British Columbia Court of Appeal affirmed the couple's four-week suspension by a school board.[45]

The court's December 1987 decision said the question was not whether the photograph of Ilze Shewan, nude from the waist up, was obscene, but whether the publication of such a photograph of a teacher in such a magazine would have an adverse effect upon the educational system, a system to which teachers owe a duty to act responsibly.

The matter arose when John Shewan's photograph was published in the February 1985 edition of *Gallery* magazine, a publication "designed to exploit sex, and to be devoted to the display of the private parts of a female form."

The Shewans had sent the picture to the magazine as part of a contest. All the contestants were women, posing nude in various positions. If the contestant's photograph was published, she would receive $50 and be eligible to win a prize.

When the Board of School Trustees of School District 34 (Abbotsford) found out about the published picture, it suspended both Mr and Mrs Shewan for six weeks.

The couple appealed their suspension to a three-person Board of Reference. The majority ruled that while the couple's actions had shown "an appalling lack of judgement," they did not amount to misconduct under

s. 122(1)(1) of the School Act. (Section 122 (1)(a) provides a school board may suspend a teacher at any time with or without pay for misconduct.) The board appealed the Board of Reference's decision to the B.C. Supreme Court where Mr Justice John Bouck rejected the Board of Reference's test for misconduct. He said the proper question was whether the teachers' conduct was within the moral standards recognized in the community where they were employed. The key ingredient was whether the act of misconduct affected the teacher in his educational capacity. Applying this test, Mr Justice Bouck concluded there has been misconduct under s. 122(1)(a). Nevertheless, he still reduced the six-week suspension to four weeks. The couple appealed.

The Shewans argued Mr Justice Bouck had exceeded his powers as an appellate judge by substituting his own view of what was misconduct for that held by the majority of the Board of Reference.

However, the Court of Appeal felt Mr Justice Bouck had not reversed the Board of Reference's findings of fact but instead had concluded, as a matter of law, that the Board had applied the wrong standard in measuring the teachers' conduct. As a result, said the appeal court, Mr Justice Bouck was entitled to make the order the Board of Reference should have made if it had applied the correct test. The Court of Appeal then turned to the main issue before it: the meaning of "misconduct" in s. 122(1)(a).

The term includes conduct both on and off the school grounds, said the court. The reason for this is that a teacher holds a position of trust, confidence, and responsibility.

"If he or she acts in an improper way, on or off the job, there may be a loss of public confidence in the teacher and in the public school system, a loss of respect by students for the teacher involved, and other teachers generally, and there may be controversy within the school and within the community which disrupts the proper carrying on of the educational system."

What conduct is necessary to achieve that purpose is not necessarily what moral conduct will be tolerated in a particular community. The minimum standard of morality which will be tolerated in a specific area is not necessarily the same standard of behavior that a school teacher must meet. The behavior of the teacher must satisfy the expectations which the community holds for the educational system. Teachers must maintain the confidence and respect of their superiors, their peers, and, in particular, the students, and those who send their children to our public schools.

The court went on to say that teachers must not only be competent, but are expected to lead by example. Any loss of confidence or respect will impair the system, and have an adverse effect upon those who participate in or rely upon it. That is why a teacher must maintain a standard of behavior which most other citizens need not observe because they do not have such public responsibilities to fulfil.

The court noted that when the matter was published there was controversy both in the school and in the community with attendant disruption of the educational system.

The court said the nature of the magazine was also relevant. It said that while Mrs Shewan's pose was modest compared to others in the magazine, it was to be inferred that she knew it was wrong to display herself in that way in that company, and that such conduct was well below the standard expected of teachers.

The court considered the Shewans' argument that Mr Justice Bouck had erred in imposing a longer suspension than the ten-day suspension the Board of Reference minority would have imposed. But the appeal court said that as the Board of Reference majority had not determined the length of suspension appropriate in the circumstances as it had not found misconduct, it was open to the court to make the order the Board of Reference should have made, or to remit the question to it. Was the penalty imposed upon the Shewans appropriate or not? It said the board was entitled to impose a suspension which would show that such conduct by other teachers would not be tolerated.

Notes

1. Somora v. Liberty School Division [1928], 2 D.L.R. 334 (Alta. D.C.).
2. The Education Act, R.S.O. 1980, c. 129 s. 10(1) para 10.
3. Re OECTA and Bishop et al. (1976), 70 D.L.R. (3d) 56, at 65 (C.A.).
4. Agassiz School Division No. 13 v. Hooge (1981), 14 Man. R. (2d) 222 at 230 (Man. Q.B.).
5. Re Porcupine Area Ambulance Service and C.U.P.E. (1974), 7 L.A.C. (2d) 182.
6. Cormier v. Board of School Trustees District 19 (1974), 8 N.B.R. (2d.) 330 (N.B.C.A.).
7. Bursa v. Lloydminster School Unit (1979), 5 Sask. R. 396. (Q.B.).
8. See Re Clark and Board of Education of Toronto, [1947] O.W.N. 878 and Re Edmonton Public School District No. 7 and ATA (1976), 72 D.L.R. (3d) 7.
9. Shaw v. Cooper (1984), 27 A.C.W.S. (2d) 326 (N.S.S.C.).
10. Ames v. Board of Trustees of Rocky Mountain School Division No. 15 (1981), 11 A.C.W.S. (2d) 72 (Alta. Q.B.).
11. The Education Act, R.S.O. 1980, c. 129, s. 1(1) 30.
12. Arnold v. Atlantic Institute of Education (1981), 29 Nfld. & P.E.I.R. 197 (P.E.I.S.C.).
13. Kaleva v. Com-Nu Enterprises Ltd. (1983), 23 A.C.W.S. (2d) 221 (Ont. Co. Ct.).
14. Wright v. Hamilton Board of Education (1977), 16 O.R. (2d) 828.
15. Corry v. Board of Trustees of Calgary School District No. 19 (1982), 37 A.R. 185, aff'd 144 D.L.R. (3d) 519.
16. R. Hanscom (No. 1) the NSTF and Treasury Board, District 31 (1976), unreported P.S.L.R.A. at page 18.
17. Board of Education for Scarborough v. Picher (1982), 37 O.R. (2d) 348.
18. Kudasik v. Board of Directors, Port Allegany School District, 455 A. 2d 261 (Pa. 1983).
19. Re Etobicoke Board of Education and OSSTF (1981), 2 L.A.C. (3d) 265.
20. Bozynski v. St. Albert Protestant Separate School District No. 6 (1982), 38 A.R. 93 (B.of R.).
21. Ibid. at p. 100.
22. Keegstra v. Board of Education County of Lacombe #14 (1983), 45 A.R. 348 (B. of R.).
23. Ibid. at 356.
24. Laws v. London Chronicle (Indicator Newspapers) Ltd., [1959] 2 All E.R. 285 (C.A.).

25. See Roe v. Weston Printing & Publishing Ltd. (1955), 37 M.P.R. 113 (NFLD.S.C.).
26. See, for example, Re United Automobile Workers and Huron Steel Products Ltd. (1967), 18 L.A.C. 220.
27. Re Board of Education for the City of Hamilton and OPSTF (1984), 13 L.A.C. (3d) 27.
28. Wheaton v. Flin Flon School Division No. 46. (1980), 4 Man. R. (2d) 420 (Man C.A.).
29. Re United Automobile Workers, Local 636, and Holland Hitch of Canada Ltd. (1972), 23 L.A.C. 378.
30. See Johnston and Ferry v. Board of Trustees, School Dist. 35 (Langley) (1979), 12 B.C.L.R./(B.C.S.C.).
31. Pliniussen v. University of Western Ontario (1983), 2 C.C.E.L.1 (Ont. Co. Ct.).
32. Re See Campbell and Stephenson (1984), 44 O.R. (2d) 656 (Ont. Div. Ct.).
33. Re Indusmin Ltd. and United Cement, Lime & Gypsum Workers (1978), 20 L.A.C. (2d) 87.
34. See, for example, Yang v. Special Charter School District No. 150 (1973).
35. See Mahoney v. Newcastle Board of School Trustees (1966), 61 D.L.R. (2d) 77 (N.B.S.C.A.D.).
36. Re Evershed and the Queen in Right of Ontario (1984), 44 O.R. (2d) 763 (Div.Ct.). Appeal dismissed (1985), 50 O.R. (2d) 198 (C.A.).
37. Re Etobicoke Board of Education and OSSTF (1981), 2 L.A.C. (3d) 265.
38. See University of Regina and C.U.P.E. (1979), 79 C.L.L.C. 199.
39. See Halton Board of Education and OPSMTF (1979), 60 (023) E.R.C.
40. See Beckwith et al. and Allen v. Colchester-East Hanok Amalgamated School Board (1978), 23 N.S.R. (2d) 268.
41. *Supra* note 24..
42. See The Education Act, R.S.O. 1980, c. 129, s. 239 (1).
43. Ibid., ss. 243 and 244.
44. (1979), 21 O.R. (2d). 255 (C.A.).
45. Board of School Trustees of School District #34 (Abbotsford) v. Shewan (1988), 8 A.C.W.S. (3d) 164. Appeal from 26 D.L.R. (4th) 54 dismissed.

9

Education and the Canadian Charter of Rights and Freedoms

On 17 April 1982, Queen Elizabeth II proclaimed the Constitution Act on Parliament Hill in Ottawa. Canadians had finally come of age. Canadians now had their own constitution, one not fashioned in a foreign land by an impersonal government and subject, theoretically, to amendment without consulting the Canadian government, but one made in Canada designed to fulfil Canadian aspirations.

More important, Canadians now had a Charter of Rights and Freedoms, modelled somewhat after the American Bill of Rights. Of course, not everyone then, or today, feel that we need a Charter of Rights and Freedoms.

The idea of a constitution which safeguarded fundamental inalienable rights against raw parliamentary power was carried to the American colonies.

Steeped in British tradition, which revered the concept of the supremacy of parliament, the early provinces of Canada gave little thought to the necessity of a Bill of Rights which would impose any limitations on their legislatures.

On 12 February 1867, the British North America Act was given its first reading in the British House of Lords and passed by that House on 26 February. The same day it was introduced into the House of Commons where it received little interest from the members. It finally passed a third reading on 8 March and was given royal assent on 29 March 1867.

By the middle of this century, it became evident that Parliament and the provincial legislatures could not be counted upon to protect fundamental freedoms.

Since the courts had no Bill of Rights to fall back on, the Supreme Court of Canada turned to the concept of *ultra vires* in determining the constitutional validity of the Bank Taxation Act, the Credit of Alberta Regulation Act, and the Accurate News and Information Act. In what became known as the *Alberta Press* case,[1] the Supreme Court of Canada struck down the first two statutes as attempts to regulate banks and banking and trade and commerce, matters that were within the exclusive jurisdiction of the Parliament of Canada.

Until the 1940s, there was little momentum in Canada for a Bill of Rights. The first political party to espouse a Bill of Rights in Canada was the Co-operative Commonwealth Federation (C.C.F.) party in 1945, moved by a C.C.F. member of the House of Commons, Alistair Stuart. The first government to enact a Bill of Rights was the C.C.F. government in Saskatchewan in 1947. In 1946 John Diefenbaker took up the cause and vigorously pursued it until his election as Prime Minister in 1957. The following year he moved the introduction of Bill C-60, a Bill of Rights. After two years of study the Canadian Bill of Rights became a reality and came into force on 10 August 1960.

Unfortunately, the Bill was only an Act of Parliament. Like other statutes passed by that legislative body, it was not constitutionally entrenched and could be amended by a simple majority. Furthermore, it was not binding on any of the provinces. Although the wording of the Bill was similar in many respects to the Charter of Rights and Freedoms, it was considered by the courts more as an instrument assisting in the interpretation of statutes rather than declaration and guarantee of fundamental rights. Indeed, in the more than two decades that span the Bill of Rights and the Charter of Rights and Freedoms, there have been few instances where the Supreme Court of Canada struck down federal legislation because it contravened the Bill of Rights.

The Canadian Charter of Rights and Freedoms is not only unique in Canada's constitutional framework, it is also somewhat foreign to the English concept of constitutional monarchy. No longer are Parliament and the provincial legislatures supreme within their own jurisdictional field. Every piece of legislation which they pass must be consistent with the provisions of the Charter otherwise they are of "no force or effect." Section 52 of the Constitutional Act admonishes Parliament and the provincial legislatures to recognize that "The Constitution of Canada is the supreme law of Canada."

Section 32

Section 32(1) of the Charter goes even further. It requires the Government of Canada and of each province to respect the rights and freedoms listed in the Charter. This was pointed out recently by our highest court in *Operation Dismantle Inc. v. The Queen*.[2] Operation Dismantle Inc. and twenty-two other labor and peace organizations sought an order from the courts prohibiting testing of the cruise missile in Canada on the grounds that it posed a threat to the lives and security of Canadians by increasing the risk of nuclear war. It was argued that by so doing, section 7 of the charter, which guarantees everyone the right to life, liberty, and security of the person, has been infringed. Counsel for the government argued that the courts had no right to scrutinize and strike down decisions made by the Cabinet.

Chief Justice Dickson of the Supreme Court of Canada disagreed. As far as he was concerned, the executive branch of the Canadian government is duty bound to act in accordance with the dictates of the Charter and the courts were duty bound to ensure that the executive did just that. However, he went on to find that in this case section 7 had not been infringed by the cabinet because it had not been established that there was, in fact, a threat to life and security of Canadian citizens. The allegation was based merely on hypothesis and speculation.

The Charter does not apply to the actions of parliament and the legislature alone but to a wide variety of quasi-governmental and non-governmental activities. Section 32(1) of the Charter states:

> (a) to the Parliament and government of Canada in respect of all matters within the authority of Parliament including all matters relating to the Yukon Territory and Northwest Territories; and

> (b) to the legislature and government of each province in respect of all matters within the authority of the legislature of each province.

Section 32(1) indicates that the Charter applies to federal and provincial governments and legislatures. The section may be interpreted as limiting the effect of the Charter to public or state actions, as opposed to the actions of private individuals.

Although cases can be found in which the Charter was applied to private individuals, the second approach to s.32 has been adopted in Canada; see **Retail, Wholesale and Department Store Union, Local 580 et al. v. Dolphin Delivery Ltd.**[3] This decision explicitly affirmed the decision of the Ontario Court of Appeal in **Blainey v. Ontario Hockey Association**[4] and implicitly affirmed a host of other cases that restricted the application of the Charter to government.

In **Dolphin Delivery Ltd.**, the appellant union sought to apply the Charter to have an injunction barring secondary picketing removed. The parties involved were purely private and the injunction had been granted under the common law, and, in particular, to prevent the common law tort of inducing a breach of contract. McIntyre J., whose discussion of the application of the Charter was approved by all members of the Court, determined that the Charter did not apply to this situation. He stated that "government" in s.32 means "the executive government of Canada and the Provinces:"[5]

> It is in my view that s.32 of the Charter specifies the actors to whom the Charter will apply. They are the legislative, executive and administrative branches of government. It will apply to those branches of government whether or not their action is invoked in public or private litigation. It would seem that legislation is the only way in which a legislature may infringe a guaranteed right or freedom. Action by the executive or administrative branches of government will generally depend upon legislation, that is, statutory authority. Such action may also depend, however, on the common law, as in the case of prerogative.

A broad approach to the notion of government was taken by Hogg in **Constitutional Law of Canada**, 2nd ed. (1985),[6] where he stated on page 671:

> It follows that any body exercising statutory authority, for example, the Governor in Council or Lieutenant Governor in Council, minister, officials, municipalities, school boards, universities, administrative tribunals and police officers, is also bound by the Charter. Action taken under statutory authority is valid only if it is within the scope of that

authority. Since neither Parliament nor a Legislature can itself pass a law in breach of the Charter, neither body can authorize action which would be in breach of the Charter.

A number of courts have followed this reasoning and applied the Charter to a body because it was exercising statutory authority. One such decision with the particularly full discussion of the issue is **Re Lavigne and Ontario Public Service Employees' Union.**[7] A community college teacher challenged a provision that required compulsory payment of union dues by non-union members that was contained in the collective agreement between the Ontario Public Service Employees Union, representing the community college teachers, and the Council of Regents, which was statutorily designated as the bargaining agent for the employer community colleges. Mr Lavigne, who was not a member of the union, argued that his rights under s.2(b) and (d) of the Charter were violated by the provision in the collective agreement. After reviewing academic commentaries and the Charter decisions of the Supreme Court of Canada, White J. opted for a "purposive" test for determining when a Crown agency is engaging in a governmental action and concluded:

> . . . I am prepared to hold that governmental action does include the entering into a contract by a Crown agency pursuant to powers granted by statute in the context of the facts at bar. To hold otherwise would be to permit "government", as identified in s.32(1) of the Charter, to impose terms in a contract that it would not impose by statute or regulation because they breach the Charter. Such an arrangement would defeat the purpose of the Charter.
>
> The Charter of Rights is concerned not only with governmental action that has as its purpose the abridgement of Charter rights, but it also regulates situations where the effect of the governmental action is to deny an individual his or her guaranteed rights or freedoms.

He set out a general purposive test:

> . . . I conclude that it is the purpose of the Charter to permit review of situations where a governmental actor acts in such a way that the effect of its action, whether such action be of a legislative or administrative nature, potentially infringes a value protected by the Charter.[8]

Justice White held that the clause in the collective agreement was subject to scrutiny under the Charter because the Council of Regents had engaged in governmental action when it agreed to include the provision in the collective agreement.

The Charter does recognize that the rights and freedoms listed in it are not absolute. There may be instances where those rights and freedoms must give way to other interests that are reasonable and can be demonstrably justified. Section 1 of the Charter, as we shall see later in more detail, recognizes that the rights and freedoms listed in it must be

> . . . subject only to such reasonable limits prescribed by law as can be justified in a free and democratic society.

What are reasonable limits? Each can only be assessed and determined in the light of the circumstances under which a particular right or freedom is sought to be curtailed. But what is clear from the section is that the rights and freedoms listed in the Charter are paramount until limits are placed on them by legislation. Those limits must also be "reasonable." They must also be "demonstrably justified" as being reasonable limits which only can be tolerated in a free and democratic society. And it is up to the government to demonstrate that the limits that it wants to impose are reasonable. It is not up to the ordinary citizen to show that the limits upon his rights and freedoms are unreasonable.

Charter Case Law

In 1983 the Supreme Court of Canada began to receive requests for leave to appeal from litigants on the losing side of Charter decisions in the provincial courts of appeal and the Federal Court of Appeal. They raised novel questions of constitutional law involving the interpretation of such broad and general concepts as "the principles of fundamental justice," limits to rights that are "unreasonable" and "demonstrably justified in a free and democratic society," "freedom of conscience," and protection against "unreasonable search or seizure."

From its very first Charter decision, **Law Society of Upper Canada v. Skapinker**,[9] rendered on 3 May 1984, it was evident that the Supreme Court had a strong sense of the heavy responsibility it was assuming as the final interpreter of a written constitution which purported to guarantee the fundamental rights and freedoms of the people. In this first decision, Mr Justice Estey wrote the court's opinion and stated:

> We are here engaged in a new task, the interpretation and application of the *Canadian Charter of Rights and Freedoms*. . . . It is part of the constitution of a nation adopted by constitutional process which, in the case of Canada in 1982, took the form of a statute of the Parliament of the United Kingdom. The adoptive mechanisms may vary from nation to nation. They lose their relevancy or shrink to mere historical curiosity value on the ultimate adoption of the instrument as the Constitution.

While the Court had long experience with interpretation of the Constitution Act, 1867, and its division of power between governments, Justice Estey acknowledged that the Charter of Rights introduces a new dimension, a new yardstick of reconciliation between the individual and the community and their respective rights, a dimension which like the balance of the Constitution remains to be interpreted and applied to the Court.

Thus, it was recognized that now it was the Judiciary that had the task of developing the law. Estey referred to the famous case of **Marbury v. Madison**[10] in which the United States Supreme Court first asserted its power to overrule laws which conflict with the constitution as authority for the kind of responsibility the Court was now assuming. For guidance in exercising this power he cited the dictum of Chief Justice Marshall for a subsequent case that "we must never forget, that it is a *constitution* we are expounding." In interpreting a constitution which is to shape and serve the Canadian community for a long time, "Narrow and technical interpretation, if not modulated by a sense of the unknown of the future can stunt the growth of the law and the community it serves."

In several cases immediately following Shapinker the court upheld various Charter claims. In one case, **Protestant School Boards**,[11] it struck down the section of Quebec's Bill 101 which closed Quebec's English school system to children of citizens who had received their English education in the English-speaking provinces. The Court found this in direct violation of the "Canada clause" in section 23(1)(b) of the Charter guaranteeing Canadian citizens the right to educate their children in English and French wherever they move in Canada.

The Court's treatment of the Charter has not altogether been in the "activist" direction. An example is the Court's response in **Operation Dismantle**[12] to the attempt by a coalition of peace groups to use the Charter to overturn the agreement of the Canadian government to test the American cruise missile in Canada. The Supreme Court decided that this was not a proper question to bring before the courts. It did not base this decision on the "political questions" doctrine developed by the United States Supreme Court, according to which questions of foreign and defence policy may be too political to be reviewed by the courts. Chief Justice Dickson, writing for the majority, said he had "no doubt that disputes of political or foreign policy nature may be properly cognizable by the courts." Here the Court was indicating that Charter claims should be rejected by the judiciary when they turn on causal connections between challenged government policies and Charter rights involving complex determinations about future behavior which cannot be satisfactorily assessed through the judicial process.

The justices clearly sense that they have a much stronger mandate from the people to give greater force and substance to the Charter than was ever the case with the Canadian Bill of Rights. They would surely all agree with Justice Wilson's statement in **Singh** that the recent adoption of the Charter by Parliament and nine of the ten provinces as part of the Canadian constitutional framework has sent a clear message to the courts that the restrictive attitude which at times characterized their approach to the Canadian Bill of Rights ought to be re-examined.[13]

The difficulty facing courts in interpreting the Charter is in determining the interplay between rights which are constitutionally protected and equally entrenched provisions limiting and overriding those rights.

Such interplay is evident in the area of education. The Charter guarantees individual rights in s.2 (among others), wherein it provides for freedom of conscience and religion and freedom of thought, belief, opinion, and expression. At the same time, it states in s.29 that "Nothing in this Charter abrogates or derogates from any rights or privileges guaranteed by or under the Constitution of Canada in respect of denominational, separate or dissentient schools." How have the courts interpreted these provisions in cases where denominational school boards, in pursuits of their religious and moral principles, terminate contracts of teachers who prefer to follow their own conscience and beliefs even in violation of the school board's principles?

Application to Boards

At least some actions of school boards have been found to be governed by the Charter. In **Re Ontario English Catholic Teachers Association and Essex County Roman Catholic School Board**,[14] there was a challenge to the Board's mandatory retirement policy. The majority judgment of Mr Justice Anderson noted that school boards owe their existence to the Education Act and that their duties and powers are defined by it. Further, boards have the power to expropriate, levy rates, and can sue and be sued. He stated at page 561:

> In my view, it is fair to conclude that a school board is created under a comprehensive statute dealing with education and has a clearly defined role within the scheme of the statute, and to conclude in consequence that the actions of a board may properly be said to be, for the purposes of the Charter, the actions of the "legislature" or "government" of Ontario.

The court, however, decided in the end that the Charter did not apply to the mandatory retirement policy because the policy was not "law" within the meaning of ss.15(1) and 52(1) of the Charter. Leave to appeal to the Ontario Court of Appeal has been granted.

The reasoning, although not necessarily the result, in Re. English Catholic Teachers Association has been called into question by the decision of the Ontario Court of Appeal in **McKinney v. Board of Governors of the University of Guelph.**[15] The Court there specifically rejected the notion that a body is governmental because it derived from statute or government in some way. The focus instead was placed on the governmental nature or functions of the body in issue. As Justice Anderson noted, however, a school board in Ontario does have certain governmental powers such as expropriation and rate levying powers. This may attract Charter scrutiny to at least some of a board's activities.

In **Casagrande v. Hinton Roman Catholic Separate School District No. 155,**[16] the Court rejected a Charter challenge to a school board policy that teachers must follow Roman Catholic doctrines in their private lives.

In **J.M.G.,**[17] the Ontario Court of Appeal assumed without deciding that a school board, teachers, and principal of a school are subject to the Charter in their actions in dealing with the students. A student had been searched by a school principal, and the Court had to address whether his ss.8 and 10(b) rights had been violated. Mr Justice Grange stated:

> The argument of the respondents is that the school system (at least the public school (system)) is an extension of government. Principals act under the authority of the government and are therefore, in those actions, subject to the **Charter**. The argument of the appellants is that a principal, when imposing discipline, is in effect the alter ego and delegate of the child's parents. As parents have a common law right and duty to discipline their children for purposes of correction they may delegate parental authority to the schoolmaster.

> I do not find it necessary to decide this difficult issue. I am prepared for the purposes of this appeal to assume that the school board direct-

ing the affairs to the school and the school itself, including the principal and other teachers, are subject to the **Charter** in their actions and dealings with the students under their care.[18]

In **Sweet**[19] the District Court rejected an argument that the detention of the accused by a teacher violated his ss.7, 9, and 10(a) rights.

The Court in **Serup v. School District No. 57 Board of Trustees**[20] rejected a Charter challenge to a school decision not to allow the applicant to review books in the school library.

It was held in **H.**[21] that the Charter applies to the actions of teachers and principals who are the employees of school boards. After reviewing the case law and the academic commentary Provincial Judge Russell noted that school boards are the creatures of provincial legislation and that they exercise a delegated legislative authority. He concluded that the Charter was therefore intended to apply to the actions of the employees of such school boards.

Section 93 of the B.N.A. Act of 1867 empowered each provincial legislature to make laws in relation to education. It also protected denominational educational interests by forbidding any law that would prejudicially affect any right or privilege with respect to denominational schools which any class of persons held by law in the province at the date of union.

As time progressed governmental limitation on the educational entitlements of the Catholic Church widened in terms of the operation of separate schools. In **Ottawa Separate School Trustees v. Mackell,**[22] the Privy Council in 1917 declared valid the Ontario Board of Education's exercise of power to regulate the operation of separate schools in the province provided it did not interfere with "a right or privilege *attached to denominational teaching*" (italics added). In **Tiny Separate School Trustees v. The King,**[23] the appellant Catholic school board claimed, among other things, the right to select courses of study for their schools and refused to accept that the Department of Education had the power to make regulations for the control of courses of study taught in separate schools. The Privy Council thought otherwise. Insisting that the provincial legislature is supreme in matters of education, the Privy Council acknowledged that the province showed in earlier statutes the intention to preserve the power to mould the educational system in the interest of the public at large, as distinguished from any section of it, *however important.* Noting that separate schools were simply a special form of common schools, and that the Council of Public Instruction determined the courses to be offered and the extent of education to be imparted, the Privy Council perceived the power of regulation by the educational authorities to be even wider than the Supreme Court of Canada thought it to be.

This precedent was dealt with by the Supreme Court of Canada regarding Bill 30. It was ultimately the view that before Confederation separate schools were free to teach students prior to university level.

The right of denominational boards to impose their own criteria for teacher firing and hiring has been attacked in two areas, under provincial human rights legislation, and the insistence on determining teacher rights through collective agreements.

The preference for members of a religious denomination violating human rights of individuals was raised in the British Columbia case **Re Caldwell and Stuart et al.**[24] A commerce teacher and a Catholic, Caldwell complained of violation of the non-discrimination section of the Human Rights Code of British Columbia by the respondent principal and school board which denied renewal of her yearly contract after she married a divorced Methodist in a civil ceremony.

Ultimately the Supreme Court of Canada dismissed her appeal. This dismissal was based in part on the Court's distinction between reasonable cause for non-renewal or firing and a bona fide qualification. Accepting that religion or marital status cannot be relied upon as reasonable cause, the Court nevertheless noted that s.8 requires equality of opportunity based on bona fide qualifications in respect of employment. It found that the special nature of the Catholic school and the unique role of teachers justify religious conformance as a bona fide qualification. By not conforming Ms Caldwell lost her bona fide qualification and also s.8 protection. The Court further ruled that s.22 of the B.C. Code protected the continuation of denominational schools and their right to preserve their religious basis by hiring staff members who accept and practice Church doctrines. In this light her dismissal did not contravene the Code.

In **Reference Re Education Act of Ontario and Minority Language Education Rights,**[25] the Ontario Court of Appeal held that the rights and privileges preserved by section 29 of the Charter are those protected by s.93 of the Constitution Act, 1867, and that there is therefore no conflict between those rights and privileges and the rights conferred by section 23 of the charter.

With regard to section 23 of the Charter, the court stated that the section enacted new rights and in effect created a code which established minority language education rights for the country. The rights conferred applied equally to the public and to the denominational systems of education. Again with reference to section 23, the court said that the quality of education to be provided the minority is also to be equal to that provided to the majority.

In **Mahe et al. v. The Queen in right of Alberta,**[26] the Alberta Court of Appeal struck down the School Act, R.S.A. 1980, c. S-3 as being inconsistent with section 23 in that it failed to accord to citizens of Canada who qualify under subsections (1) and (2) the right to exercise a degree of exclusive management and control over French-language instruction for their children. Having regard to section 29 of the Charter the Alberta court found that the pre-Confederation rights and privileges relating to the language of instruction in Alberta schools do not constitute rights or privileges in respect of denominational, separate, or dissentient schools within the meaning of section 29 and therefore could not limit the application of section 23. In this case it was the application of section 23 to a combined elementary and junior high school in Edmonton, Alberta. There were 242 students whose parents' first language was French, unlike of course schools with French immersion.

Does the "equality" section of the Charter, section 15, apply with respect to denominational rights in education? In **Casagrande,**[27] the Alberta Court of Queen's Bench found that section 15 had no application to a separate school board's dismissal of a teacher on the ground that she had engaged in conduct prohibited by the teachings and doctrine of the Catholic Church.

The court stated that section 29 in effect immunizes from Charter review the right to dismiss for cause, which formed part of the constitutional right to establish separate schools granted to Roman Catholics in Alberta by s.17 of the Alberta Act, 1905 (Can.), c.3.

In **Reference Re an Act to Amend the Education Act,**[28] the Supreme Court of Canada held on 25 June 1987 that section 29 rendered immune from Charter review not only the rights and privileges protected by s.93(1) of the Constitution Act, 1867, but also rights and privileges conferred by legislation passed pursuant to the province's plenary power in relation to education under the opening words of s.93. The protection of the latter class of rights and privileges lay not in the guaranteed nature of the rights and privileges conferred by the legislation but in the guaranteed nature of the province's plenary power to enact the legislation. Thus the 1986 legislation, Bill 30, in Ontario providing for full funding for the separate school system to the end of high school was constitutionally valid.

Since it was never intended that the Charter could be used to invalidate other provisions of the Constitution, particularly a provision such as s.93 which represented a fundamental part of the Confederation compromise, this section was not required in order to immunize from Charter review legislation in relation to denominational, separate, or dissentient schools. It was included for greater certainty, simply to emphasize that the special treatment guaranteed by the Constitution to such schools was not impaired by the Charter.

Also, since both rights and privileges protected by s.93(1) of the Constitution Act, 1867, and legislation enacted pursuant to the province's plenary power under the opening words of s.93 in relation to denominational, separate, or dissentient schools are immune from Charter review, the Supreme Court of Canada stated that section 15 had no application to the legislation providing full funding to Roman Catholic separate high schools. The court went on to say that Canada was founded upon the recognition of special or unequal educational rights for specific religious groups in Ontario and Quebec. It suggested that the educational rights granted specifically to the Protestants in Quebec and the Roman Catholics in Ontario at Confederation render it impossible to treat all Canadians equally.

This case is a good example of the impact of the Charter on education. Before 1982 of course "Education," under the division of powers pursuant to section 93, was clearly provincial and to challenge either provincial or federal legislation one would have to show that the legislation in question was outside the powers of or *ultra vires* the legislature or Parliament.

Under s.23, which has been alluded to, parents in English Canada have the right to instruction for their children in French if they satisfy three conditions:

(1) Canadian citizenship;
(2) (a) parents must have learned French first and still understand it; or
(b) the primary school instruction of children must have been in English or French primary or secondary schools in Canada;
(3) the numbers of children entitled to the right must be "sufficient to warrant" public funding.

Section 23 is silent as to what numbers are sufficient to warrant minority language educational rights.

It is evident therefore that the adoption of the Charter has removed the question of the language of education from the exclusive jurisdiction of the provinces and elevated it to a matter of fundamental rights, enshrined in the constitution for the benefit of all of Canada.

It can readily be seen that a "battle" has developed since the Charter between the "Canada Clause" in section 23 of the Charter and the "Quebec clause" in section 72 of the Quebec Charter of the French language.

The Supreme Court of Canada found in the Protestant School Board of Greater Montreal[29] case that the language of education provisions of the Charter of French Language, R.S.Q. 1977, c.5, was inconsistent with section 23 and, assuming without deciding that 2.1 applies to the rights that this section confers, they cannot be saved by s.1. Since this section was specifically and deliberately adopted by the framers of the Charter to remedy the kind of language of education regime created by the Quebec legislation, the legislation could not possibly constitute a legitimate limit on rights within the meaning of s.1. The legislation, moreover, collided directly with this section in purporting to redefine the classes of persons entitled under the Charter to have their children instructed in English. The court stated that Section 1 cannot legitimize legislation that collides directly with a right guaranteed by the Charter or that constitutes exceptions or amendments to those rights.

In **Marchand v. Simcoe County Board of Education et al.,**[30] it was held that it was the potential rather than the actual enrolment of minority language students that determines entitlement to minority language instruction and minority language facilities provided out of public funds. Once numbers warrant the provision of minority language instruction and educational facilities out of public funds, the instruction and facilities to be provided must be equivalent to the instruction and facilities provided to majority language students. A mandatory order refusing the board to provide such instruction and facilities was awarded.

In **Jones v. The Queen,**[31] the Supreme Court of Canada held that the provisions of the Alberta School Act, R.S.A. 1980, c. S-3, which required every child of a certain age to attend public school unless excused for certain reasons, such as where a child is under efficient instruction at home as certified by the public school authorities or attending a private school approved under provincial legislation, did not offend the guarantee to freedom of religion.

The accused, Pastor Jones, the pastor-principal of Western Baptist Academy in Calgary, who had taught his children and other children in his church basement, claimed that the authority over his children and his duty to attend to their education came from God and that it would be sinful for him to request the state to permit him to do God's will. The Court said, however, that the School Act was a flexible piece of legislation which sought to ensure only that all children receive an adequate education. It did not offend the accused's freedom of religion that he was required under the statute to recognize a secular role for school authorities. Even assuming, the court indicated, that the legislation affected the accused's beliefs, not every effect of legislation on religious beliefs or practices is offensive to the guarantees provided. Three justices, Dickson C.J.C., Lamer and La

Forest JJ. held that while the School Act had a purely secular goal, if its effect was to interfere with the accused's religious activities or convictions then it raised another issue.

Assuming the sincerity of Jones's convictions that to apply for certification would involve acknowledging that the government rather than God has the final authority over the education of his children, then the effect of the School Act did constitute some interference with the freedom of religion of the accused. It was not for the court to question the validity of Jones's religious beliefs, notwithstanding that few shared it. Nevertheless, the state also has an important interest in the education of its citizens and it may, in advancing its compelling interest in the education of the young, place reasonable limits on the freedom of those who, like the accused, believe that they should themselves attend to the education of their children and should do so in conformity with their religious convictions.

A requirement that a person who gives instruction at home or elsewhere have that instruction certified as being efficient was considered to be a demonstrably justified limitation within the meaning of s.1. A further requirement that the person in question apply for certification constitutes a minimal or peripheral instrusion on religion. To permit anyone to ignore it on the basis of religious conviction would create an unwarranted burden on the operation of the legitimate legislative scheme to assure a reasonable standard of education.

Jones argued further that the provisions of the School Act violated section 7 of the Charter. The court said that the provision under which he was charged in this case did not *per se* violate the claim to liberty and would do so only if those charged within its administration used it as a device for unduly infringing on such liberty. That, however, is not what occurred in this case. In her dissenting opinion, Justice Bertha Wilson held that the accused's right to liberty as guaranteed by this section was infringed.

Justice Wilson indicated that the effect of the legislative scheme is that the accused was precluded at trial from introducing any evidence of efficient instruction other than the certificate from the public school authorities. The government, according to Justice Wilson, had not established that this was a reasonable limitation within the meaning of s.1.

Re Zylberberg[32] also dealt with section 2(a) of the Charter. Here the Court found that section 28(1) of Ont. Reg. 262/80, made under the Education Act, did not infringe this paragraph in requiring that a public school be opened or closed each school day with religious exercises consisting of the reading of the scriptures or other suitable readings and the repeating of the Lord's Prayer or other suitable prayers. By s.28(10) of the regulation, no pupil shall be required to take part in any religious exercises. Having regard to the exemption provided by s.28(10), the regulation does not compel or coerce religious observance so as to infringe freedom of religion. An appeal to the Ontario Court of Appeal is pending at this writing.

In **Serup v. School District #57 Board of Trustees,**[33] the court dealt with "freedom of expression" under section 2(b) of the Charter. Here the court found that there was no infringement of freedom of expression in placing conditions on a parent's access to her child's school library for the purpose of determining the suitability of the books that are found there. Alternatively, if there is an infringement, it was justified under section

154

1 of the Charter in view of the potential for interference by non-students with the educational function of the school.

Section 11(d) of the Charter states that "any person has the right to be presumed innocent until proven guilty. . . ." Section 122(1)(b) of the B.C. School Act, R.S.B.C. 1979, c.375, authorizing a school board to suspend a teacher where the teacher has been charged with a criminal offence and where the board believed that under the circumstances he should not continue with his duties, did not offend this section since section 122(1)(b) did not presume that the teacher was guilty of the charges against him. Additionally, the court found that his life, liberty, or security of the program was threatened pursuant to section 7 of the Charter.

What about the relationship between trade unions and its members?

In **Tomen v. Federation of Women Teachers' Association of Ontario,**[34] Mr Justice Ewaschuck of the Supreme Court of Ontario rejected an argument that a by-law of the Ontario Teachers' Federation compelling membership of women public school teachers in the Federation of Women Teachers' Associations of Ontario was governed by the Charter. The applicants argued that the by-law was not merely private law because it controls the collective bargaining process of elementary and secondary schools. The Court, however, looked to see if the by-law was a "governmental matter," reasoning to the contrary.

In **Cromer and B.C. Teachers' Federation**[35] it was assumed that the Charter applied to the B.C. Teachers' Federation's Code of Ethics, which was made under a by-law of the federation pursuant to s.142 of the B.C. School Act, which authorized the federation to make laws governing the suspension and expulsion of members.

The court disposed of the case along the lines of matters of public concern vis-à-vis matters of personal interest. Cromer, a teacher and a member of the British Columbia Teachers' Federation, was charged by another teacher, Sauve, with criticizing her in breach of cl.5 of the Federation's Code of Ethics.

At a hearing before the judicial committee of the BCTF, Cromer objected that the charge was not proper because the application of cl.5 of the Code of Ethics would be a violation of her freedom of expression right under s.2(b) of the Canadian Charter of Rights and Freedoms. The judicial committee decided that the charge was proper. Cromer's appeal to a judge in chamber for judicial review was dismissed. The British Columbia Court of Appeal agreed to review the case.

Lambert J.A. stated that freedoms in general and the freedom of expression in particular is not absolute, is subject to the careful weighting and balancing of competing interests for all purposes or remains subject to the same balancing process against other and often compelling values.

The Court found that the Code of Ethics was designed to avoid disharmony among teaching colleagues and to promote the teaching milieu of the educational process. Criticism was not precluded but that it had to follow set procedures.

Cromer's freedom of speech rights to make personal criticisms about another teacher did not override the public interest good incorporated in the Code of Ethics designed to ensure harmonious working relationships amongst teaching staffs to deliver education most efficiently.

Legal Rights

Like many words in our language, the word *right* has several different meanings. In one sense, *right* refers to a state, condition, or situation which it is felt should be present.

In a second sense, *right* is used in the sense of a "legal right." Legal rights have been defined in various ways, but generally two important elements are present: (i) there is the capability of one individual to demand and require another to behave in a certain way; and (ii) legal enforceability. As *Black's Law Dictionary* phrases it, a legal right is "the capability in one man of controlling, with the assent and assistance of the state, the actions of others." A legal right, then, is a genuine entitlement, or a valid claim, that one person may make upon others.

Legal rights have their basis in law and are derived from a variety of legal sources. The common law provides certain rights such as those accorded to children in the *in loco parentis* doctrine. Contracts and contractual arrangements such as those found in collective agreements provide rights to the contractual parties. In addition, enactments of legally competent jurisdictions, together with regulations and orders-in-council provided for by statutes, provide legal rights that are referred to as statutory rights. Agencies established by statute, like departments of education, school boards, teachers' federations, and so on, have their areas of legal competence defined by the legislation establishing them, and are the sources of other legal rights. The Constitution itself, as we have seen, provides us with a further set of legal rights which are referred to as constitutional rights.

By definition, the possession of a legal right by a person implies a duty on the part of another. If a child, for example, has a statutory right to attend school then someone has the associated obligation to provide the facilities and services that this right implies. Thus a direct relationship exists between a right and a duty in the sense that the existence of one necessarily implies the existence of the other. A right implies a duty, and similarly a duty implies a right.

Rights may be stated in two equivalent ways: the first by a proposition invoking a right, the second by a proposition that invokes a duty. Thus a legislative statement of a duty such as "No teacher shall administer corporal punishment" is equivalent to a rights statement such as "Every pupil has the right not to be subject to corporal punishment."

Both our Charter and the U.S. Constitution contain textual provisions guaranteeing equality rights. The U.S. Fourteenth Amendment simply prohibits the denial by government of "the equal protection of the laws" to any person. However, the judicially developed equal protection doctrine has spawned what many U.S. constitutional writers refer to as the second American Revolution and has been used to dismantle the separate but equal system, to desegregate school systems, to require race and gender-conscious affirmative action programs, to aid traditional victims of societal discrimination, to strike down exclusionary zoning practices, and to redraw legislative apportionments.[36]

Equality

The Charter's provisions on equality rights can be found in Sections 15, 27, and 28, although Section 15 has become the most frequently litigated section. Section 15(1) appears to be broader, guaranteeing to the individual the right to be "equal before and under the law" and to the "equal protection and equal benefit of law." Section 15(2) recognizes the legitimacy of valid affirmative action programs. Section 27 recognizes as an interpretive guide to the Charter the principle of multiculturalism, and Section 28 guarantees sexual equality.

These equality provisions appear implicitly to incorporate a doctrine similar to the U.S. "suspect classification" standard of protection in that the rights are afforded protection against discrimination on the basis of "in particular: race, national, or ethnic origin, colour, religion, sex, age, or mental or physical disability." The words "in particular" would appear to leave it open for the court to scrutinize discrimination on any other suspect basis. While the cases have not yet found discrimination on another ground, no case has rejected the argument that there could be behavior which could be violative of s.15 on the basis of a classification not enumerated in the section. Furthermore, s.1 would seem to require that all government classifications be "reasonable."

In **Blainey**[37] the Ontario Court of Appeal stated that section 15(1) of the Charter, read as a whole, constitutes a compendious expression of a positive right to equality in both the substance and the administration of the law. It does not, however, require that every person in every instance be treated in precisely the same way. Its purpose, the court stated, is to require that those who are similarly situated be similarly treated, and the interests of true equality may well require differentiation in treatment. The court further indicated that this subsection does not reach private activity, but is confined to governmental action. Discriminatory actions by individuals are left to regulation by the common law, and of course, statutes and human rights codes. Similarly, the right to the equal protection and equal benefit of the law guaranteed by section 15(1), like all other rights and freedoms guaranteed by the Charter, is not absolute. A law which denies that right may nevertheless be constitutional if it can be brought within s.1.

Section 1

Critics have pointed to Section 1 as a potential source of subjective judicial remaking on the grounds that it allows courts to expand, or more likely, to contract the Charter's guaranteed rights on the basis of their personal perceptions of what is justifiable in a free and democratic society.

Section 1 states:

> The Canadian Charter of Rights and Freedoms guarantees the rights and freedoms set out in it subject only to such reasonable limit prescribed by law as can be demonstrably justified in a free and democratic society.

A leading case on the interpretation and application of s.1 is the decision of the Supreme Court of Canada in **Oakes.**[38] Chief Justice Dickson held there that s.1 has a dual nature:

> It is important to observe at the outset that s.1 has two functions: first, it constitutionally guarantees the rights and freedoms set out in the provisions which follow; and, second, it states explicitly the exclusive justificatory criteria (outside of s.33 of the Constitution Act, 1982) against which limitations on those rights and freedoms must be measured.

Each step in the application of s.1 must be taken in light of the reason why the allegedly infringed right is constitutionally entrenched. In **Big M Drug Mart,**[39] the Supreme Court affirmed that the basis of Charter interpretation is the "purposive" approach. Chief Justice Dickson stated, citing **Hunter v. Southam**[40] (S.C.C.), that,

> (T)he proper approach to the definition of the rights and freedoms guaranteed by the **Charter** (is) a purposive one. The meaning of a right or freedom guaranteed by the Charter (is) to be ascertained by an analysis of the **purpose** of such a guarantee; it is to be understood, in other words, in the light of the interests it was meant to protect. [emphasis in original]

The Supreme Court has subsequently affirmed that the purposive approach is the central element of Charter interpretation.

In Big M. Drug Mart, Dickson C.J.C. outlined the nature of this inquiry as follows:

> In my view, this analysis is to be undertaken, and the purpose of the right or freedom in question is to be sought by reference to the character and the larger objects of the Charter itself, to the language chosen to articulate the specific right or freedom, to the historical origins of the concepts enshrined, and where applicable, to the meaning and purpose of the other specific rights and freedoms with which it is associated within the text of the Charter. The interpretation should be, as the judgement in Southam emphasizes, a generous one rather than a legalistic one, aimed at fulfilling the purpose of the guarantee and securing for individuals the full benefit of the Charter's protection. At the same time it is important not to over-shoot the actual purpose of the right or freedom in question, but to recall that the Charter was not enacted in a vacuum, and must therefore, as this Court's decision in Law Society of Upper Canada v. Skapinker (1984), 9 D.L.R. (4th) 161, illustrates, be placed in its proper linguistic, philosophic and historical contexts.

Perhaps the most important issue of contextual interpretation is the significance of the existence of s.1. in the Charter for the interpretation of the specific rights and freedoms guaranteed therein. The central problem of constitutional adjudication under the Charter is the balancing of individual rights against the interests of society as a whole.

The grammatical structure of the Charter makes it difficult to argue that s.1 does not have universal applications. As stated in Oakes, s.1 is the only express constitutional guarantee of the rights and freedoms in the following provisions, and it states the exclusive justificatory criteria against which limitations on the rights and freedoms must be measured. The case law suggests that courts may properly resort to a wide variety of external sources as evidence of the purpose of particular rights.

It has been established that the courts may examine historical facts in a very broad context to determine why a particular right has been considered essential to the maintenance of freedom and democracy. In the *Reference Re Education Act of Ontario* (Ont. C.A.), the Court drew an analogy to the "mischief rule" of statutory interpretation.

One approach to the purpose of the right, approved and applied in Big M. Drug Mart, is a consideration of the results evident in history where the specific right has not been respected. Similarly, in Bryant (Ont. C.A.), Mr Justice Blair introduced a lengthy review of the historical context in which the right to trial by jury developed by saying:

> Trial by jury is an institution unique to common law countries. It is more than a mere incident of common law procedure. It had been described as a pillar of the constitution and praised as a palladium of liberty. . . . The true significance of the right to trial by jury can only be understood by reference to its history.

In **Reference Re S.94(2) of the Motor Vehicle Act (B.C.)**,[42] the Supreme Court of Canada directly addressed the issue of the significance of testimony before the Special Joint Committee as to the drafters' intentions and beliefs concerning the scope of 2.7 of the Charter. The Court held, adopting what it described as the recent trend towards a flexible standard of admissibility in constitutional matters, that parliamentary speeches, debates, and the proceedings of the Special Joint Committee were prima facie admissible as evidence in a purposive analysis of the Charter.

Section 1 of the Charter makes it clear that the rights and freedoms guaranteed therein are not absolute but rather are subject to such reasonable limits prescribed by law as can be demonstrably justified in a free and democratic society.

It must be remembered that Section 1 applies in one way or another to all of the rights declared in the Charter, and it may be the Charter's most important section.

Section 1 gives rise to two general questions: What is the relationship between Section 1 and the sections setting out rights and freedoms? and, What is the nature of the standards established by Section 1?

There are really two competing approaches. The first, the one-stage approach, assumes that Section 1 is a part of every section creating a right or is a guide to be used in evaluating the limits inherent in the various rights. In other words, one takes Section 1 into account while applying the section creating the right. The second approach, or the two-stage approach, involves first determining whether, apart from Section 1, a course of conduct infringes a right and, if it does, to move to a second stage at which Section 1 is used to determine whether the infringement is justified in the circumstances.

The one-stage approach is undermined by the way the Charter is organized. The fact that the limits appear in a separate section makes it natural to think of them as applying after it had been decided that a right seems to have been violated. Thinking in terms of one stage may have more practical effects. For example, section 28 provides:

> Notwithstanding anything in this Charter, **the rights and freedoms referred to in it** are guaranteed equally to male and female persons.

Using the one-stage approach, it is possible that the rights and freedoms referred to in the charter are rights that have been defined after taking into account Section 1 limits.

The two-stage approach has its own problems. Difficulty is caused in part by the fact that many sections which create rights themselves contain explicit limitations that seem to overlap Section 1. For example, Section 8 prohibits only "unreasonable" searches. Does Section 1 provide some further limitation on this right?

At one stage or another one must consider the limitations on rights described in Section 1. The experience to date tends to refute the allegations that the section will nullify rights more or less completely. Indeed, Section 1 may impose certain requirements that would not have been imposed without it. There is a two-stage procedure to be followed in determining whether a guaranteed fundamental right has been denied. An applicant must establish on the balance of probabilities a prima facie infringement of a fundamental right. Once this is done, the party seeking to uphold the limit has a positive obligation to establish that the limit is reasonable and demonstrably justified.

The second major stage in the test of reasonable justification under s.1 is the inquiry into whether the infringement is proportional to the goal.

A limit obviously cannot be justified if, once the purpose of the law has been determined, there is no evidence that the impugned law tends to advance it. Several laws have been struck down on this basis under the Charter. Although the overall goal of the legislation in question might be approved, the courts have held that the infringement of the right does not make the achievement of the goal any more probable.

In **Re Ontario English Catholic Teachers Association et al. and Essex County Roman Catholic Separate School Board**,[43] the Divisional Court of Ontario held that Section 15 of the Charter had no application to the termination by a school board of a teacher's contract of employment on the basis of the board's mandatory retirement policy. Section 15 relates to the rights and liabilities of the individual in relation to law, in the sense of a rule of conduct made binding upon a subject by the state. Neither the board's policy nor the resolution terminating the teacher's employment may be regarded as law in that sense.

The Charter in this case did not apply because the board owed its existence, duties, and powers to the Education Act, R.S.O. 1980, c.129, so that its actions could be said to be the actions of the legislative or government of the province of Ontario.

The purpose of the Charter is to protect the individual against actions or activities that impinge on the individual because they have behind them the power of the state. The relationship required is that of the subject to the state. The Charter does not apply unless the action or activity under review has the nature and quality of law. In particular, the Charter was not intended to restrict the power of government in matters of contract.

The relationship between the teacher and the board in this case was contractual relationship, that of employee to employer, and neither the board's mandatory retirement policy nor the resolution terminating the teacher's employment has the nature and quality of law. The fact that an action constitutes the exercise of a statutory power of decision within the meaning of s.1(f) and 2(1) of the **Judicial Review Procedure Act,** R.S.O. 1980, c.224, was irrelevant to the application of the Charter. In any event, the court said, s.15(1) could not be applied, since it addresses only the rights and liabilities of the individual in relation to the law.

Future Application

The Charter, as we have seen, does not confer rights of action as between private citizens. Such rights must be determined by the ordinary law, subject to the proviso that the statutory component of the ordinary law may be invalid to the extent that it purports to restrict constitutional rights.

With regard to the applicability of the Charter, even though the Charter does not apply to private action and therefore applies to governmental action, the courts have not yet indicated what constitutes governmental action. By the end of 1987 the Court of Appeal in British Columbia had indicated that the effect of the Charter is to do away eventually with mandatory retirement while the Ontario Court of Appeal has stated the opposite. In both instances here we are speaking of professors at postsecondary institutions, not the subject matter of this publication. Suffice to say, the matter ultimately will be dealt with by the Supreme Court of Canada. In particular, the British Columbia Human Rights Act was contrary to s.15(1) of the Charter.

As with the Charter, the ultimate source of some of the most important rights in the American Bill of Rights is the English common law tradition. The Bill has had an obvious influence in some respects on the drafting of the Charter. Where there is a clear identity of interest between specific rights in both documents, our courts have used American jurisprudence, relying on the lengthy American experience with constitutional adjudication, to help elucidate the purpose of rights guaranteed under the Charter.

However, it is also clear that American law cannot be applied automatically to the interpretation of Charter rights or to any other Canadian or provincial set of facts.

Another very important difference between the Charter and the Bill of Rights is the fact that the former document does not contain provisions comparable to ss.1 and 33 of the Charter.

It should also be noted that the nature of American federalism, in particular the division of powers between federal and state governments, has had a profound effect on the interpretation of the American Bill of Rights which, unlike the Charter, is not uniformly applicable to all sovereign powers under the Constitution. Depending on the state, local constitutional interpretations may differ markedly from federal interpretations. Because American law is not binding on Canadian courts one way or the other, it is suggested that constitutional interpretations from jurisdictions other than the federal system may also be useful in some cases in shedding light on the purpose of particular rights.

What remedies are available on challenges under the Charter? There are several possible conclusions which might be reached as a court goes through the necessary stages of analysis in a Charter challenge. These are:

(a) The impugned law might be held to be inconsistent with the fundamental nature of the right. No s.1 question arises in such a case.

(2) The right might be infringed, but the source of the infringement not be prescribed by law.

(3) The impugned law might be held to have a legislative purpose which is not inconsistent with the right, but which is not sufficiently compelling to justify an infringement of the right under s.1.

(4) The purpose of the law might justify infringement, but the particular form of the law might be unacceptable as being unreasonable in view of the object to be achieved.

A law may be unconstitutional, as being violative of a guaranteed right or freedom, in which case it is, to the extent of the inconsistency, of "no force or effect." This is in the nature of a declaratory judgment. Section 24 permits a person whose rights have been infringed to apply for a remedy from a court of competent jurisdiction.

All Charter litigation involves a choice between the competing interests of various individuals or groups in society. Is this because the state never acts in vain? When the state intervenes to regulate behavior it does so in order to advance the interests of identifiable individuals in society. If the Charter is used to restrict the state's ability to so act, the loser is not the state *per se* but rather those individuals who would have benefitted from the state regulation. What the courts are asked to do in Charter litigation is to balance those competing interests and to make a choice between them. As we gain more experience under the Charter I think it is useful and important to keep in mind the advice of Judge Learned Hand who many years ago pointed out the fallacy in looking to constitutions and to courts to protect individual freedom.

I often wonder whether we do not rest our hopes too much upon constitutions, laws, and courts. These are false hopes; believe me, these are false hopes. Liberty lies in the hearts of men and women; when it dies there, no constitution, no law, no courts can save it; no constitution, no law, no court can even do much to help it. While it lies there it needs no constitution, no law, no court to save it.

Notes

1. Reference re Alberta Statutes (1938), S.C.R. 100.
2. Operation Dismantle Inc. v. R. [1985] I.S.C.R. 441.
3. Retail, Wholesale and Department Store Union, Local 580 et al. v. Dolphin Delivery Ltd., [1987] 1 W.W.R. 577, [1986] 2 S.C.R. 573.
4. Re Blainey and Ontario Hockey Association (1986), 54 O.R. (2d) 513, leave to appeal refused (1986) 58 O.R. (2d) 274 (S.C.C.).

5. *Supra,* note 3 at 597-598.
6. Peter W. Hogg, *Constitutional Law in Canada,* 2nd ed. (Toronto: Carswell, 1985).
7. Re. Lavigne and Ontario Public Service Employees' Union (1986), 55 O.R. (2d), 449.
8. Ibid., at 480.
9. Law Society of Upper Canada v. Skapinker [1984] 1 S.C.R. 357.
10. Marbury v. Madison (1803) 5 U.S. (1 Cranch) 137.
11. A-G Que v. Association of Protestant School Boards [1984] 2 S.C.R. 66.
12. *Supra,* footnote 2.
13. Singh et al. v. Minister of Employment and Immigration [1985] 1 S.C.R. 177.
14. (1987), 58 O.R. (2d) 545, (Div. Ct.).
15. Re McKinney and Board of Governors of the University of Guelph et al. (1986), 57 O.R. (2d) 1..
16. (1987), 38 D.L.R. (4th) 382 (Alta. Q.B.).
17. (1986), 56 O.R. (2d) 705, leave to appeal refused (1987),59 O.R. (2d) 286 (S.C.C.).
18. Ibid., at 708.
19. (1986) 17 W.C.B. 395 (Ont. Dist. Ct.).
20. Serup v. School district No. 57 Board of Trustees (1987), 39 D.L.R. (4th) 754 (B.C.S.C.).
21. H. (1985), 43 Alta. L.R. (2d) 250 (Prov. Ct. Youth Div.).
22. Ottawa Separate School Trustees v. Mackell [1917] A.C. 62.
23. Tiny Separate School Trustees v. The King (1928) A.C. 363.
24. Re Caldwell and Stuart et al. [1984] 2 S.C.R. 603.
25. Reference Re Education Act of Ontario and Minority Language Education Rights (1984), 10 D.L.R., (4th) 491 (C.A.).
26. (1985), 22 D.L.R. (4th) 24.
27. *Supra,* note 16.
28. [1987] 1 S.C.R. 1148.
29. *Supra,* note 11.
30. Marchard v. Simcoe County Board of Education (1986), 55 O.R. (2d) 638 (Ont. H.C.S.), (1988), 61 O.R. (2d) 651.
31. Jones v. The Queen [1986] 2 S.C.R. 284.
32. Re Zylberberg et al. and Director of Education of Sudbury Board of Education (1986) 29 D.L.R. 4th 709, 55 O.R. (2d) 749 (Div. Ct.).
33. *Supra,* note 20.
34. (1988), 61 O.R. (2d) 489.
35. (1987) 5 W.W.R. 638 (B.C.C.A.).
36. See Frank C. Munro, "The Original Understandings of Equal Protection of the Laws", 50 *Columbia Law Review,* 131 (1950).
37. *Supra,* note 4.
38. R.v. Oakes [1986] 1 S.C.R. 103.
39. R.v. Big M. Drug Mart Ltd., [1985] 1 S.C.R. 295.
40. Hunter v. Southam Inc. [1984] 2 S.C.R. 145.
41. *Supra,* note 39.
42. Re British Columbia Motor Vehicle Act [1985] 2 S.C.R. 486.
43. *Supra,* note 14.

10

Conclusion

It is perhaps self-evident that our citizens are demanding greater accountability from public education and are certainly becoming more
knowledgeable in using legal tools to challenge any perceived arbitrary
practices.

School personnel will always have the most difficulty in situations where
there are no guidelines and no legislation or regulations to lead us. It is
here that you must make judgements based on your professional training
and general knowledge of the law as it relates to education.

Contrary to what may be the popular opinion, the scales of justice have
not been tipped against educators. School personnel have the authority
as well as the duty to make and enforce regulations that are necessary
to operate their schools and to maintain a proper environment.

One lesson to be learned repeatedly is that practices and policies that
are arbitrary or unjustifiably violate protected individual rights will not
be tolerated by the courts. Educators should sit down and identify and
effectively change those policies that may well generate legal interventions. Only with an increased awareness and understanding of basic legal
principles can all of us in the educational process develop more respect
for the law and those responsibilities that accompany legal rights.

Appendix A

Education Act

Revised Statutes of Ontario, 1980
Chapter 129

as amended by
1981, Chapter 47, ss. 17 to 21; 1982, Chapter 20,
s. 2; 1982, Chapter 32; 1984, Chapter 48, s. 21;
1984, Chapter 55, s. 216; 1984, Chapter 60;
1986, Chapter 19, s. 2; 1986, Chapter 21;
1986, Chapter 29; 1986, Chapter 64, s. 12 and
1987, Chapter 17, s. 3

Education Act

1.—(1) In this Act and the regulations, except where otherwise provided in the Act or regulations,

1. "adjoining" means touching at any point;

2. "average daily enrolment" for a calendar year means the average daily enrolment calculated in accordance with the regulations; R.S.O. 1980, c. 129, s. 1 (1), pars. 1, 2.

2a. "band" and "council of the band" have the same meaning as in the *Indian Act* (Canada); 1982, c. 32, s. 1 (1), *part.*

3. "board" means a board of education, public school board, secondary school board, Roman Catholic separate school board or Protestant separate school board;

4. "board of education" includes a divisional board;

5. "city" includes a separated town and the portion of a city that is in one school division;

6. "combined separate school zone" means a union of two or more separate school zones;

7. "county" includes a provisional county and united counties;

8. "county combined separate school board" means a separate school board established for a county combined separate school zone;

9. "county combined separate school zone" means a union of the separate school zones whose centres are within an area designated by the regulations that includes a county or all or part of a regional municipality that is not in a territorial district;

10. "county municipality" means a municipality, other than a city, that forms part of a county or regional municipality that is not in the territorial districts; R.S.O. 1980, c. 129, s. 1 (1), pars. 3-10.

10a. "credit" means recognition granted to a pupil by a principal as *prima facie* evidence that the pupil has successfully completed a quantity of work that,

    i. has been specified by the principal in accordance with the requirements of the Minister, and

    ii. is acceptable to the Minister as partial fulfilment of the requirements for the Ontario secondary school diploma, the secondary school graduation diploma or the secondary school honour graduation diploma, as the case may be; 1982, c. 32, s. 1 (1), *part*; 1984, c. 60, s. 1.

11. "current expenditure" means an expenditure for operating purposes or a permanent improvement from funds other than those arising from the sale of a debenture, from a capital loan or from a loan pending the sale of a debenture;

12. "current revenue" means all amounts earned by a board, together with the amounts to which it becomes entitled, other than by borrowing, that may be used to meet its expenditures;

13. "debt charge" means the amount of money necessary annually,

    i. to pay the principal due on long-term debt not payable from a sinking fund,

    ii. to provide a fund for the redemption of debentures payable from a sinking fund, and

    iii. to pay the interest due on all debt referred to in subparagraphs i and ii;

14. "defined city" means,

    i. the City of Hamilton,

    ii. the City of London, and

    iii. the City of Windsor;

15. "district combined separate school board" means a separate school board established for a district combined separate school zone;

16. "district combined separate school zone" means a union of the separate school zones whose centres are within an area in the territorial districts that is designated by the regulations;

17. "district municipality" means a municipality, except a city, in a territorial district;

18. "district school area" means a school section in the territorial districts that is not a school division or a school section designated under section 70;

19. "divisional board" means a divisional board of education;   R.S.O. 1980, c. 129, s. 1 (1), pars. 11-19.

19a. "education authority" means a corporation that is incorporated by two or more bands or councils of bands for the purpose of providing for the educational needs of the members of such bands;   1982, c. 32, s. 1 (1), *part*.

20. "elementary school" means a public school, Roman Catholic separate school or Protestant separate school;

21. "exceptional pupil" means a pupil whose behavioural, communicational, intellectual, physical or multiple exceptionalities are such that he is considered to need placement in a special education program by a committee, established under subparagraph iii of paragraph 5 of subsection 10 (1), of the board,

    i. of which he is a resident pupil,

    ii. that admits or enrols the pupil other than pursuant to an agreement with another board for the provision of education, or

    iii. to which the cost of education in respect of the pupil is payable by the Minister;   R.S.O. 1980. c. 129, s. 1 (1), pars. 20, 21.

22. "guardian" means a person who has lawful custody of a child, other than the parent of the child; 1982, c. 20, s. 2 (1).

23. "head office" of a board means the place at which the minute book, financial statements and records, and seal of the board are ordinarily kept;   R.S.O. 1980, c. 129, s. 1 (1), par. 23.

23a. "Indian" has the same meaning as in the *Indian Act* (Canada); 1982, c. 32, s. 1 (1), *part.*

24. "intermediate division" means the division of the organization of a school comprising the first four years of the program of studies immediately following the junior division;

25. "judge" means the judge of the county or district court of the county or district in which the head office of the board is situate;

26. "junior division" means the division of the organization of an elementary school comprising the first three years of the program of studies immediately following the primary division;

27. "locality" means a part of territory without municipal organization that is deemed to be a district municipality for the purposes of a divisional board or of a district combined separate school board;

28. "Minister" means the Minister of Education;

29. "Ministry" means the Ministry of Education;

30. "municipality" means a city, town, village, township or improvement district;

31. "occasional teacher" means a teacher employed to teach as a substitute for a permanent, probationary or temporary teacher who has died during the school year or who is absent from his regular duties for a temporary period that is less than a school year and that does not extend beyond the end of a school year;

32. "parcel of land" means a parcel of land that by the *Assessment Act* is required to be separately assessed;

33. "part-time teacher" means a teacher employed by a board on a regular basis for other than full-time duty;

34. "permanent improvement" includes,

     i. a school site and an addition or an improvement to a school site,

ii. a building used for instructional purposes and any addition, alteration or improvement thereto,

iii. an administration office, a residence for teachers or caretakers and a storage building for equipment and supplies, and any addition, alteration or improvement thereto,

iv. furniture, furnishings, library books, instructional equipment and apparatus, and equipment required for maintenance of the property,

v. a bus or other vehicle, including watercraft, for the transportation of pupils,

vi. the obtaining of a water supply or an electrical power supply on the school property or the conveying of a water supply or an electrical power supply to the school from outside the school property,

vii. initial payments or contributions for past service pensions to a pension plan for officers and other employees of the board;

35. "permanent teacher" means a teacher employed by a board under a permanent teacher's contract made in accordance with the regulations and includes a teacher whose contract is deemed to include the terms and conditions contained in the form of contract prescribed in the regulations for a permanent teacher;   R.S.O. 1980, c. 129, s. 1 (1), pars. 24-35.

35a. "Planning and Implementation Commission" means the Planning and Implementation Commission continued under section 136r;   1986, c. 21, s. 1, *part.*

36. "polling list" means a polling list as defined in the *Municipal Elections Act*;

37. "population" means the population as determined by the latest census taken under section 14 or 15 of the *Assessment Act*;

38. "primary division" means the division of the organization of an elementary school comprising junior kindergarten, kindergarten and the first three years of the program of studies immediately following kindergarten;

39. "principal" means a teacher appointed by a board to perform in respect of a school the duties of a principal under this Act and the regulations;

40. "private school" means an institution at which instruction is provided at any time between the hours of 9 a.m. and 4 p.m. on any school day for five or more pupils who are of or over compulsory school age in any of the subjects of the elementary or secondary school courses of study and that is not a school as defined in this section;

41. "probationary teacher" means a teacher employed by a board under a probationary teacher's contract made in accordance with the regulations;

42. "provincial supervisory officer" means a supervisory officer employed by the Minister;   R.S.O. 1980, c. 129, s. 1 (1), pars. 36-42.

42a. "public board" means a board of education or a secondary school board established under section 69;   1986, c. 21, s. 1, *part.*

43. "public school elector", in respect of an area for which one or more members of a board are to be elected by public school electors, means a public school elector under the *Municipal Elections Act*, who is qualified to vote at the election for such members in such area;

44. "regulations" means the regulations made under this Act;

45. "reserve fund" means a reserve fund established under section 165 of the *Municipal Act*;

46. "Roman Catholic" includes a Catholic of the Greek or Ukrainian Rite in union with the See of Rome; R.S.O. 1980, c. 129, s. 1 (1), pars. 43-46.

46a. "Roman Catholic school board" means a separate school board that has made an election under section 136a or 136f that has been approved by the Minister;   1986, c. 21, s. 1, *part.*

47. "rural separate school" means a separate school for Roman Catholics in a township or territory without municipal organization that is not part of a county or district combined separate school zone;

48. "rural separate school zone" means a separate school zone in respect of a rural separate school; R.S.O. 1980, c. 129, s. 1 (1), pars. 47, 48.

48a. "salary" means all payments and benefits paid or provided to or for the benefit of a person who is designated under section 136-1;   1986, c. 21, s. 1, *part.*

49. "school" means,

   i. the body of public school pupils or separate school pupils or secondary school pupils that is organized as a unit for educational purposes under the jurisdiction of the appropriate board, or

   ii. the body of pupils enrolled in any of the elementary or secondary school courses of study in an educational institution operated by the Government of Ontario,

and includes the teachers and other staff members associated with such unit or institution and the lands and premises used in connection therewith;

50. "school day" means a day that is within a school year and is not a school holiday;

51. "school division" means the area in which a divisional board has jurisdiction;

52. "school section" means the area in which a public school board or board of education has jurisdiction for public school purposes;

53. "school site" means land or interest therein or premises required by a board for a school, school playground, school garden, teacher's residence, caretaker's residence. gymnasium, offices, parking areas or for any other school purpose;

54. "school year" means the period prescribed as such by, or approved as such under, the regulations;

55. "secondary school" means a school that is under the jurisdiction of a secondary school board;

56. "secondary school district" means the area in which a secondary school board or a board of education has jurisdiction for secondary school purposes;

57. "secretary" and "treasurer" includes a secretary-treasurer;

58. "senior division" means the division of the organization of a secondary school comprising the three years of the program of studies following the intermediate division;

59. "separated town" means a town separated for municipal purposes from the county in which it is situated;   R.S.O. 1980, c. 129, s. 1 (1), pars. 49-59.

59a. "separate school board" means a board that operates a separate school for Roman Catholics;   1986, c. 21, s. 1, *part.*

60. "separate school elector", in respect of an area for which one or more members of a board are to be elected by separate school electors, means a separate school elector under the *Municipal Elections Act*, who is qualified to vote at the election of such members in such area;   R.S.O. 1980, c. 129, s. 1 (1), par. 60.

61. "separate school supporter" means a Roman Catholic ratepayer,

      i. in respect of whom notice of school support has been given in accordance with section 119 and notice of withdrawal of support has not been given under section 120,

     ii. who is shown as a separate school supporter on the school support list as prepared or revised by the assessment commissioner under section 15 of the *Assessment Act*, or

    iii. who is declared to be a separate school supporter as a result of a final decision rendered in proceedings commenced under the *Assessment Act*,

and includes the Roman Catholic spouse of such ratepayer;   R.S.O. 1980, c. 129, s. 1 (1), par. 61; 1981, c. 47, s. 17.

62. "separate school zone" means the area in which property may be assessed to support a separate school or schools for Roman Catholics under the jurisdiction of one separate school board;

63. "special education program" means, in respect of an exceptional pupil, an educational program that is based on and modified by the results of continuous assessment and evaluation and that includes a plan containing specific objectives and an outline of educational services that meets the needs of the exceptional pupil;

64. "special education services" means facilities and resources, including support personnel and equipment, necessary for developing and implementing a special education program;

65. "supervisory officer" means a person who is qualified in accordance with the regulations governing supervisory officers and who is employed,

    i. by a board, or

    ii. in the Ministry and designated by the Minister,

to perform such supervisory and administrative duties as are required of supervisory officers by this Act and the regulations; R.S.O. 1980, c. 129. s. 1 (1), pars. 62-65.

65a. "support staff" means staff other than supervisory officer staff or teaching staff; 1986, c. 21, s. 1, *part.*

66. "teacher" means a person who holds a valid certificate of qualification or a letter of standing as a teacher in an elementary or a secondary school in Ontario; R.S.O. 1980, c. 129, s. 1 (1), par. 66; 1982, c. 32, s. 1 (2).

67. "temporary teacher" means a person employed to teach under the authority of a letter of permission;

68. "trainable retarded child" or "trainable retarded pupil" means an exceptional pupil whose intellectual functioning is below the level at which he could profit from a special education program for educable retarded pupils;

69. "urban municipality" means a city, town or village;

70. "urban school section" means a school section, except a school division or a district school area, that includes a municipality;

71. "urban separate school" means a separate school for Roman Catholics in an urban municipality;

72. "urban separate school zone" means a separate school zone established in an urban municipality that does not form part of a county or district combined separate school zone;

73. "vocational school" includes a special vocational school.   R.S.O. 1980, c. 129, s. 1 (1), pars. 67-73.

(2) Where by or under this Act any authority or right is vested in, or any obligation is imposed upon, or any reimbursement may be made to, a parent or guardian of a pupil, such authority, right, obligation or reimbursement shall, where the pupil is an adult, be vested in or imposed upon or made to the pupil, as the case may be.

(3) Where any question arises touching the validity of any proceeding with respect to the formation, alteration or dissolution of a school section or touching any by-law with respect to any of such matters, the question shall be raised, heard and determined upon a summary application to the judge, and no proceeding or by-law with respect to the formation, alteration or dissolution of a school section is invalid or shall be set aside because of failure to comply with the provisions of any Act applicable to the proceeding or by-law, unless, in the opinion of the judge before whom the proceeding or by-law is called in question, the proceeding or by-law, if allowed to stand, would cause substantial injustice to be done to any person affected thereby.

(4) This Act does not adversely affect any right or privilege respecting separate schools enjoyed by separate school boards or their supporters under the predecessors of this Act as they existed immediately prior to the 1st day of January, 1975. R.S.O. 1980, c. 129, s. 1 (2-4).

(5) Until altered under the authority of this or any other Act, all school jurisdictions and boards, including the names of the boards, as they existed on the 31st day of July, 1981, are continued subject to the provisions of this Act.   1982, c. 32, s. 1 (3).
. . .

10.—(1) Subject to the approval of the Lieutenant Governor in Council, the Minister may make regulations in respect of schools or classes established under this Act, or any predecessor of this Act, and with respect to all other schools supported in whole or in part by public money,

1. for the establishment, organization, administration and government thereof;

2. governing the admission of pupils;

3. prescribing the manner in which records in respect of pupils of elementary and secondary schools shall be established and maintained, including the forms to be used therefor and the type of information that shall be kept and recorded, and providing for the retention, transfer and disposal of such records;

4. providing for the disposition of records established prior to the 1st day of September, 1972, in respect of pupils;

5. governing the provision, establishment, organization and administration of,

     i. special education programs,

     ii. special education services, and

     iii. committees to identify exceptional pupils and to make and review placements of exceptional pupils,

and, subject to paragraph 7 of section 149, prescribing generally or with application to a particular board, the date by which and the extent to which such programs and services shall be established;

6. governing procedures with respect to parents or guardians for appeals in respect of identification and placement of exceptional pupils in special education programs;

7. defining and governing evening classes;

8. requiring boards to purchase books for the use of pupils;

9. prescribing the accommodation and equipment of buildings and the arrangement of premises;

10. defining and governing programs of recreation, camping, physical education and adult education; R.S.O. 1980, c. 129, s. 10 (1), pars. 1-10.

11. governing the granting, suspending and cancelling of certificates of qualification, and letters of

standing; R.S.O. 1980, c. 129, s. 10 (1), par. 11; 1982, c. 32, s. 4 (1).

11a. providing for the issuing of teacher's qualifications record cards and governing the professional qualifications that may be recorded on such record cards; 1982, c. 32, s. 4 (2).

12. governing the granting to a board of a letter of permission and a temporary letter of approval and providing for the withdrawal of such letters;

13. prescribing the form of contract that shall be used for every contract entered into between a board and a permanent teacher or a probationary teacher for the services of the teacher, and prescribing in the form of contract the terms and conditions of the contract;

14. governing the establishment and operation of public and secondary schools on lands held by the Crown in right of Canada or Ontario or by an agency thereof, or on other lands that are exempt from taxation for school purposes, and providing for the payment of moneys to assist in the cost of establishment and maintenance of such schools;

15. governing the payment of the cost of education at elementary and secondary schools of pupils who,

    i. reside in the territorial districts, or on lands held by the Crown in right of Canada or Ontario or by an agency thereof, or on other lands that are exempt from taxation for school purposes,

    ii. are wards of or in the care of a children's aid society, or

    iii. are admitted to a centre, facility, home, hospital or institution that is approved, designated, established, licensed or registered under any Act;

16. providing for assistance in the payment of board, lodging and transportation costs of elementary and secondary school pupils;

17. prescribing the fees to be paid to presiding officers and examiners in connection with examinations and

by whom and in what manner such fees and other expenses in connection with such examinations shall be borne and paid;

18. governing the provision of religious exercises and religious education in public and secondary schools and providing for the exemption of pupils from participating in such exercises and education and of a teacher from teaching, and a public school board or a secondary school board from providing, religious education in any school or class;

19. prescribing the language or languages in which any subject or subjects shall be taught in any year of the primary, junior, intermediate or senior division;

20. providing for and governing the exchange of teachers between Ontario and other parts of Canada and between Ontario and other jurisdictions;

21. governing school libraries;

22. listing the textbooks that are selected and approved by the Minister for use in schools;

23. respecting observation and practice teaching by student teachers; R.S.O. 1980, c. 129, s. 10 (1), pars. 12-23.

24. prescribing the powers, duties and qualifications, and governing the appointment of, teachers, supervisors, directors, supervisory officers, heads of departments, principals, superintendents, residence counsellors, school attendance counsellors and other officials; R.S.O. 1980, c. 129, s. 10 (1), par. 24; 1982, c. 32, s. 4 (3).

25. prescribing the duties of pupils;

26. governing the operation of schools for trainable retarded children;

27. prescribing the qualifications and experience required for the purpose of qualifying a person to teach;

28. prescribing forms and providing for their use;

29. governing the transportation of pupils;

30. regulating the practice and procedure to be followed at any hearing provided for by or under this Act;

31. governing the assignment by a board of duties to directors of education and other supervisory officers and prescribing the procedures in respect thereof, and defining any word or expression used in such regulation;

32. prescribing the practices and procedures to be followed by a board in the case of suspension or dismissal of a director of education or other supervisory officer;   R.S.O. 1980, c. 129, s. 10 (1), pars. 25-32.

33. notwithstanding paragraph 26 of subsection 150 (1), prohibiting or regulating and controlling any program or activity of a board that is or may be in competition with any business or occupation in the private sector and providing that such regulations have general application or application to a particular board.   1982, c. 32, s. 4 (4).

(2) REPEALED: 1986, c. 64, s. 12 (1).

(3) Subject to the approval of the Lieutenant Governor in Council, the Minister may make regulations,

(a) providing for the apportionment and distribution of moneys appropriated or raised by the Legislature for educational purposes;

(b) prescribing the conditions governing the payment of legislative grants;

(c) for the purposes of legislative grants,

(i) defining any word or expression,

(ii) requiring the approval of the Minister to any amount of money, enrolment or rate used in determining the amount of such grants,

(iii) prescribing the portions of any expenditure to which such grants apply, and

(iv) respecting the application of any part of such grants;

(d) providing an assessment equalization factor,

(i) for each municipality, including, for public and secondary school purposes, any part of territory without municipal organization that is deemed to be attached thereto for such purposes and, for public school purposes, any part of territory without municipal organization that is deemed to be annexed thereto for public school purposes,

(ii) for each part of territory without municipal organization that is deemed to be a district municipality for the purposes of Part III,

(iii) for each part of territory without municipal organization that is deemed to be a district municipality for the purposes of Part IV,

(iv) for each public school section that comprises only territory without municipal organization, and

(v) for each separate school zone that comprises only territory without municipal organization,

and may determine the assessment roll to which each such factor applies;

(e) prescribing the method of calculating the amount of the fee receivable by a board in respect of elementary or secondary school pupils or any class or group thereof, where the board provides education for one or more pupils in respect of whom a fee is payable under this Act, and defining any word or expression used in such regulation;

(f) prescribing the method of calculating average daily enrolment.

(4) A regulation made in any year under subsection (3) may be made to apply in its operation to that year, to a previous year, or to both.

(5) Subject to the approval of the Lieutenant Governor in Council and to section 134, the Minister may make regulations governing estimates that a board is required to prepare and

adopt and expenditures that may be made by a board for any purpose.

(6) Subject to the approval of the Lieutenant Governor in Council, the Minister may make regulations,

(a) prescribing and governing the school year, school terms and school holidays;

(b) authorizing a board to vary one or more school terms or school holidays as designated by the regulations; and

(c) permitting a board to designate, and to implement with the prior approval of the Minister, a school year, school terms and school holidays for one or more schools under its jurisdiction that are different from those prescribed by the regulations.

(7) Subject to the approval of the Lieutenant Governor in Council, the Minister may make regulations prescribing the conditions under which, and establishing the procedures by which, a child who is otherwise required to attend school under Part II and who has attained the age of fourteen years may be excused from attendance at school or required to attend school only part-time.   R.S.O. 1980, c. 129, s. 10 (3-7).

(8) Subject to the approval of the Lieutenant Governor in Council, the Minister may make regulations,

(a) prescribing the fee to be paid to the Ministry for a transcript of standing obtained in Ontario by a pupil;

(b) prescribing the fee to be paid to the Ministry for duplicates of certificates of qualification, letters of standing and Ontario Teacher's Qualifications Record Cards;

(c) prescribing the fee to be paid to the Ministry by a teacher for the preparation at his request of a statement of standing obtained, or a description of courses completed, at a teacher education institution in Ontario, and the forwarding thereof to a certification authority outside Ontario or to an educational institution;

(d) prescribing the conditions under which fees shall be paid to the Ministry for the evaluation of academic certificates, transcripts and other documents of educational standing, and prescribing the amounts of the fees;

(e) prescribing the fees to be paid for duplicates of diplomas and certificates granted to pupils;

(f) prescribing the fees to be paid for courses provided by the Ministry for teachers, principals and supervisory officers or any class thereof;

(g) prescribing the terms and conditions upon which students may be admitted to a teachers' college, remain therein and be dismissed therefrom;

(h) requiring the payment of a tuition fee by students attending a teachers' college, fixing the amount and manner of payment thereof and prescribing the conditions under which a student is entitled to a refund of the fee or part thereof. R.S.O. 1980, c. 129, s. 10 (8); 1982, c. 32, s. 4 (5); 1984, c. 60, s. 4.

(9) A regulation made under this section may be made to apply to The Metropolitan Toronto School Board. R.S.O. 1980, c. 129, s. 10 (9).

. . .

15.—(1) No private school shall be operated in Ontario unless notice of intention to operate the private school has been submitted in accordance with this section.

(2) Every private school shall submit annually to the Ministry on or before the 1st day of September a notice of intention to operate a private school.

(3) A notice of intention to operate a private school shall be in such form and shall include such particulars as the Minister may require.

(4) Every person concerned in the management of a private school that is operated in contravention of subsection (1) is guilty of an offence and on conviction is liable to a fine of not more than $25 for every day such school is so operated.

(5) The principal, headmaster or person in charge of a private school shall make a return to the Ministry furnishing such statistical information regarding enrolment, staff, courses of study and other information as and when required by the Minister, and any such person who fails to make such return within sixty days of the request of the Minister is guilty of an offence and on conviction is liable to a fine of not more than $100.

(6) The Minister may direct one or more supervisory officers to inspect a private school, in which case each such supervisory officer may enter the school at all reasonable hours and conduct an inspection of the school and any records or documents relating thereto, and every person who prevents or obstructs or attempts to prevent or obstruct any such entry or inspection is guilty of an offence and on conviction is liable to a fine of not more than $200.   R.S.O. 1980, c. 129, s. 15 (1-6).

(7) The Minister may, on the request of any person operating a private school, provide for inspection of the school in respect of the standard of instruction in the subjects leading to the Ontario secondary school diploma, the secondary school graduation diploma and to the secondary school honour graduation diploma, and may determine and charge a fee for such inspection.   R.S.O. 1980, c. 129, s. 15 (7); 1984, c. 60, s. 5.

(8) The Minister may, on the request of a person operating a private school or of a person in charge of a conservation authority school or field centre, provide for the inspection of a teacher in such school or centre who requires the recommendation of a supervisory officer for certification purposes.

(9) Every person who knowingly makes a false statement in a notice of intention to operate a private school or an information return under this section is guilty of an offence and on conviction is liable to a fine of not more than $200.   R.S.O. 1980, c. 129, s. 15 (8, 9).

• • •

SCHOOL ATTENDANCE

17. In sections 20, 22, 25, 27 and 29, "guardian", in addition to having the meaning ascribed in section 1, includes any person who has received into his home another person's child who is of compulsory school age and is resident with him or in his care.   R.S.O. 1980, c. 129, s. 17; 1982, c. 20, s. 2 (2).

18. A board may close or authorize the closing of a school or class for a temporary period where such closing appears unavoidable because of,

    (a) failure of transportation arrangements; or

    (b) inclement weather, fire, flood, the breakdown of the school heating plant, the failure of an essential utility or a similar emergency.   R.S.O. 1980, c. 129, s. 18.

19. Where the head of the council of a municipality in which a school is situate proclaims a school day as a civic holiday for the municipality, the board may, by resolution, close any of the schools under its jurisdiction on such day.   R.S.O. 1980, c. 129, s. 19.

20.—(1) Unless excused under this section,

(a) every child who attains the age of six years on or before the first school day in September in any year shall attend an elementary or secondary school on every school day from the first school day in September in that year until he attains the age of sixteen years; and

(b) every child who attains the age of six years after the first school day in September in any year shall attend an elementary or secondary school on every school day from the first school day in September in the next succeeding year until the last school day in June in the year in which he attains the age of sixteen years.

(2) A child is excused from attendance at school if,

(a) he is receiving satisfactory instruction at home or elsewhere;

(b) he is unable to attend school by reason of sickness or other unavoidable cause;

(c) transportation is not provided by a board for the child and there is no school that he has a right to attend situated,

    (i) within 1.6 kilometres from his residence measured by the nearest road if he has not attained the age of seven years on or before the first school day in September in the year in question, or

    (ii) within 3.2 kilometres from his residence measured by the nearest road if he has attained the age of seven years but not the age of ten years on or before the first school day in September in the year in question, or

    (iii) within 4.8 kilometres from his residence measured by the nearest road if he has attained the age of ten years on or before the first school day in September in the year in question;

(d) he has obtained a secondary school graduation diploma or has completed a course that gives him equivalent standing;

(e) he is absent from school for the purpose of receiving instruction in music and the period of absence does not exceed one-half day in any week;

(f) he is suspended, expelled or excluded from attendance at school under any Act or under the regulations;

(g) he is absent on a day regarded as a holy day by the church or religious denomination to which he belongs; or

(h) he is absent or excused as authorized under this Act and the regulations.

(3) The fact that a child is blind, deaf or mentally handicapped is not of itself an unavoidable cause under clause (2) (b).

(4) Where a child under compulsory school age has been enrolled as a pupil in an elementary school, this section applies during the period for which the child is enrolled as if he were of compulsory school age.

(5) The parent or guardian of a child who is required to attend school under this section shall cause the child to attend school as required by this section.

(6) Nothing in this section requires the child of a Roman Catholic separate school supporter to attend a public school or a Protestant separate school, or requires the child of a public school supporter to attend a Roman Catholic separate school. R.S.O. 1980, c. 129, s. 20.

• • •

22.—(1) A principal may suspend a pupil for a fixed period, not in excess of a period determined by the board, because of persistent truancy, persistent opposition to authority, habitual neglect of duty, the wilful destruction of school property, the use of profane or improper language, or conduct injurious to the moral tone of the school or to the physical or mental well being of others in the school and, where a pupil has been suspended, the principal shall notify forthwith in writing the pupil, his teachers, the parent or guardian of the pupil, the board, the appropriate school attendance counsellor and the appropriate supervisory officer of the suspension, the reasons therefor and the right of appeal under subsection (2).

(2) The parent or guardian of a pupil who has been suspended or the pupil, where he is an adult, may, within seven days of the commencement of the suspension, appeal to the board against the suspension and the board, after hearing the appeal or where no appeal is made, may remove, confirm or modify the suspension and, where the board considers it appropriate, may order that any record of the suspension be expunged.

(3) A board may expel a pupil from its schools on the ground that his conduct is so refractory that his presence is injurious to other pupils where,

    (a) the principal and the appropriate supervisory officer so recommend;

    (b) the pupil and his parent or guardian have been notified in writing of,

        (i) the recommendation of the principal and the supervisory officer, and

        (ii) the right of the pupil where he is an adult and otherwise of his parent or guardian to make representations at a hearing to be conducted by the board;

    (c) the teacher or teachers of the pupil have been notified; and

    (d) such hearing has been conducted.

(4) The parties to a hearing under this section shall be the parent or guardian of the pupil or the pupil, where he is an adult, the principal of the school that the pupil attends and, in the case of an expulsion, the appropriate supervisory officer.

(5) A board may at its discretion readmit to school a pupil who has been expelled.   R.S.O. 1980, c. 129, s. 22.

23.—(1) The Lieutenant Governor in Council may appoint an officer, to be known as the Provincial School Attendance Counsellor, who shall, under the direction of the Minister, superintend and direct the enforcement of compulsory school attendance.

(2) Where the parent or guardian of a child considers that the child is excused from attendance at school under subsection 20 (2), and the appropriate school attendance counsellor or the Provincial School Attendance Counsellor is of the opinion that the child should not be excused from attendance, the

Provincial School Attendance Counsellor shall direct that an inquiry be made as to the validity of the reason or excuse for non-attendance and the other relevant circumstances, and for such purpose shall appoint one or more persons who are not employees of the board that operates the school that the child has the right to attend to conduct a hearing and to report to him the result of the inquiry and may, by order in writing signed by him, direct that the child,

(a) be excused from attendance at school; or

(b) attend school,

and a copy of the order shall be delivered to the board and to the parent or guardian of the child.

(3) The Provincial School Attendance Counsellor has all the powers of a school attendance counsellor and may exercise such powers anywhere in Ontario.   R.S.O. 1980, c. 129, s. 23.

24.—(1) Every board shall appoint one or more school attendance counsellors.

(2) Two or more boards may appoint the same school attendance counsellor or counsellors.

(3) Where the office of a school attendance counsellor becomes vacant, it shall be filled forthwith by the board.

(4) Notice of the appointment of a school attendance counsellor shall be given in writing by the board to the Provincial School Attendance Counsellor and to the supervisory officers concerned.

(5) A school attendance counsellor appointed by a board has jurisdiction and is responsible for the enforcement of compulsory school attendance in respect of every child who is required to attend school and who,

(a) is qualified to be a resident pupil of the board; or

(b) is or has been enrolled during the current school year in a school operated by the board, except a child who is under the jurisdiction of a person appointed under section 119 of the *Indian Act* (Canada).   R.S.O. 1980, c. 129, s. 24.

25.—(1) Where a school attendance counsellor has reasonable and probable grounds for believing that a child is illegally absent from school, he may, at the written request of the parent or guardian of the child or of the principal of the school that the child is required to attend, take the child to his parent or guardian or to the school from which he is absent provided that, if exception is taken to his entering a dwelling place, he shall not enter therein.   R.S.O. 1980, c. 129, s. 25 (1); 1982, c. 32, s. 7.

(2) A school attendance counsellor shall report to the board that appointed him as required by the board.

(3) A school attendance counsellor is responsible to the appropriate supervisory officer, and shall carry out the instructions and directions of the Provincial School Attendance Counsellor.

(4) A school attendance counsellor shall inquire into every case of failure to attend school within his knowledge or when requested so to do by the appropriate supervisory officer or the principal of a school or a ratepayer, and shall give written warning of the consequences of such failure to the parent or guardian of a child who is not attending school as required, and shall also give written notice to the parent or guardian to cause the child to attend school forthwith, and shall advise the parent or guardian in writing of the provisions of subsection 23 (2).   R.S.O. 1980, c. 129, s. 25 (2-4).

26. A board may make or obtain a complete census of all persons in the area in which the board has jurisdiction who have not attained the age of twenty-one years.   R.S.O. 1980, c. 129, s. 26.

27.—(1) The principal of every elementary and secondary school shall,

    (a) report to the appropriate school attendance counsellor and supervisory officer the names, ages and residences of all pupils of compulsory school age who have not attended school as required;

    (b) furnish the school attendance counsellor with such other information as the counsellor requires for the enforcement of compulsory school attendance; and

    (c) report in writing to the school attendance counsellor every case of expulsion and readmission of a pupil.

(2) Where a child of compulsory school age has not attended school as required and there is no school attendance counsellor having jurisdiction in respect of the child, the appropriate supervisory officer shall notify the parent or guardian of the child of the requirements of section 20. R.S.O. 1980, c. 129, s. 27.

. . .

29.—(1) A parent or guardian of a child of compulsory school age who neglects or refuses to cause the child to attend school is, unless the child is legally excused from attendance, guilty of an offence and on conviction is liable to a fine of not more than $100.   R.S.O. 1980, c. 129, s. 29 (1).

(2) The court may, in addition to or instead of imposing a fine, require a person convicted of an offence under subsection (1) to submit to the Treasurer of Ontario a personal bond, in a form prescribed by the court, in the penal sum of $200 with one or more sureties as required, conditioned that the person shall cause the child to attend school as required by this Part, and upon breach of the condition the bond is forfeit to the Crown.   R.S.O. 1980, c. 129, s. 29 (2); 1982, c. 32, s. 8.

(3) A person who employs during school hours a child who is required to attend school under section 20 is guilty of an offence and on conviction is liable to a fine of not more than $100.

(4) Subsections (1) and (3) apply with necessary modifications to a corporation and, in addition, every director and officer of the corporation who authorizes, permits or acquiesces in the contravention is guilty of an offence and on conviction is liable to the same penalty as the corporation.

(5) A child who is required by law to attend school and who refuses to attend or who is habitually absent from school is guilty of an offence and on conviction is liable to the penalties provided for children adjudged to be juvenile delinquents under the *Juvenile Delinquents Act* (Canada), and the child and his parent or guardian may be summoned to appear before the Provincial Court (Family Division), and the court has the same powers to deal with such child and his parent or guardian, including the imposition and payment of fines, as it has with respect to a juvenile delinquent and his parent or guardian under the *Juvenile Delinquents Act* (Canada), and subsection 237 (2) applies in any proceeding under this section.

(6) Proceedings in respect of offences under subsection (5) shall be proceeded with only in accordance with such subsection.

(7) Where, in proceedings under this section, it appears to the court that the child may have been excused from attendance at school under subsection 20 (2), the court may refer the matter to the Provincial School Attendance Counsellor who shall direct that an inquiry shall be made as provided in subsection 23 (2) which subsection shall apply with necessary modifications except that the Provincial School Attendance Counsellor shall, in lieu of making an order, submit a report to the court.   R.S.O. 1980, c. 129, s. 29 (3-7).

30.—(1) Prosecutions under section 29 shall be instituted by the school attendance counsellor concerned and prosecutions under subsection 29 (1) shall be instituted in the Provincial Court (Family Division) or the Unified Family Court. R.S.O. 1980, c. 129, s. 30 (1); 1982, c. 32, s. 9.

(2) In prosecutions under section 29, a certificate as to the attendance or non-attendance at school of any child, signed or purporting to be signed by the principal of the school, is *prima facie* evidence of the facts stated therein without any proof of the signature or appointment of the principal.

(3) Where a person is charged under section 29 in respect of a child who is alleged to be of compulsory school age and the child appears to the court to be of compulsory school age, the child shall, for the purposes of such prosecution, be deemed to be of compulsory school age unless the contrary is proved.

(4) An order made under subsection 23 (2) shall be admitted in evidence in a prosecution only where the prosecution is in respect of the school year for which the order was made. R.S.O. 1980, c. 129, s. 30 (2-4).
. . .

34.—(1) In this section,

(a) "board" includes The Metropolitan Toronto School Board;

(b) "hard to serve pupil" means a pupil who, under this section, is determined to be unable to profit by instruction offered by a board due to a mental handicap or a mental and one or more additional handicaps;

(c) "school" includes a school or class for trainable retarded pupils.

(2) Where a principal considers that an exceptional pupil who attends his school is, because of a mental or a mental and

one or more additional handicaps, unable to profit by instruction offered by the board, or where the parent or guardian of a pupil considers that the pupil is, because of a mental or a mental and one or more additional handicaps, unable to profit by instruction offered by the board, the principal shall refer the matter to the appropriate supervisory officer who shall refer the matter to the board, and the board shall appoint a committee of three persons consisting of a supervisory officer, a principal and a legally qualified medical practitioner who has expertise in respect of the mental or other handicap of the pupil, none of whom is a person to whom the matter has been previously referred.

(3) The committee referred to in subsection (2) shall,

    (a) in accordance with subsection (4), inquire into the alleged inability of the pupil to profit by instruction offered by the board;

    (b) inquire into the handicap or handicaps of the pupil; and

    (c) determine whether the pupil can profit by instruction offered by the board or determine that the pupil is a hard to serve pupil,

and the committee shall make a written report of its findings and of its determination to the board and to the parent or guardian of the pupil.

(4) The committee shall, for the purposes of its inquiry, study all existing reports in respect of the pupil, hear the teachers, the parent or guardian of the pupil, where reasonably possible the pupil, and any other person who may be able to contribute information bearing upon the matter and may, with the consent of the parent or guardian of the pupil, and of the pupil where he is an adult and capable of giving such consent, obtain and consider in respect of the pupil, the report of an assessment conducted by a person considered by the committee to be competent for the purpose.

(5) Any costs incurred in respect of an assessment or examination under this section, or in respect of the obtaining of other evidence required by the committee under subsection (3) or under subsection (6) shall be paid by the board referred to in subsection (2).

(6) Where the parent or guardian of a person in respect of whom a determination has been made under clause (3) (c), or the person, where he is an adult,

(a) believes that by reason of improvement in the condition of the person or other cause the person has become able to profit by instruction; and

(b) furnishes to a supervisory officer of the board in whose jurisdiction the person resides, evidence or information to establish such belief,

the board shall appoint a committee constituted in accordance with subsection (2) that shall review the determination in respect of the person last made under this section and confirm or alter such determination and for such purpose the committee has the powers and duties of a committee under subsection (3), which subsection applies with necessary modifications to such a review.

(7) Where a committee under subsection (3) or subsection (6) determines that a pupil is a hard to serve pupil, the committee shall so notify the board and the board shall consider the recommendation and determine that the pupil is a hard to serve pupil or that the pupil is considered to need placement in a special education program, as the case may be, and shall notify the parent or guardian of the pupil in writing of its determination.

(8) Where the board determines that the pupil is considered to need placement in a special education program, the board shall refer the matter to the appropriate committee established under subparagraph iii of paragraph 5 of subsection 10 (1) that shall determine, designate or design an appropriate special education program for the exceptional pupil.

(9) Where the board determines that the pupil is a hard to serve pupil and the parent or guardian of the pupil agrees with the said determination, the board shall assist the parent or guardian to locate a placement suited to the needs of the pupil and reimburse the parent or guardian for any expenses incurred by the parent or guardian in locating such placement.

(10) Where,

(a) the board determines that a pupil is a hard to serve pupil and the parent or guardian of the pupil disagrees with such determination and believes that the pupil is able to profit by instruction; or

(b) the board locates a placement under subsection (9) and the parent or guardian disagrees with the placement,

the parent or guardian of the pupil may, within fifteen days of the receipt of the notice under subsection (7) or any time prior to the implementation of the placement under subsection (9), notify the board in writing of the disagreement and the board shall forthwith refer the matter to the secretary of a Special Education Tribunal established under subsection 35 (1), by forwarding all the documentation outlining the special education programs and special education services that have been provided to the pupil and all existing reports and relevant material in respect of the pupil.

(11) The board shall reimburse the parent or guardian for any expenses he incurs in connection with the referral to and subsequent hearing by the Tribunal referred to in subsection (10), provided that such expenses are approved by the Tribunal.

(12) The Special Education Tribunal shall consider the referral and, after a hearing and review of the report of the committee referred to in subsection (3) and the determination of the board, shall find that,

    (a)   the pupil is a hard to serve pupil;

    (b)   the pupil is considered to need placement in a special education program; or

    (c)   the proposed placement under subsection (9) is or is not suited to the needs of the pupil,

and so notify in writing the parent or guardian of the pupil, the board and the Minister.

(13) Where the Tribunal finds that the pupil is considered to need placement in a special education program, the board shall provide a special education program and special education services for the pupil and the board shall, within sixty days of receipt of the notice under subsection (12), inform the Minister of the special education services that have been provided for the pupil.

(14) Where, under subsection (12), the Tribunal finds that the pupil is a hard to serve pupil or that the placement under subsection (9) is not suited to the needs of the pupil, the board shall assist the parent or guardian to locate a placement or a new placement, as the case may be, suited to the needs of the pupil and reimburse the parent or guardian for any expenses incurred by the parent or guardian in locating such placement.

(15) Where, pursuant to an application by the board or by the pupil or on his behalf for judicial review under the *Judicial Review Procedure Act*, the finding of the Special Education Tribunal is set aside, the determination of the board under

subsection (7) shall be referred to a Special Education Tribunal for a new hearing conducted by members of the Tribunal other than those who first heard the matter if the board or the parent or guardian of the pupil, as the case may be, makes application therefor to the secretary of the Special Education Tribunal by registered mail within fifteen days after the date of the order of the court setting aside the finding of the Special Education Tribunal and the provisions of subsections (11), (12), (13) and (14) apply with necessary modifications in respect of a hearing by the Special Education Tribunal under this subsection.

(16) A placement of a hard to serve pupil under subsection (9) or (14) shall be made in Ontario, except where no placement suited to the needs of the pupil is available in Ontario, a placement may be made outside Ontario.

(17) Where a hard to serve pupil is placed under subsection (9) or (14), Ontario shall pay the cost, if any, of such placement. R.S.O. 1980, c. 129, s. 34.

35.—(1) For the purposes of section 34, the Lieutenant Governor in Council shall establish one or more tribunals known as Special Education Tribunals, provincial or regional, and appoint a secretary of such tribunals.

(2) The Lieutenant Governor in Council may by order,

(a) establish the procedures that shall apply; and

(b) authorize Special Education Tribunals to fix and assess costs,

with respect to matters dealt with by Special Education Tribunals. R.S.O. 1980, c. 129, s. 35.

36.—(1) Where a parent or guardian of a pupil has exhausted all rights of appeal under the regulations in respect of the identification or placement of the pupil as an exceptional pupil and is dissatisfied with the decision in respect of the identification or placement, the parent or guardian may apply to the secretary of a Special Education Tribunal for a hearing for leave to appeal to a regional tribunal established by the Minister under subsection (2) in respect of the identification or placement.

(2) Where leave to appeal is granted under subsection (1), a regional tribunal shall be established by the Minister to hear the appeal of the parent or guardian.

(3) Notwithstanding subsection (1), a Special Education Tribunal may with the consent of the parties before it in lieu of granting leave to appeal to a regional tribunal hear and dispose of the appeal of the parent or guardian.

(4) The Lieutenant Governor in Council may make regulations governing the provision, establishment, organization and administration of a regional tribunal and regulating and controlling the practice and procedure before such tribunal including the costs of persons before such tribunal.

(5) The decision of a Special Education Tribunal or of a regional tribunal under this section is final and binding upon the parties to any such decision.

(6) The tribunal hearing the appeal may,

    (a)   dismiss the appeal; or

    (b)   grant the appeal and make such order as it considers necessary with respect to the identification or placement of the pupil.   R.S.O. 1980, c. 129, s. 36.

. . .

149. Every board shall,

1. appoint a secretary and a treasurer or a secretary-treasurer who, in the case of a board of not more than five elected members, may be a member of the board;

2. take proper security from the treasurer or secretary-treasurer;

3. give the necessary orders on the treasurer for payment of all moneys expended for school purposes and of such other expenses for promoting the interests of the schools under the jurisdiction of the board as may be authorized by this Act or the regulations and by the board;

4. fix the times and places for the meetings of the board and the mode of calling and conducting them, and ensure that a full and correct account of the proceedings thereat is kept;

5. establish and maintain a head office and notify the Ministry of its location and address and notify the Ministry of any change in the location or address of the head office within ten days of such change;

6. provide instruction and adequate accommodation during each school year for the pupils who have a right to attend a school under the jurisdiction of the board;

7. before the 1st day of September, 1985, provide or enter into an agreement with another board to provide in accordance with the regulations special education programs and special education services for its exceptional pupils in the English language or, where the pupil is enrolled in a school or class established under Part XI, the French language, as the case may be;

8. keep the school buildings and premises in proper repair and in a proper sanitary condition, provide suitable furniture and equipment and keep it in proper repair, and protect the property of the board;

9. make provision for insuring adequately the buildings and equipment of the board and for insuring the board and its employees and volunteers who are assigned duties by the principal against claims in respect of accidents incurred by pupils while under the jurisdiction or supervision of the board;

10. ensure that every school under its charge is conducted in accordance with this Act and the regulations;

11. keep open its schools during the whole period of the school year determined under the regulations, except where it is otherwise provided under this Act;

12. appoint for each school that it operates a principal and an adequate number of teachers, all of whom shall be qualified according to this Act and the regulations;

13. provide, without charge, for the use of the pupils attending the school or schools operated by the board, the textbooks that are required by the regulations to be purchased by the board;

14. where it furnishes transportation for pupils in a vehicle that is owned by the board, provide and carry with an insurer licensed under the *Insurance Act* for each such vehicle at least the amount of

insurance that is required to be provided in respect of such a vehicle by the licensee of a school vehicle under the *Public Vehicles Act*;

15. ascertain and report to the Ministry at least once in each year in the manner required by the Minister the names and ages of all children of compulsory school age within its jurisdiction who are not enrolled in any school or private school and the reasons therefor;

16. transmit to the Minister all reports and returns required by this Act and the regulations;

17. issue to an employee, upon the termination of his employment with the board, a statement of the sick leave credits standing to his credit with the board at the time of such termination;

18. do anything that a board is required by the Minister to do under subsection 8 (1). R.S.O. 1980, c. 129, s. 149; 1982, c. 32, s. 39.

150.—(1) A board may,

1. establish committees composed of members of the board to make recommendations to the board in respect of education, finance, personnel and property;

1a. establish committees that may include persons who are not members of the board in respect of matters other than those referred to in paragraph 1; 1982, c. 32, s. 40 (1).

2. subject to Part X, appoint and remove such officers and servants and, subject to Part IX, appoint and remove such teachers, as it considers expedient, determine the terms on which such officers, servants and teachers are to be employed, prescribe their duties and fix their salaries, except that in the case of a secretary of a board who is a member of the board, the board may pay only such compensation for his services as is approved by the electors at a meeting of the electors;

3. permit a principal to assign to a person who volunteers to serve without remuneration such duties in respect of the school as are approved by the board and to terminate such assignment;

4. appoint supervisors of the teaching staff for positions that are provided for in any Act or regulation administered by the Minister and every appointee shall hold the qualifications and perform the duties required in the Act or regulations;

5. appoint one or more,

    i. psychiatrists who are on the register of specialists in psychiatry of The Royal College of Physicians and Surgeons of Canada or of the College of Physicians and Surgeons of Ontario,

    ii. psychologists who are legally qualified medical practitioners or hold a certificate of registration under the *Psychologists Registration Act*; R.S.O. 1980, c. 129, s. 150 (1), pars. 2-5.

6. determine the number and kind of schools to be established and maintained and the attendance area for each school, and close schools in accordance with policies established by the board from guidelines issued by the Minister; R.S.O. 1980, c. 129, s. 150 (1), par. 6; 1982, c. 32, s. 40 (2).

7. provide instruction in courses of study that are prescribed or approved by the Minister, developed from curriculum guidelines issued by the Minister or approved by the board where the Minister permits the board to approve courses of study;

8. in lieu of purchasing a computer or system of computer programming, enter into an agreement for the use thereof by the board;

9. operate the school ground as a park or playground and rink during the school year or in vacation or both, and provide and maintain such equipment as it considers advisable, and provide such supervision as it considers proper, provided the proper conduct of the school is not interfered with;

10. organize and carry on gymnasium classes in school buildings for pupils or others during the school year or in vacation or both, and provide supervision and training for such classes, provided the proper conduct of the school is not interfered with;

11. purchase milk to be consumed by the pupils in the schools under the jurisdiction of the board during school days in accordance with the terms and conditions prescribed by the regulations;

12. provide school supplies, other than the textbooks that it is required to provide under paragraph 13 of section 149, for the use of pupils;

13. establish and maintain school libraries and resource centres;

14. establish kindergartens and junior kindergartens;

15. provide that the signature of the treasurer and of any other person authorized to sign cheques issued by the treasurer may be written or engraved, lithographed, printed or otherwise mechanically reproduced on cheques;

16. pay the travelling expenses and membership fees of any member of the board, or of any teacher or officer of the board, incurred in attending meetings of an educational association and may make grants and pay membership fees to any such organization;

17. pay the costs, or any part thereof, incurred by any member of the board or by any teacher, officer or other employee of the board in successfully defending any legal proceeding brought against him,

   i. for libel or slander in respect of any statements relating to the employment, suspension or dismissal of any person by the board published at a meeting of the board or of a committee thereof, or

   ii. for assault in respect of disciplinary action taken in the course of duty;

18. invest funds received from an insurance claim, gift, legacy or sale of property in such securities as a trustee may invest in under the *Trustee Act*;

19. invest moneys not required immediately by the board in,

   i. bonds, debentures or other evidences of indebtedness of, or guaranteed by, the Government of Canada or the Province of Ontario, or any other province of Canada,

ii. debentures, notes or guaranteed investment certificates of or term deposits with any trust company or loan corporation that is registered under the *Loan and Trust Corporations Act*,

iii. term deposits, deposit receipts, deposit notes, certificates of deposit, acceptances and other similar instruments issued, accepted, guaranteed or endorsed by any chartered bank to which the *Bank Act* (Canada) applies,

iv. promissory notes of a municipality as defined in the *Municipal Affairs Act*, and promissory notes of a metropolitan municipality, a regional municipality, the District Municipality of Muskoka and the County of Oxford, and

v. term deposits accepted by a credit union as defined in the *Credit Unions and Caisses Populaires Act*,

provided that the investments become due and payable by the day on which the moneys are required by the board, and all interest thereon shall be credited to the fund from which the moneys are invested;

20. notwithstanding any other Act, borrow, for any purpose for which the board has authority to spend money, any moneys in any fund established by the board that are not immediately required by the board for the purposes of such fund, but such borrowing shall not extend beyond the term of office of the members of the board and, where secondary school moneys are borrowed for public school purposes or public school moneys are borrowed for secondary school purposes, the board shall pay interest to the fund from which such moneys are borrowed at a rate not less than that being earned by the fund at the date of borrowing;

21. subject to the provisions of this Act and the regulations, fix the fees to be paid by or on behalf of pupils, and the times of payment thereof, and when necessary enforce payment thereof by action in the

small claims court, and exclude any pupil by or on behalf of whom fees that are legally required to be paid are not paid after reasonable notice;

22. permit the school buildings and premises and school buses owned by the board to be used for any educational or other lawful purpose;

23. provide for surgical treatment of children attending the school who suffer from minor physical defects, where in the opinion of the teacher and, where a school nurse and medical officer are employed, of the nurse and medical officer, the defect interferes with the proper education of the child, and include in the estimates for the current year the funds necessary for cases where the parents are not able to pay, provided that no such treatment shall be undertaken without the consent of the parents or guardian of the child;

24. establish and maintain cadet corps;

25. provide for the promotion and encouragement of athletics and for the holding of school games;

26. provide, during the school year or at other times, activities and programs on or off school premises, including field trips, and exercise jurisdiction over those persons participating therein;

27. appoint one or more teachers qualified in guidance according to the regulations to collect and distribute information regarding available occupations and employments, and to offer such counsel to the pupils as will enable them to plan intelligently for their educational and vocational advancement;

28. conduct free lectures open to the public and include in the estimates for the current year the expenses thereof;

29. establish summer schools for pupils;

30. establish and conduct during the school year courses for teachers;

31. establish evening classes;

32. erect and maintain any wall or fence considered necessary by the board for enclosure of the school premises;

33. contribute toward the support of school fairs;

34. authorize such school activities as pertain to the welfare of the pupils and exercise jurisdiction in respect thereof;

35. operate a cafeteria for the use of the staff and pupils;

36. institute a program of records management that will, subject to the regulations in respect of pupil records,

    i. provide for the archival retention by the board or the Archivist of Ontario of school registers, minute books of the board and its predecessors, documents pertaining to boundaries of school sections, separate school zones and secondary school districts, original assessment and taxation records in the possession of the board and other records considered by the board to have enduring value or to be of historical interest, and

    ii. establish, with the written approval of the auditor of the board, schedules for the retention, disposition and eventual destruction of records of the board and of the schools under its jurisdiction other than records retained for archival use;

37. employ and pay teachers, when so requested in writing by a charitable organization having the charge of children of school age, for the education of such children, whether such children are being educated in premises within or beyond the limits of the jurisdiction of the board, and pay for and furnish school supplies for their use;   R.S.O. 1980, c. 129, s. 150 (1), pars. 7-37.

38. with the approval of the Minister, conduct an education program in a centre, facility, home, hospital or institution that is approved, designated, established, licensed or registered under any Act and in which the Ministry does not conduct an education program;   1984, c. 60, s. 10.

39. provide for maternity leave for a teacher, not exceeding two years for each pregnancy;

40. establish, subject to the regulations, special educa-

tion programs to provide special education services for children who require such services;

41. when requested by the board of a cerebral palsy treatment centre school, a crippled children's treatment centre school, a hospital school or a sanatorium school, and with the approval of the Minister, by agreement, assume the assets and liabilities of such board and continue to operate such a school, and, upon the effective date of the agreement between the two boards, the board making the request is dissolved;

42. where a recreation committee or a joint recreation committee has been appointed for territory without municipal organization within the jurisdiction of the board, exercise the powers and duties of a municipal council with respect to preparing estimates of the sums required during the year for the purposes of the committee or joint committee, and levying rates and collecting taxes for such purposes on the rateable property supporting the board in such territory, and where such a joint recreation committee has been appointed, apportion the costs of such committee by agreement with the other board concerned;

43. with the approval of the Minister, enter into an agreement with a university, college of a university, or the board of governors of a polytechnical institute or of a college of applied arts and technology, in respect of the provision, maintenance and use of educational or recreational facilities on the property of either of the parties to the agreement;

44. pass a resolution referred to in subsection 83 (2) of the *Municipal Elections Act*;

45. provide for insurance against risks that may involve pecuniary loss or liability on the part of the board, and for paying premiums therefor.   R.S.O. 1980, c. 129, s. 150 (1), pars. 39-45.

(2) In addition to any other remedy possessed by a board in territory without municipal organization for the recovery of rates imposed under the authority of this Act, the board, with the approval of the Minister, may bring an action in a court of competent jurisdiction for the recovery of any rates in arrear against the person assessed therefor.   R.S.O. 1980, c. 129, s. 150 (2).
. . .

183.—(1) The meetings of a board and, subject to subsection (1a), meetings of a committee of the board, including a committee of the whole board, shall be open to the public, and no person shall be excluded from a meeting that is open to the public except for improper conduct.

(1a) A meeting of a committee of a board, including a committee of the whole board, may be closed to the public when the subject-matter under consideration involves,

    (a) the security of the property of the board;

    (b) the disclosure of intimate, personal or financial information in respect of a member of the board or committee, an employee or prospective employee of the board or a pupil or his parent or guardian;

    (c) the acquisition or disposal of a school site;

    (d) decisions in respect of negotiations with employees of the board; or

    (e) litigation affecting the board.   1982, c. 32, s. 51.

(2) The presiding officer may expel or exclude from any meeting any person who has been guilty of improper conduct at the meeting.

(3) Any person may, at all reasonable hours, at the head office of the board inspect the minute book, the audited annual financial report and the current accounts of a board, and, upon the written request of any person and upon the payment to the board at the rate of 25 cents for every 100 words or at such lower rate as the board may fix, the secretary shall furnish copies of them or extracts therefrom certified under his hand.   R.S.O. 1980, c. 129, s. 183 (2, 3).

Board Meetings

184.—(1) A board shall be deemed to be constituted when a majority of the members to be elected or appointed has been elected or appointed.

(2) A board that is elected at a regular election under the *Municipal Elections Act* and a board that is appointed or elected other than at a regular election under the *Municipal Elections Act* shall hold its first meeting not later than seven days after the day on which the term of office of the board commences on such date and at such time and place as the board determines and, failing such determination, at 8 p.m. at the

head office of the board on the first Wednesday following the commencement of the term of office.

(3) Notwithstanding subsection (2), on the petition of a majority of the members of a newly elected or appointed board, the appropriate supervisory officer may provide for calling the first meeting of the board at some other time and date.

(4) At the first meeting in December of each year, the chief executive officer shall preside until the election of the chairman or, if there is no chief executive officer or in his absence, the members present shall designate who shall preside at the election of the chairman and if a member of the board is so designated, he may vote at the election of the chairman.

(5) At the first meeting in December of each year and at the first meeting after a vacancy occurs in the office of chairman, the members shall elect one of themselves to be chairman, and the chairman shall preside at all meetings.

(6) Subsequent meetings of the board shall be held at such time and place as the board considers expedient.

(7) The members of the board may also elect one of themselves to be vice-chairman and he shall preside in the absence of the chairman.

(8) In the case of an equality of votes at the election of a chairman or vice-chairman, the candidates shall draw lots to fill the position of chairman or vice-chairman, as the case may be.

(9) If at any meeting there is no chairman or vice-chairman present, the members present may elect one of themselves to be chairman for that meeting.

(10) In the absence of the secretary from any meeting, the chairman or other member presiding may appoint any member or other person to act as secretary for that meeting.

(11) The presence of a majority of all the members constituting a board is necessary to form a quorum, except that when a board of education is dealing with matters that affect public schools exclusively, the presence of a majority of the members elected to the board of education by the public school electors is necessary to form a quorum.

(12) Subject to subsection 55 (4), the presiding officer, except where he is the chief executive officer of the board and is not a member, may vote with the other members of the

board upon all motions, and any motion on which there is an equality of votes is lost.

(13) Special meetings of the board may be called by the chairman and in such other manner as the board may determine. R.S.O. 1980, c. 129, s. 184.

. . .

230.—(1) A full-time or part-time teacher who is employed by a board and who is not an occasional teacher shall be employed as a permanent or a probationary teacher.

(2) A memorandum of every contract of employment between a board and a permanent teacher or a probationary teacher shall be made in writing in the form of contract prescribed by the regulations, signed by the parties, sealed with the seal of the board and executed before the teacher enters upon his duties, but if for any reason such memorandum is not so made, or has not been amended to incorporate any change made in the form of contract so prescribed, every contract shall be deemed to include the terms and conditions contained in the form of contract prescribed for a permanent teacher. R.S.O. 1980, c. 129, s. 230.

231.—(1) Unless otherwise expressly agreed and subject to subsections (2) to (5), a teacher is entitled to be paid his salary in the proportion that the total number of school days for which he performs his duties in the school year bears to the total number of school days in the school year.

(2) Subject to subsection (3), a permanent, probationary or temporary teacher is entitled to his salary for a total of twenty school days in any one school year in respect of his absence from duty on account of his sickness certified to by a physician or on account of acute inflammatory condition of his teeth or gums certified to by a licentiate of dental surgery, but a board may in its discretion pay the teacher his salary for more than twenty days absence from duty on account of such sickness or such tooth or gum condition.

(3) A part-time teacher is entitled to his salary for 10 per cent of the periods of instruction and supervision specified in the agreement for his employment in any one school year in respect of his absence from duty on account of his sickness certified to by a physician or on account of acute inflammatory condition of his teeth or gums certified to by a licentiate of dental surgery, but a board may in its discretion pay the part-time teacher his salary for more than 10 per cent of the periods of instruction and supervision in respect of his absence from duty on account of such sickness or such tooth or gum condition.

(4) Every teacher is entitled to his salary notwithstanding his absence from duty in any case where, because of exposure to a communicable disease, he is quarantined or otherwise prevented by the order of the medical health authorities from attending upon his duties.

(5) A teacher is entitled to his salary notwithstanding his absence from duty by reason of a summons to serve as a juror, or a subpoena as a witness in any proceeding to which he is not a party or one of the persons charged, provided that the teacher pays to the board any fee, exclusive of travelling allowances and living expenses, that he receives as a juror or as a witness.

(6) If it appears to the judge on the trial of an action for the recovery of a teacher's salary that there was not reasonable ground for the board disputing its liability or that the failure of the board to pay was from an improper motive, he may award as a penalty a sum not exceeding three months salary.

(7) For the purposes of subsection (6), the failure of a board to pay a teacher's salary may be extended by a judge to include failure to pay a teacher's salary when an agreement for his employment has been made by the board but no written memorandum has been made and executed as required by section 230, if the judge is satisfied upon the evidence that the refusal of the board to pay the salary by reason of the absence of a memorandum in writing is without merit.   R.S.O. 1980, c. 129, s. 231.

232. A board shall not offer to a teacher, and no teacher shall accept, a contract as a probationary teacher for a period greater than,

(a) two years where the teacher has less than three years' experience; and

(b) one year where the teacher has three or more years' experience,

as a teacher in an elementary or secondary school in Ontario before the commencement of the contract.   R.S.O. 1980, c. 129, s. 232.

233.—(1) Except as otherwise provided in this Act, no person shall be employed or act as a teacher in an elementary or secondary school unless he is qualified as prescribed by the regulations.

(2) Subject to this Act, a certificate of qualification as a

teacher may be awarded only to a person of good moral character and physically fit to perform the duties of a teacher, who passes the examinations prescribed by, and otherwise complies with, the regulations.

(3) All certificates of qualification are valid for such periods as the regulations prescribe.   R.S.O. 1980, c. 129, s. 233.

234. Notwithstanding the other provisions of this Part and notwithstanding anything in the contract between the board and the teacher, where a permanent or probationary teacher is employed by a board and a matter arises that in the opinion of the Minister adversely affects the welfare of the school in which the teacher is employed,

(a)   the board or the teacher may, with the consent of the Minister, give the other party thirty days written notice of termination, and the contract is terminated at the expiration of thirty days from the date the notice is given; or

(b)   the board may, with the consent of the Minister, give the teacher written notice of immediate termination together with one-tenth of the teacher's yearly salary in addition to the amount to which he would otherwise be entitled, and the contract thereupon is terminated.   R.S.O. 1980, c. 129, s. 234.

Duties

235.—(1) It is the duty of a teacher and a temporary teacher,

(a)   to teach diligently and faithfully the classes or subjects assigned to him by the principal;

(b)   to encourage the pupils in the pursuit of learning;

(c)   to inculcate by precept and example respect for religion and the principles of Judaeo-Christian morality and the highest regard for truth, justice, loyalty, love of country, humanity, benevolence, sobriety, industry, frugality, purity, temperance and all other virtues;

(d)   to assist in developing co-operation and co-ordination of effort among the members of the staff of the school;

(e)   to maintain, under the direction of the principal, proper order and discipline in his classroom and while on duty in the school and on the school ground;

(f) in instruction and in all communications with the pupils in regard to discipline and the management of the school,

(i) to use the English language, except where it is impractical to do so by reason of the pupil not understanding English, and except in respect of instruction in a language other than English when such other language is being taught as one of the subjects in the course of study, or

(ii) to use the French language in schools or classes in which French is the language of instruction except where it is impractical to do so by reason of the pupil not understanding French, and except in respect of instruction in a language other than French when such other language is being taught as one of the subjects in the course of study;

(g) to conduct his class in accordance with a timetable which shall be accessible to pupils and to the principal and supervisory officers;

(h) to participate in professional activity days as designated by the board under the regulations;

(i) to notify such person as is designated by the board if he is to be absent from school and the reason therefor;

(j) to deliver the register, the school key and other school property in his possession to the board on demand, or when his agreement with the board has expired, or when for any reason his employment has ceased; and

(k) to use and permit to be used as a textbook in a class that he teaches in an elementary or a secondary school,

(i) in a subject area for which textbooks are approved by the Minister, only textbooks that are approved by the Minister, and

(ii) in all subject areas, only textbooks that are approved by the board. R.S.O. 1980, c. 129, s. 235 (1); 1982, c. 32, s. 58.

(2) A teacher who refuses, on demand or order of the board that operates the school concerned, to deliver to the board any school property in his possession forfeits any claim that he may have against the board.

(3) Teachers may organize themselves for the purpose of conducting professional development conferences and seminars. R.S.O. 1980, c. 129, s. 235 (2, 3).

236. It is the duty of a principal of a school, in addition to his duties as a teacher,

(a) to maintain proper order and discipline in the school;

(b) to develop co-operation and co-ordination of effort among the members of the staff of the school;

(c) to register the pupils and to ensure that the attendance of pupils for every school day is recorded either in the register supplied by the Minister in accordance with the instructions contained therein or in such other manner as is approved by the Minister;

(d) to establish and maintain, and to retain, transfer and dispose of, in the manner prescribed by the regulations, a record in respect of each pupil enrolled in the school;

(e) to prepare a timetable, to conduct the school according to such timetable and the school year calendar or calendars applicable thereto, to make the calendar or calendars and the timetable accessible to the pupils, teachers and supervisory officers and to assign classes and subjects to the teachers;

(f) to hold, subject to the approval of the appropriate supervisory officer, such examinations as he considers necessary for the promotion of pupils or for any other purpose and report as required by the board the progress of the pupil to his parent or guardian where the pupil is a minor and otherwise to the pupil;

(g) subject to revision by the appropriate supervisory officer, to promote such pupils as he considers proper and to issue to each such pupil a statement thereof;

(h) to ensure that all textbooks used by pupils are those approved by the board and, in the case of subject areas for which the Minister approves textbooks, those approved by the Minister;

(i) to furnish to the Ministry and to the appropriate supervisory officer any information that it may be in his power to give respecting the condition of the school premises, the discipline of the school, the progress of the pupils and any other matter affecting the interests of the school, and to prepare such reports for the board as are required by the board;

(j) to give assiduous attention to the health and comfort of the pupils, to the cleanliness, temperature and ventilation of the school, to the care of all teaching materials and other school property, and to the condition and appearance of the school buildings and grounds;

(k) to report promptly to the board and to the municipal health officer or to the school medical officer where one has been appointed, when he has reason to suspect the existence of any infectious or contagious disease in the school, and of the unsanitary condition of any part of the school building or the school grounds;

(l) to refuse admission to the school of any person who he believes is infected with or exposed to communicable diseases requiring quarantine and placarding under regulations made pursuant to the *Public Health Act* until furnished with a certificate of a medical officer of health or of a legally qualified medical practitioner approved by him that all danger from exposure to contact with such person has passed;

(m) subject to an appeal to the board, to refuse to admit to the school or classroom a person whose presence in the school or classroom would in his judgment be detrimental to the physical or mental well-being of the pupils; and

(n) to maintain a visitor's book in the school when so determined by the board. R.S.O. 1980, c. 129, s. 236.

Pupil Records

237.—(1) In this section, except in subsection (12), "record" in respect of a pupil means a record maintained or retained by the principal of a school in accordance with the regulations.

(2) A record is privileged for the information and use of supervisory officers and the principal and teachers of the school for the improvement of instruction of the pupil, and such record,

    (a)   subject to subsections (3) and (5), is not available to any other person; and

    (b)   except for the purposes of subsection (5), is not admissible in evidence for any purpose in any trial, inquest, inquiry, examination, hearing or other proceeding, except to prove the establishment, maintenance, retention or transfer of the record,

without the written permission of the parent or guardian of the pupil or, where the pupil is an adult, the written permission of the pupil.

(3) A pupil, and his parent or guardian where the pupil is a minor, is entitled to examine the record of such pupil.

(4) Where, in the opinion of a pupil who is an adult, or of the parent or guardian of a pupil who is a minor, information recorded upon the record of the pupil is,

    (a)   inaccurately recorded; or

    (b)   not conducive to the improvement of instruction of the pupil,

such pupil, parent or guardian, as the case may be, may, in writing, request the principal to correct the alleged inaccuracy in, or to remove the impugned information from, such record.

(5) Where the principal refuses to comply with a request under subsection (4), the pupil, parent or guardian who made the request may, in writing, require the principal to refer the request to the appropriate supervisory officer who shall either require the principal to comply with the request or submit the record and the request to a person designated by the Minister, and such person shall hold a hearing at which the principal and the person who made the request are the parties to the proceedings, and the person so designated shall, after the hearing, decide the matter, and his decision is final and binding upon the parties to the proceedings.

(6) Nothing in subsection (2) prohibits the use by the principal of the record in respect of a pupil to assist in the preparation of,

(a) a report required by this Act or the regulations; or

(b) a report,

    (i) for an educational institution or for the pupil or former pupil, in respect of an application for further education, or

    (ii) for the pupil or former pupil in respect of an application for employment,

where a written request is made by the former pupil, the pupil where he is an adult, or the parent or guardian of the pupil where the pupil is a minor.

(7) Nothing in this section prevents the compilation and delivery of such information as may be required by the Minister or by the board.

(8) No action shall be brought against any person in respect of the content of a record.

(9) Except where the record has been introduced in evidence as provided in this section, no person shall be required in any trial or other proceeding to give evidence in respect of the content of a record.

(10) Except as permitted under this section, every person shall preserve secrecy in respect of the content of a record that comes to his knowledge in the course of his duties or employment, and no such person shall communicate any such knowledge to any other person except,

(a) as may be required in the performance of his duties; or

(b) with the written consent of the parent or guardian of the pupil where the pupil is a minor; or

(c) with the written consent of the pupil where the pupil is an adult.

(11) For the purposes of this section, "guardian" includes a person, society or corporation who or that has custody of a pupil.

(12) This section, except subsections (3), (4) and (5), applies with necessary modifications to a record established and maintained in respect of a pupil or retained in respect of a former pupil prior to the 1st day of September, 1972.

(13) Nothing in this section prevents the use of a record in respect of a pupil by the principal of the school attended by the pupil or the board that operates the school for the purposes of a disciplinary proceeding instituted by the principal in respect of conduct for which the pupil is responsible to the principal.   R.S.O. 1980, c. 129, s. 237.

Boards of Reference

238. In sections 239 to 248,

(a) "contract" means a contract of employment between a teacher and a board;

(b) "employed" means employed as a permanent teacher by a board;

(c) "judge" means a judge of a county or district court;

(d) "teacher" means a person qualified to teach in an elementary or secondary school and employed by a board on the terms and conditions contained in the form of contract prescribed for a permanent teacher.   R.S.O. 1980, c. 129, s. 238.

239.—(1) The dismissal of a teacher, or the termination of the contract of a teacher, by a board shall be by notice in writing, which shall state the reasons therefor, in accordance with the terms of the contract.

(2) Where a teacher is employed by a board, the termination of the contract by the teacher shall be by notice in writing in accordance with the terms of the contract.

(3) Where a teacher is dismissed or the contract of a teacher is terminated by the board or the teacher, the teacher or board if not in agreement with the dismissal or termination may at any time within twenty-one days after receiving the notice referred to in subsection (1) or (2), as the case may be, apply in writing by registered letter to the Minister for a Board of Reference, stating the disagreement.

(4) The applicant shall send a copy of the application by registered mail to the other party to the disagreement on the same day as the application is sent to the Minister.   R.S.O. 1980, c. 129, s. 239.

240.—(1) A board shall not make a permanent appointment to take the place of a teacher who is dismissed or whose contract has been terminated in a manner not agreeable to the teacher until,

    (a)   the time prescribed for applying for a Board of Reference has elapsed and the teacher has not applied for a Board of Reference and sent a copy of the application to the board, as provided in section 239;

    (b)   the board has received from the teacher notice in writing that no application will be made under section 239;

    (c)   the board has received from the Minister notice in writing that an application made by the teacher under section 239 has been withdrawn;

    (d)   the board has received from the Minister notice in writing that he has refused an application made by the teacher under section 239;

    (e)   the board has received from the Minister notice in writing that the teacher, being the applicant, has failed to comply with the requirements of subsection 241 (3); or

    (f)   the board has received from the Minister a copy of the direction of the Board of Reference under section 244 directing the discontinuance of the contract,

whichever first occurs.

(2) A teacher who terminates a contract in a manner not agreeable to the board shall not enter into a contract with another board after the teacher has received notice of the application of the board for a Board of Reference until,

    (a)   the teacher has received from the Minister notice in writing that an application made by the board under section 239 has been withdrawn;

    (b)   the teacher has received from the Minister notice in writing that he has refused an application made by the board under section 239;

    (c)   the teacher has received from the Minister notice in writing that the board, being the applicant, has failed to comply with the requirements of subsection 241 (3); or

(d) the teacher has received from the Board of Reference a copy of the direction of the Board of Reference under section 244 directing the discontinuance of the contract,

whichever first occurs.   R.S.O. 1980, c. 129, s. 240.

241.—(1) Upon receipt of an application for a Board of Reference, the Minister shall cause notice of the application to be sent by registered mail to the other party to the disagreement and shall within thirty days of sending the notice inquire into the disagreement and shall, within the same time,

(a) refuse to grant the Board of Reference; or

(b) grant the Board of Reference and appoint a judge to act as chairman thereof.

(2) Where, under subsection (1), a judge is appointed after the expiry of thirty days referred to therein to act as chairman of a Board of Reference, the failure to make the appointment within the thirty-day period does not invalidate the Board of Reference or the appointment of the judge as chairman thereof, provided the Board of Reference is granted in accordance with subsection (1).

(3) Upon appointing a judge to act as chairman of a Board of Reference, the Minister shall cause notice thereof to be sent by registered mail to the board and teacher involved in the disagreement and the notice shall require each of them to name to the Board of Reference a representative who is not the teacher involved or a member of the board and to send or cause to be sent by hand or by registered mail to the Minister a notice of such nomination within twelve days of the sending of the notice by the Minister.

(4) If the applicant fails to comply with the requirements of subsection (3), the application shall be deemed to be abandoned and the Minister shall cause notice thereof to be sent by registered mail to the other party to the disagreement.

(5) If the respondent fails to comply with the requirements of subsection (3), the Minister shall direct the continuance of the contract.

(6) If the representative of the board or the teacher, having been named, fails to appear at the hearing, the chairman of the Board of Reference shall name a representative for the board or teacher, as the case may be.

(7) Where the Minister grants a Board of Reference, the appiicant shall be deemed to have met the conditions precedent to the granting of a Board of Reference.

(8) Where, after the hearing has commenced, the representative of the board or of the teacher dies, for any reason is unable to continue to act or withdraws from the Board of Reference, the other representative shall withdraw and the decision of the Board of Reference shall be made by the chairman.

(9) Where, before the hearing has commenced, the chairman of a Board of Reference dies, disqualifies himself, for any reason is unable to act or is prohibited from acting, the Minister shall appoint another judge to act as chairman and the Board of Reference shall proceed in accordance with this Part except that for the purposes of section 242 the date of appointment of the chairman is the date of appointment of the chairman appointed to act under this section.

(10) Where, after the hearing has commenced and before the chairman of a Board of Reference reports to the Minister and to the parties,

    (a)   the chairman dies, disqualifies himself, for any reason is unable to continue as chairman, or is prohibited from acting; or

    (b)   the Board of Reference is prohibited from acting or proceeding,

the Board of Reference is terminated and, where, within ninety days after the death, disqualification, inability to continue or prohibition referred to in clause (a) or (b), the person who applied for the Board of Reference requests the Minister in writing to grant another Board of Reference, the Minister may grant a new Board of Reference, in which case the provisions of this Part apply with necessary modifications except that the representatives named to the new Board of Reference shall not be the representatives named to the Board of Reference terminated under this subsection and the determination and direction of the costs under section 247 may include the costs, if any, incurred in respect of the Board of Reference terminated under this subsection.

(11) Where a new Board of Reference is granted under subsection (10), the hearing shall proceed as if the hearing by the Board of Reference terminated under subsection (10) had not commenced.   R.S.O. 1980, c. 129, s. 241.

242. The chairman of the Board of Reference shall, within thirty days of his appointment, and upon reasonable notice thereof to the parties, convene the Board of Reference in any appropriate and convenient court house or municipal or school building and at such time as he may appoint.   R.S.O. 1980, c. 129, s. 242.

243. The Board of Reference shall inquire into the matter in dispute and for such purposes the chairman has the powers of a commission under Part II of the *Public Inquiries Act*, which Part applies to such inquiry as if it were an inquiry under that Act.   R.S.O. 1980, c. 129, s. 243.

244.—(1) A Board of Reference shall direct the continuance of the contract or the discontinuance of the contract.

(2) The chairman of a Board of Reference shall, within seven days after,

(a) the application for the Board of Reference is withdrawn; or

(b) the matter in dispute has been settled by the parties to the Board of Reference; or

(c) the completion of the hearing and the receipt of any written submissions required by him,

report to the Minister and the parties the disposition of the application.   R.S.O. 1980, c. 129, s. 244.

245. Where, pursuant to an application for judicial review under the *Judicial Review Procedure Act*, the report or the direction of a Board of Reference is set aside, the Minister may grant a new Board of Reference if the board or teacher applies therefor to the Minister by registered mail within fifteen days after the date of the order of the court setting aside the report or direction, and the provisions of sections 238 to 248 apply with necessary modifications in respect of the new Board of Reference.   R.S.O. 1980, c. 129, s. 245.

246.—(1) The direction of the Board of Reference under section 244 is binding upon the board and the teacher.

(2) If a board fails to comply with the direction of the Board of Reference under section 244, the Minister may direct that any portion of the amounts then or thereafter payable to the board under the authority of any Act of the Legislature shall not be paid to the board until it has complied with the direction.

(3) If a teacher fails to comply with the direction of the Board of Reference under section 244, the Minister may sus-

pend the certificate of qualification of the teacher for such period as he considers advisable.   R.S.O. 1980, c. 129, s. 246.

247. Subject to the regulations made under section 248, the chairman of the Board of Reference shall determine and direct the costs to be paid by either or both parties in the disagreement, and every such order may be enforced in the same manner as an order as to costs made in an action in a county or district court.   R.S.O. 1980, c. 129, s. 247.

248. The Lieutenant Governor in Council may make regulations,

   (a) fixing the remuneration of members of Boards of Reference and defining, prescribing and limiting other items of expense, including travelling and living expenses, which shall be included in the costs of a Board of Reference;

   (b) regulating the practice and procedure to be followed upon any reference; and

   (c) respecting any matter necessary or advisable to carry out effectively the intent and purpose of sections 239 to 247.   R.S.O. 1980, c. 129, s. 248.

. . .

TRANSITIONAL PROVISIONS

278.—(1) Where the Lieutenant Governor in Council designates a date for the purposes of subsections 32 (5) and (6), subsection 39 (3), subsection 47 (1) and subsection 209 (3) or any of them, such designation may have general application or may relate to such board or boards as may be set out in the designation.

(2) Where the Lieutenant Governor in Council designates a date for the purposes of subsection 32 (5) and subsection 209 (3) in respect of a divisional board, subsection 55 (5) ceases to apply to such divisional board.

(3) Effective the date designated by the Lieutenant Governor in Council for the purposes of subsection 39 (3), or the 31st day of December, 1984, whichever occurs first, in relation to The Metropolitan Separate School Board and The Metropolitan Toronto School Board, subsection 39 (4) ceases to operate and the cost of operation of schools for trainable retarded children operated by The Metropolitan Toronto School Board shall be included in the estimates of such board for public elementary school purposes.   R.S.O. 1980, c. 129, s. 278.

Appendix B

Young Offenders Act

An Act respecting young offenders

1. This Act may be cited as the *Young Offenders Act.* 1980-81-82-83, c. 110, s. 1.

INTERPRETATION

2. (1) In this Act,

"adult" means a person who is neither a young person nor a child;

"alternative measures" means measures other than judicial proceedings under this Act used to deal with a young person alleged to have committed an offence;

"child" means a person who is or, in the absence of evidence to the contrary, appears to be under the age of twelve years;

"disposition" means a disposition made under section 20 or sections 28 to 33 and includes a confirmation or a variation of a disposition;

"offence" means an offence created by an Act of Parliament or by any regulation, rule, order, by-law or ordinance made thereunder other than an ordinance of the Yukon Territory or the Northwest Territories;

"ordinary court" means the court that would, but for this Act, have jurisdiction in respect of an offence alleged to have been committed;

"parent" includes, in respect of another person, any person who is under a legal duty to provide for that other person or any person who has, in law or in fact, the custody or control of that other person;

"pre-disposition report" means a report on the personal and family history and present environment of a young person made in accordance with section 14;

"progress report" means a report made in accordance with section 28 on the performance of a young person against whom a disposition has been made;

"provincial director" means a person, a group or class of persons or a body appointed or designated by or pursuant to an Act of the legislature of a province or by the Lieutenant Governor in Council of a province or his delegate to perform in that province, either generally or in a specific case, any of the duties or functions of a provincial director under this Act;

"review board" means a review board established or designated by a province for the purposes of section 30;

"young person" means a person who is or, in the absence of evidence to the contrary, appears to be twelve years of age or more, but under eighteen years of age and, where the context requires, includes any person who is charged under this Act with having committed an offence while he was a young person or is found guilty of an offence under this Act;

"youth court" means a court established or designated by or under an Act of the legislature of a province, or designated by the Governor in Council or the Lieutenant Governor in Council of a province, as a youth court for the purposes of this Act;

"youth court judge" means a person appointed to be a judge of a youth court;

"youth worker" means a person appointed or designated, whether by title of youth worker or probation officer or by any other title, by or pursuant to an Act of the legislature of a province or by the Lieutenant Governor in Council of a province or his delegate, to perform, either generally or in a specific case, in that province any of the duties or functions of a youth worker under this Act.

(2) Unless otherwise provided, words and expressions used in this Act have the same meaning as in the *Criminal Code*. 1980-81-82-83, c. 110, s. 2.

3. (1) It is hereby recognized and declared that

(*a*) while young persons should not in all instances be held accountable in the same manner or suffer the same consequences for their behaviour as adults, young persons who commit offences should nonetheless bear responsibility for their contraventions;

(*b*) society must, although it has the responsibility to take reasonable measures to prevent criminal conduct by young persons, be afforded the necessary protection from illegal behaviour;

(*c*) young persons who commit offences require supervision, discipline and control, but, because of their state of dependency and level of development and maturity, they also have special needs and require guidance and assistance;

(*d*) where it is not inconsistent with the protection of society, taking no measures or taking measures other than judicial proceedings under this Act should be considered for dealing with young persons who have committed offences;

(*e*) young persons have rights and freedoms in their own right, including those stated in the *Canadian Charter of Rights and Freedoms* or in the *Canadian Bill of Rights*, and in particular a right to be heard in the course of, and to participate in, the processes that lead to decisions that affect them, and young persons should have special guarantees of their rights and freedoms;

(*f*) in the application of this Act, the rights and freedoms of young persons include a right to the least possible interference with freedom that is consistent with the protection of society, having regard to the needs of young persons and the interests of their families;

(*g*) young persons have the right, in every instance where they have rights or freedoms that may be affected by this Act, to be informed as to what those rights and freedoms are; and

(*h*) parents have responsibility for the care and supervision of their children, and, for that reason, young persons should be removed from parental supervision either partly or entirely only when measures that provide for continuing parental supervision are inappropriate.

(2) This Act shall be liberally construed to the end that young persons will be dealt with in accordance with the principles set out in subsection (1). 1980-81-82-83, c. 110, s. 3.

ALTERNATIVE MEASURES

4. (1) Alternative measures may be used to deal with a young person alleged to have committed an offence instead of judicial proceedings under this Act only if

(*a*) the measures are part of a program of alternative measures authorized by the Attorney General or his delegate or authorized by a person, or a person within a class of persons, designated by the Lieutenant Governor in Council of a province;

(*b*) the person who is considering whether to use such measures is satisfied that they would be appropriate, having regard to the needs of the young person and the interests of society;

(*c*) the young person, having been informed of the alternative measures, fully and freely consents to participate therein;

(*d*) the young person has, before consenting to participate in the alternative measures, been advised of his right to be represented by counsel and been given a reasonable opportunity to consult with counsel;

(*e*) the young person accepts responsibility for the act or omission that forms the basis of the offence that he is alleged to have committed;

(*f*) there is, in the opinion of the Attorney General or his agent, sufficient evidence to proceed with the prosecution of the offence; and

(*g*) the prosecution of the offence is not in any way barred at law.

(2) Alternative measures shall not be used to deal with a young person alleged to have committed an offence if the young person

(*a*) denies his participation or involvement in the commission of the offence; or

(*b*) expresses his wish to have any charge against him dealt with by the youth court.

(3) No admission, confession or statement accepting responsibility for a given act or omission made by a young person alleged to have committed an offence as a condition of his being dealt with by alternative measures shall be admissible in evidence against him in any civil or criminal proceedings.

(4) The use of alternative measures in respect of a young person alleged to have committed an offence is not a bar to proceedings against him under this Act, but

(*a*) where the youth court is satisfied on a balance of probabilities that the young person has totally complied with the terms and conditions of the alternative measures, the youth court shall dismiss any charge against him; and

(*b*) where the youth court is satisfied on a balance of probabilities that the young person has partially complied with the terms and conditions of the alternative measures, the youth court may dismiss any charge against him if, in the opinion of the court, the prosecution of the charge would, having regard to the circumstances, be unfair, and the youth court may consider the young person's performance with respect to the alter-native measures before making a disposition under this Act.

(5) Subject to subsection (4), nothing in this section shall be construed to prevent any person from laying an information, obtaining the issue or confirmation of any process or proceeding with the prosecution of any offence in accordance with law. 1980-81-82-83, c. 110, s. 4.

JURISDICTION

5. (1) Notwithstanding any other Act of Parliament but subject to the *National Defence Act* and section 16, a youth court has exclusive jurisdiction in respect of any offence alleged to have been committed by a person while he was a young person and any such person shall be dealt with as provided in this Act.

(2) No proceedings in respect of an offence shall be commenced under this Act after the expiration of the time limit set out in any other Act of Parliament or any regulation made thereunder for the institution of proceedings in respect of that offence.

(3) Proceedings commenced under this Act against a young person may be continued, after he becomes an adult, in all respects as if he remained a young person.

(4) A youth court judge, for the purpose of carrying out the provisions of this Act, is a justice and a magistrate and has the jurisdiction and powers of a summary conviction court under the *Criminal Code*.

(5) A youth court is a court of record. 1980-81-82-83, c. 110, s. 5.

6. Subject to section 8, any proceeding that may be carried out before a justice under the *Criminal Code*, other than a plea, a trial or an adjudication, may be carried out before a justice in respect of an offence alleged to have been committed by a young person, and any process that may be issued by a justice under the *Criminal Code* may be issued by a justice in respect of an offence alleged to have been committed by a young person. 1980-81-82-83, c. 110, s. 6.

222

DETENTION PRIOR TO DISPOSITION

7. (1) A young person who is arrested and detained prior to the making of a disposition in respect of the young person under section 20 shall, subject to subsection (2), be detained in a place of temporary detention designated as such by the Lieutenant Governor in Council of the appropriate province or his delegate or in a place within a class of places so designated.

(2) Subsection (1) does not apply in respect of the arrest of a young person or in respect of any temporary restraint of a young person in the hands of a peace officer after the arrest of the young person but prior to his detention in custody.

(3) No young person who has been arrested shall be detained prior to the making of a disposition in respect of the young person under section 20 in any part of a place in which an adult who has been charged with or convicted of an offence against any law of Canada or a province is detained or held in custody unless a youth court judge or, where a youth court judge is, having regard to the circumstances, not reasonably available, a justice authorizes the detention, being satisfied that

(a) the young person cannot, having regard to his own safety or the safety of others, be detained in a place of detention for young persons; or

(b) no place of detention for young persons is available within a reasonable distance.

(4) Where a youth court judge or a justice is satisfied that

(a) a responsible person is willing and able to take care of and exercise control over a young person who has been arrested, and

(b) the young person is willing to be placed in the care of that person,

and where that person undertakes in writing to take care of and to be responsible for the attendance of the young person in court when required, the young person may be placed in the care of that person instead of being detained in custody.

(5) In any province for which the Lieutenant Governor in Council has designated a person or a group of persons whose authorization is required before a young person who has been arrested may be detained prior to his appearance before a youth court judge or a justice, no young person shall be so detained unless that authorization is first obtained.

(6) A young person who is detained in custody in accordance with this section may, during the period of detention, be transferred by the provincial director or his delegate from one place of temporary detention to another.

(7) Any person who fails to comply with subsection (1), (3) or (5) is guilty of an offence punishable on summary conviction. 1980-81-82-83, c. 110, s. 7.

8. (1) No order may be made under section 515 of the *Criminal Code* by a court, judge or justice, other than a youth court judge, for the release from or the detention in custody of a young person against whom proceedings have been taken under this Act unless, having regard to the circumstances, a youth court judge is not reasonably available.

(2) Where an order is made under section 515 of the *Criminal Code* in respect of a young person by a justice who is not a youth court judge, an application may, at any time after the order is made, be made to a youth court for the release from or detention in custody of the young person, as the case may be, and the youth court shall hear the matter as an original application.

(3) An application under subsection (2) for release from custody shall not be heard unless the young person has given the prosecutor at least two clear days notice in writing of the application.

(4) An application under subsection (2) for detention in custody shall not be heard unless the prosecutor has given the young person at least two clear days notice in writing of the application.

(5) The requirement for a notice under subsection (3) or (4) may be waived by the prosecutor or by the young person or his counsel, as the case may be.

(6) An application under section 520 or 521 of the *Criminal Code* for a review of an order made in respect of a young person by a youth court judge who is a judge of a superior, county

or district court shall be made to a judge of the court of appeal.

(7) No application may be made under section 520 or 521 of the *Criminal Code* for a review of an order made in respect of a young person by a justice who is not a youth court judge.

(8) Where a young person against whom proceedings have been taken under this Act is charged with an offence referred to in section 522 of the *Criminal Code*, a youth court judge, but no other court, judge or justice, may release the young person from custody under that section.

(9) A decision made by a youth court judge under subsection (8) may be reviewed in accordance with section 680 of the *Criminal Code* and that section applies, with such modifications as the circumstances require, to any decision so made. 1980-81-82-83, c. 110, s. 8.

NOTICES TO PARENTS

9. (1) Subject to subsections (3) and (4), where a young person is arrested and detained in custody pending his appearance in court, the officer in charge at the time the young person is detained shall, as soon as possible, give or cause to be given, orally or in writing, to a parent of the young person notice of the arrest stating the place of detention and the reason for the arrest.

(2) Subject to subsections (3) and (4), where a summons or an appearance notice is issued in respect of a young person, the person who issued the summons or appearance notice, or, where a young person is released on giving his promise to appear or entering into a recognizance, the officer in charge, shall, as soon as possible, give or cause to be given, in writing, to a parent of the young person notice of the summons, appearance notice, promise to appear or recognizance.

(3) Where the whereabouts of the parents of a young person

(*a*) who is arrested and detained in custody,

(*b*) in respect of whom a summons or an appearance notice is issued, or

(*c*) who is released on giving his promise to appear or entering into a recognizance

are not known or it appears that no parent is available, a notice under this section may be given to an adult relative of the young person who is known to the young person and is likely to assist him or, if no such adult relative is available, to such other adult who is known to the young person and is likely to assist him as the person giving the notice considers appropriate.

(4) Where a young person described in paragraph (3)(*a*), (*b*) or (*c*) is married, a notice under this section may be given to the spouse of the young person instead of a parent.

(5) Where doubt exists as to the person to whom a notice under this section should be given, a youth court judge or, where a youth court judge is, having regard to the circumstances, not reasonably available, a justice may give directions as to the person to whom the notice should be given, and a notice given in accordance with those directions is sufficient notice for the purposes of this section.

(6) Any notice under this section shall, in addition to any other requirements under this section, include

(*a*) the name of the young person in respect of whom it is given;

(*b*) the charge against the young person and the time and place of appearance; and

(*c*) a statement that the young person has the right to be represented by counsel.

(7) Subject to subsection (10), a notice under this section given in writing may be served personally or may be sent by mail.

(8) Subject to subsection (9), failure to give notice in accordance with this section does not affect the validity of proceedings under this Act.

(9) Failure to give notice in accordance with subsection (2) in any case renders invalid any subsequent proceedings under this Act relating to the case unless

(*a*) a parent of the young person against whom proceedings are held attends court with the young person; or

(*b*) notice has been dispensed with pursuant to paragraph (10)(*b*).

(10) Where there has been a failure to give a notice in accordance with this section and none of the persons to whom such notice may be given attends court with a young person, a youth court judge or a justice before whom proceedings are held against the young person may

(*a*) adjourn the proceedings and order that the notice be given in such manner and to such person as he directs; or

(*b*) dispense with the notice where, in his opinion, having regard to the circumstances, notice may be dispensed with.

(11) A notice under subsection (1) or (2) may be in Form 1 and a notice under subsection (3) may be in Form 2. 1980-81-82-83, c. 110, s. 9.

10. (1) Where a parent does not attend proceedings before a youth court in respect of a young person, the court may, if in its opinion the presence of the parent is necessary or in the best interest of the young person, by order in writing require the parent to attend at any stage of the proceedings.

(2) An order made under subsection (1) may be in Form 3 and a copy of the order shall be served by a peace officer or by a person designated by a youth court by delivering it personally to the parent to whom it is directed, unless the youth court authorizes service by registered mail.

(3) A parent who is ordered to attend a youth court pursuant to subsection (1) and who fails without reasonable excuse, the proof of which lies on that parent, to comply with the order

(*a*) is guilty of contempt of court;

(*b*) may be dealt with summarily by the court; and

(*c*) is liable to the punishment provided for in the *Criminal Code* for a summary conviction offence.

(4) Section 10 of the *Criminal Code* applies where a person is convicted of contempt of court under subsection (3).

(5) If a parent who is ordered to attend a youth court pursuant to subsection (1) does not attend at the time and place named in the order or fails to remain in attendance as required and

it is proved that a copy of the order was served on the parent, a youth court may issue a warrant to compel the attendance of the parent.

RIGHT TO COUNSEL

11. (1) A young person has the right to retain and instruct counsel without delay at any stage of proceedings against him and prior to and during any consideration of whether, instead of commencing or continuing judicial proceedings against him under this Act, to use alternative measures to deal with him.

(2) Every young person who is arrested or detained shall, forthwith on his arrest or detention, be advised by the arresting officer or the officer in charge, as the case may be, of his right to be represented by counsel and shall be given an opportunity to obtain counsel.

(3) Where a young person is not represented by counsel

(*a*) at a hearing at which it will be determined whether to release the young person or detain him in custody prior to disposition of his case,

(*b*) at a hearing held pursuant to section 16,

(*c*) at his trial, or

(*d*) at a review of a disposition held before a youth court or a review board under this Act,

the justice before whom, or the youth court or review board before which, the hearing, trial or review is held shall advise the young person of his right to be represented by counsel and shall give the young person a reasonable opportunity to obtain counsel.

(4) Where a young person at his trial or at a hearing or review referred to in subsection (3) wishes to obtain counsel but is unable to do so, the youth court before which the hearing, trial or review is held or the review board before which the review is held

(*a*) shall, where there is a legal aid or an assistance program available in the province where the hearing, trial or review is held, refer the young person to that program for the appointment of counsel; or

(*b*) where no legal aid or assistance program is available or the young person is unable to obtain counsel through such a program, may, and on the request of the young person shall, direct that the young person be represented by counsel.

(5) Where a direction is made under paragraph (4)(*b*) in respect of a young person, the Attorney General of the province in which the direction is made shall appoint counsel, or cause counsel to be appointed, to represent the young person.

(6) Where a young person at a hearing before a justice who is not a youth court judge at which it will be determined whether to release the young person or detain him in custody prior to disposition of his case wishes to obtain counsel but is unable to do so, the justice shall

(*a*) where there is a legal aid or an assistance program available in the province where the hearing is held,

(i) refer the young person to that program for the appointment of counsel, or

(ii) refer the matter to a youth court to be dealt with in accordance with paragraph (4)(*a*) or (*b*); or

(*b*) where no legal aid or assistance program is available or the young person is unable to obtain counsel through such a program, refer the matter to a youth court to be dealt with in accordance with paragraph (4)(*b*).

(7) Where a young person is not represented by counsel at his trial or at a hearing or review referred to in subsection (3), the justice before whom or the youth court or review board before which the proceedings are held may, on the request of the young person, allow the young person to be assisted by an adult whom the justice, court or review board considers to be suitable.

(8) In any case where it appears to a youth court judge or a justice that the interests of a young person and his parents are in conflict or that it would be in the best interest of the young person to be represented by his own counsel, the judge or justice shall ensure that the young person is represented by counsel independent of his parents.

(9) A statement that a young person has the right to be represented by counsel shall be included in any appearance notice or summons issued to the young person, any warrant to arrest the young person, any promise to appear given by the young person, any recognizance entered into before an officer in charge by the young person or any notice of a review of a disposition given to the young person. 1980-81-82-83, c. 110, s. 11.

12. (1) Where a young person against whom an information is laid first appears before a youth court judge or a justice, the judge or justice shall

(*a*) cause the information to be read to him; and

(*b*) where the young person is not represented by counsel, inform him of his right to be so represented.

(2) A young person may waive the requirement under paragraph (1)(*a*) where the young person is represented by counsel.

(3) Where a young person is not represented in youth court by counsel, the youth court shall, before accepting a plea,

(*a*) satisfy itself that the young person understands the charge against him; and

(*b*) explain to the young person that he may plead guilty or not guilty to the charge.

(4) Where the youth court is not satisfied that a young person understands the charge against him, as required under paragraph (3)(*a*), the court shall enter a plea of not guilty on behalf of the young person and shall proceed with the trial in accordance with subsection 19(2). 1980-81-82-83, c. 110, s. 12.

13. (1) For the purpose of

(*a*) considering an application under section 16,

(*b*) determining whether to direct that an issue be tried whether a young person is, on account of insanity, unfit to stand trial, or

(*c*) making or reviewing a disposition under this Act,

a youth court may, at any stage of proceedings against a young person,

(*d*) with the consent of the young person and the prosecutor, or

226

(e) on its own motion or on the application of either the young person or the prosecutor, where the court has reasonable grounds to believe that the young person may be suffering from a physical or mental illness or disorder, a psychological disorder, an emotional disturbance, a learning disability or mental retardation and where the court believes a medical, psychological or psychiatric report in respect of the young person might be helpful in making any decision pursuant to this Act,

by order require that the young person be examined by a qualified person and that the person who conducts the examination report the results thereof in writing to the court.

(2) Where a youth court makes an order for an examination under subsection (1) for the purpose of determining whether to direct that an issue be tried whether a young person is, on account of insanity, unfit to stand trial, the examination shall be carried out by a qualified medical practitioner.

(3) For the purpose of an examination under this section, a youth court may remand the young person who is to be examined to such custody as it directs for a period not exceeding eight days or, where it is satisfied that observation is required for a longer period to complete an examination or assessment and its opinion is supported by the evidence of, or a report in writing of, at least one qualified person, for a longer period not exceeding thirty days.

(4) Where a youth court receives a report made in respect of a young person pursuant to subsection (1),

(a) the court shall, subject to subsection (6), cause a copy of the report to be given to

(i) the young person,

(ii) a parent of the young person, if the parent is in attendance at the proceedings against the young person,

(iii) counsel, if any, representing the young person, and

(iv) the prosecutor; and

(b) the court may cause a copy of the report to be given to a parent of the young person not in attendance at the proceedings against the young person if the parent is, in the opinion of the court, taking an active interest in the proceedings.

(5) Where a report is made in respect of a young person pursuant to subsection (1), the young person, his counsel or the adult assisting him pursuant to subsection 11(7) and the prosecutor shall, subject to subsection (6), on application to the youth court, be given an opportunity to cross-examine the person who made the report.

(6) A youth court may withhold the whole or any part of a report made in respect of a young person pursuant to subsection (1) from

(a) a private prosecutor where disclosure of the report or part thereof, in the opinion of the court, is not necessary for the prosecution of the case and might be prejudicial to the young person; or

(b) the young person, his parents or a private prosecutor where the person who made the report states in writing that disclosure of the report or part thereof would be likely to be detrimental to the treatment or recovery of the young person or would be likely to result in bodily harm to, or be detrimental to the mental condition of, a third party.

(7) A youth court may, at any time before an adjudication in respect of a young person charged with an offence, where it appears that there is sufficient reason to doubt that the young person is, on account of insanity, capable of conducting his defence, direct that an issue be tried as to whether the young person is then on account of insanity unfit to stand trial.

(8) Where a youth court directs the trial of an issue under subsection (7), it shall proceed in accordance with section 615 of the *Criminal Code* in so far as that section may be applied.

(9) A report made pursuant to subsection (1) shall form part of the record of the case in respect of which it was requested.

(10) Notwithstanding any other provision of this Act, a qualified person who is of the opinion that a young person held in detention or committed to custody is likely to endanger his own life or safety or to endanger the life of, or cause bodily harm to, another person may immediately so advise any person who has the care and custody of the young person whether or not the same information is contained in a report made pursuant to subsection (1).

(11) In this section, "qualified person"

means a person duly qualified by provincial law to practice medicine or psychiatry or to carry out psychological examinations or assessments, as the circumstances require, or, where no such law exists, a person who is, in the opinion of the youth court, so qualified, and includes a person or a person within a class of persons designated by the Lieutenant Governor in Council of a province or his delegate.

(12) An order under subsection (1) may be in Form 5. 1980-81-82-83, c. 110, s. 13.

PRE-DISPOSITION REPORT

14. (1) Where a youth court deems it advisable before making a disposition under section 20 in respect of a young person who is found guilty of an offence it may, and where a youth court is required under this Act to consider a pre-disposition report before making an order or a disposition in respect of a young person it shall, require the provincial director to cause to be prepared a pre-disposition report in respect of the young person and to submit the report to the court.

(2) A pre-disposition report made in respect of a young person shall, subject to subsection (3), be in writing and shall include

(*a*) the results of an interview with the young person and, where reasonably possible, the results of an interview with the parents of the young person;

(*b*) the results of an interview with the victim in the case, where applicable and where reasonably possible; and

(*c*) such information as is applicable to the case including, where applicable,

(i) the age, maturity, character, behaviour and attitude of the young person and his willingness to make amends,

(ii) any plans put forward by the young person to change his conduct or to participate in activities or undertake measures to improve himself,

(iii) the history of previous findings of delinquency under the *Juvenile Delinquents Act*, chapter J-3 of the Revised Statutes of Canada, 1970, or previous findings of guilt under this Act or any other Act of Parliament or any regulation made thereunder or under an Act of the legislature of a province or a by-law or ordinance of a municipality, the history of community or other services rendered to the young person with respect to those findings and the response of the young person to previous sentences or dispositions and to services rendered to him,

(iv) the history of alternative measures used to deal with the young person and the response of the young person thereto,

(v) the availability of community services and facilities for young persons and the willingness of the young person to avail himself of those services or facilities,

(vi) the relationship between the young person and his parents and the degree of control and influence of the parents over the young person, and

(vii) the school attendance and performance record and the employment record of the young person.

(3) Where a pre-disposition report cannot reasonably be committed to writing, it may, with leave of the youth court, be submitted orally in court.

(4) A pre-disposition report shall form part of the record of the case in respect of which it was requested.

(5) Where a pre-disposition report made in respect of a young person is submitted to a youth court in writing, the court

(*a*) shall, subject to subsection (7), cause a copy of the report to be given to

(i) the young person,

(ii) a parent of the young person, if the parent is in attendance at the proceedings against the young person,

(iii) counsel, if any, representing the young person, and

(iv) the prosecutor; and

(*b*) may cause a copy of the report to be given to a parent of the young person not in attendance at the proceedings against the young person if the parent is, in the opinion of the court, taking an active interest in the proceedings.

(6) Where a pre-disposition report made in respect of a young person is submitted to a youth court, the young person, his counsel or the adult assisting him pursuant to subsection

228

11(7) and the prosecutor shall, subject to subsection (7), on application to the youth court, be given the opportunity to cross-examine the person who made the report.

(7) Where a pre-disposition report made in respect of a young person is submitted to a youth court, the court may, where the prosecutor is a private prosecutor and disclosure of the report or any part thereof to the prosecutor might, in the opinion of the court, be prejudicial to the young person and is not, in the opinion of the court, necessary for the prosecution of the case against the young person,

(a) withhold the report or part thereof from the prosecutor, if the report is submitted in writing; or

(b) exclude the prosecutor from the court during the submission of the report or part thereof, if the report is submitted orally in court.

(8) Where a pre-disposition report made in respect of a young person is submitted to a youth court, the court

(a) shall, on request, cause a copy or a transcript of the report to be supplied to

(i) any court that is dealing with matters relating to the young person, and

(ii) any youth worker to whom the young person's case has been assigned; and

(b) may, on request, cause a copy or a transcript of the report, or a part thereof, to be supplied to any person not otherwise authorized under this section to receive a copy or a transcript of the report if, in the opinion of the court, the person has a valid interest in the proceedings.

(9) A provincial director who submits a pre-disposition report made in respect of a young person to a youth court may make the report, or any part thereof, available to any person in whose custody or under whose supervision the young person is placed or to any other person who is directly assisting in the care or treatment of the young person.

(10) No statement made by a young person in the course of the preparation of a pre-disposition report in respect of the young person is admissible in evidence against him in any civil or criminal proceedings except in proceedings under section 16 or 20 or sections 28 to 32. 1980-81-82-83, c. 110, s. 14.

1980-81-82-83, c. 110, s. 14.

DISQUALIFICATION OF JUDGE

15. (1) Subject to subsection (2), a youth court judge who, prior to an adjudication in respect of a young person charged with an offence, examines a pre-disposition report made in respect of the young person, or hears an application under section 16 in respect of the young person, in connection with that offence shall not in any capacity conduct or continue the trial of the young person for the offence and shall transfer the case to another judge to be dealt with according to law.

(2) A youth court judge may, in the circumstances referred to in subsection (1), with the consent of the young person and the prosecutor, conduct or continue the trial of the young person if the judge is satisfied that he has not been predisposed by information contained in the pre-disposition report or by representations made in respect of the application under section 16. 1980-81-82-83, c. 110, s. 15.

TRANSFER TO ORDINARY COURT

16. (1) At any time after an information is laid against a young person alleged to have, after attaining the age of fourteen years, committed an indictable offence other than an offence referred to in section 553 of the *Criminal Code* but prior to adjudication, a youth court may, on application of the young person or his counsel, or the Attorney General or his agent, after affording both parties and the parents of the young person an opportunity to be heard, if the court is of the opinion that, in the interest of society and having regard to the needs of the young person, the young person should be proceeded against in ordinary court, order that the young person be so proceeded against in accordance with the law ordinarily applicable to an adult charged with the offence.

(2) In considering an application under subsection (1) in respect of a young person, a youth court shall take into account

(a) the seriousness of the alleged offence and the circumstances in which it was allegedly committed;

(*b*) the age, maturity, character and background of the young person and any record or summary of previous findings of delinquency under the *Juvenile Delinquents Act*, chapter J-3 of the Revised Statutes of Canada, 1970, or previous findings of guilt under this Act or any other Act of Parliament or any regulation made thereunder;

(*c*) the adequacy of this Act, and the adequacy of the *Criminal Code* or other Act of Parliament that would apply in respect of the young person if an order were made under subsection (1), to meet the circumstances of the case;

(*d*) the availability of treatment or correctional resources;

(*e*) any representations made to the court by or on behalf of the young person or by the Attorney General or his agent: and

(*f*) any other factors that the court considers relevant.

(3) In considering an application under subsection (1), a youth court shall consider a pre-disposition report.

(4) Notwithstanding subsections (1) and (3), where an application is made under subsection (1) by the Attorney General or his agent in respect of an offence alleged to have been committed by a young person while the young person was being proceeded against in ordinary court pursuant to an order previously made under that subsection or serving a sentence as a result of proceedings in ordinary court, the youth court may make a further order under that subsection without a hearing and without considering a pre-disposition report.

(5) Where a youth court makes an order or refuses to make an order under subsection (1), it shall state the reasons for its decision and the reasons shall form part of the record of the proceedings in the youth court.

(6) Where a youth court refuses to make an order under subsection (1) in respect of an alleged offence, no further application may be made under this section in respect of that offence.

(7) Where an order is made under subsection (1), proceedings under this Act shall be discontinued and the young person against whom the proceedings are taken shall be taken before the ordinary court.

(8) Where an order is made under subsection (1) that a young person be proceeded against in ordinary court in respect of an offence, that court has jurisdiction only in respect of that offence or an offence included therein.

(9) Subject to subsection (11), an order made in respect of a young person under subsection (1) or a refusal to make such an order shall, on application of the young person or his counsel or the Attorney General or his agent made within thirty days after the decision of the youth court, be reviewed by the superior court and that court may, in its discretion, confirm or reverse the decision of the youth court.

(10) A decision made in respect of a young person by a superior court under subsection (9) may, on application of the young person or his counsel or the Attorney General or his agent made within thirty days after the decision of the superior court, with the leave of the court of appeal, be reviewed by that court, and the court of appeal may, in its discretion, confirm or reverse the decision of the superior court.

(11) In any province where the youth court is a superior court, a review under subsection (9) shall be made by the court of appeal of the province.

(12) A court to which an application is made under subsection (9) or (10) may at any time extend the time within which the application may be made.

(13) A person who proposes to apply for a review under subsection (9) or (10) or for leave to apply for a review under subsection (10) shall give notice of his application for a review or for leave to apply for a review in such manner and within such period of time as may be directed by rules of court.

(14) An order made under subsection (1) may be in Form 6. 1980-81-82-83, c. 110, s. 16.

17. (1) Where a youth court hears an application for a transfer to ordinary court under section 16, it shall

(*a*) where the young person is not represented by counsel, or (*b*) on application made by or on behalf of the young person or the prosecutor, where the young person is represented by counsel,

make an order directing that any information respecting the offence presented at the hearing shall not be published in any newspaper or broadcast before such time as

(*c*) an order for a transfer is refused or set aside on review and the time for all reviews against the decision has expired or all proceedings in respect of any such review have been completed; or

(*d*) the trial is ended, if the case is transferred to ordinary court.

(2) Every one who fails to comply with an order made pursuant to subsection (1) is guilty of an offence punishable on summary conviction.

(3) In this section, "newspaper" has the meaning set out in section 297 of the *Criminal Code*. 1980-81-82-83, c. 110, s. 17.

TRANSFER OF JURISDICTION

18. Notwithstanding subsections 478(1) and (3) of the *Criminal Code*, where a young person is charged with an offence that is alleged to have been committed in one province, he may, if the Attorney General of the province where the offence is alleged to have been committed consents, appear before a youth court of any other province and,

(*a*) where the young person signifies his consent to plead guilty and pleads guilty to that offence, the court shall, if it is satisfied that the facts support the charge, find the young person guilty of the offence alleged in the information; and

(*b*) where the young person does not signify his consent to plead guilty and does not plead guilty, or where the court is not satisfied that the facts support the charge, the young person shall, if he was detained in custody prior to his appearance, be returned to custody and dealt with according to law. 1980-81-82-83, c. 110, s. 18.

ADJUDICATION

19. (1) Where a young person pleads guilty to an offence charged against him and the youth court is satisfied that the facts support the charge, the court shall find the young person guilty of the offence.

(2) Where a young person pleads not guilty to an offence charged against him, or where a young person pleads guilty but the youth court is not satisfied that the facts support the charge, the court shall proceed with the trial and shall, after considering the matter, find the young person guilty or not guilty or make an order dismissing the charge, as the case may be. 1980-81-82-83, c. 110, s. 19.

DISPOSITIONS

20. (1) Where a youth court finds a young person guilty of an offence, it shall consider any pre-disposition report required by the court, any representations made by the parties to the proceedings or their counsel or agents and by the parents of the young person and any other relevant information before the court, and the court shall then make any one of the following dispositions, or any number thereof that are not inconsistent with each other:

(*a*) by order direct that the young person be discharged absolutely, if the court considers it to be in the best interests of the young person and not contrary to the public interest;

(*b*) impose on the young person a fine not exceeding one thousand dollars to be paid at such time and on such terms as the court may fix;

(*c*) order the young person to pay to any other person at such time and on such terms as the court may fix an amount by way of compensation for loss of or damage to property, for loss of income or support or for special damages for personal injury arising from the commission of the offence where the value thereof is readily ascertainable, but no order shall be made for general damages;

(*d*) order the young person to make restitution to any other person of any property obtained by the young person as a result of the commission of the offence within such time as the court may fix, if the property is owned by that other person or was, at the time of the offence, in his lawful possession;

(*e*) if any property obtained as a result of the commission of the offence has been sold to an innocent purchaser, where restitution of the property to its owner or any other person has been made or ordered, order the young person to pay the purchaser, at such time and on such terms as the court may fix, an amount not exceeding the amount paid by the purchaser for the property;

(*f*) subject to section 21, order the young person to compensate any person in kind or by way of personal services at such time and on such terms as the court may fix for any loss, damage or injury suffered by that person in respect of which an order may be made under paragraph (*c*) or (*e*);

(*g*) subject to section 21, order the young person to perform a community service at such time and on such terms as the court may fix;

(*h*) make any order of prohibition, seizure or forfeiture that may be imposed under any Act of Parliament or any regulation made thereunder where an accused is found guilty or convicted of that offence;

(*i*) subject to section 22, by order direct that the young person be detained for treatment, subject to such conditions as the court considers appropriate, in a hospital or other place where treatment is available, where a report has been made in respect of the young person pursuant to subsection 13(1) that recommends that the young person undergo treatment for a condition referred to in paragraph 13(1)(*e*);

(*j*) place the young person on probation in accordance with section 23 for a specified period not exceeding two years;

(*k*) subject to section 24, commit the young person to custody, to be served continuously or intermittently, for a specified period not exceeding

(i) two years from the date of committal, or

(ii) where the young person is found guilty of an offence for which the punishment provided by the *Criminal Code* or any other Act of Parliament is imprisonment for life, three years from the date of committal; and

(*l*) impose on the young person such other reasonable and ancillary conditions as it deems advisable and in the best interest of the young person and the public.

(2) A disposition made under this section shall come into force on the date on which it is made or on such later date as the youth court specifies therein.

(3) No disposition made under this section, except an order made under paragraph (1)(*h*) or (*k*), shall continue in force for more than two years and, where the youth court makes more than one disposition at the same time in respect of the same offence, the combined duration of the dispositions, except in respect of an order made under paragraph (1)(*h*) or (*k*), shall not exceed two years.

(4) Where more than one disposition is made under this section in respect of a young person with respect to different offences, the continuous combined duration of those dispositions shall not exceed three years.

(5) A disposition made under this section shall continue in effect, in accordance with the terms thereof, after the young person against whom it is made becomes an adult.

(6) Where a youth court makes a disposition under this section, it shall state its reasons therefor in the record of the case and shall

(*a*) provide or cause to be provided a copy of the disposition, and

(*b*) on request, provide or cause to be provided a transcript or copy of the reasons for the disposition

to the young person in respect of whom the disposition was made, his counsel, his parents, the provincial director, where the provincial director has an interest in the disposition, the prosecutor and, in the case of a custodial disposition made under paragraph (1)(*k*), the review board, if any has been established or designated.

(7) No disposition shall be made in respect of a young person under this section that results in a punishment that is greater than the maximum punishment that would be applicable to an adult who has committed the same offence.

(8) Part XXIII of the *Criminal Code* does not apply in respect of proceedings under this Act except for subsections 727(2) to (5) and 736(2) and sections 749, 750 and 751, which provisions apply with such modifications as the circumstances require.

(9) Section 787 of the *Criminal Code* does not apply in respect of proceedings under this Act.

(10) A disposition made under this section, other than a probation order, may be in Form 7.

(11) A probation order made under this section may be in Form 8 and the youth court shall specify in the order the period for which it is to remain in force. 1980-81-82-83, c. 110, s. 20.

. . .

YOUTH WORKERS

37. The duties and functions of a youth worker in respect of a young person whose case has been assigned to him by the provincial director or his delegate include

(*a*) where the young person is bound by a probation order that requires him to be under supervision, supervising the young person in complying with the conditions of the probation order or in carrying out any other disposition made together with it;

(*b*) where the young person is found guilty of any offence, giving such assistance to him as he considers appropriate up to the time the young person is discharged or the disposition of his case terminates;

(*c*) attending court when he considers it advisable or when required by the youth court to be present;

(*d*) preparing, at the request of the provincial director or his delegate, a pre-disposition report or a progress report; and

(*e*) performing such other duties and functions as the provincial director requires. 1980-81-82-83, c. 110, s. 37.

PROTECTION OF PRIVACY OF YOUNG PERSONS

38. (1) No person shall publish by any means any report

(*a*) of an offence committed or alleged to have been committed by a young person, unless an order has been made under section 16 with respect thereto, or

(*b*) of any hearing, adjudication, disposition or appeal concerning a young person who committed or is alleged to have committed an offence

in which the name of the young person, a child or a young person aggrieved by the offence or a child or a young person who appeared as a witness in connection with the offence, or in which any information serving to identify the young person or child, is disclosed.

(2) Every one who contravenes subsection (1)

(*a*) is guilty of an indictable offence and liable to imprisonment for a term not exceeding two years; or

(*b*) is guilty of an offence punishable on summary conviction.

(3) Where an accused is charged with an offence under paragraph (2)(*a*), a magistrate has absolute jurisdiction to try the case and his jurisdiction does not depend on the consent of the accused. 1980-81-82-83, c. 110, s. 38.

. . .

EVIDENCE

56. (1) Subject to this section, the law relating to the admissibility of statements made by persons accused of committing offences applies in respect of young persons.

(2) No oral or written statement given by a young person to a peace officer or other person who is, in law, a person in authority is admissible against the young person unless

(*a*) the statement was voluntary;

(*b*) the person to whom the statement was given has, before the statement was made, clearly explained to the young person, in language appropriate to his age and understanding, that

(i) the young person is under no obligation to give a statement,

(ii) any statement given by him may be used as evidence in proceedings against him,

(iii) the young person has the right to consult another person in accordance with paragraph (*c*), and

(iv) any statement made by the young person is required to be made in the presence of the person consulted, unless the young person desires otherwise;

(*c*) the young person has, before the statement was made, been given a reasonable opportunity to consult with counsel or a parent, or in the absence of a parent, an adult relative, or in the absence of a parent and an adult relative, any other appropriate adult chosen by the young person; and

(*d*) where the young person consults any person pursuant to paragraph (*c*), the young person has been given a reasonable opportunity to make the statement in the presence of that person.

(3) The requirements set out in paragraphs (2)(*b*), (*c*) and (*d*) do not apply in respect of oral statements where they are made spontaneously by the young person to a peace officer or other person in authority before that person has had a reasonable opportunity to comply with those requirements.

(4) A young person may waive his rights under paragraph (2)(*c*) or (*d*) but any such waiver shall be made in writing and shall contain a statement signed by the young person that he has been apprised of the right that he is waiving.

(5) A youth court judge may rule inadmissible in any proceedings under this Act a statement given by the young person in respect of whom the proceedings are taken if the young person satisfies the judge that the statement was given under duress imposed by any person who is not, in law, a person in authority. 1980-81-82-83, c. 110, s. 56.

57. (1) In any proceedings under this Act, the testimony of a parent as to the age of a person of whom he is a parent is admissible as evidence of the age of that person.

(2) In any proceedings under this Act,

(*a*) a birth or baptismal certificate or a copy thereof purporting to be certified under the hand of the person in whose custody those records are held is evidence of the age of the person named in the certificate or copy; and

(*b*) an entry or record of an incorporated society that has had the control or care of the person alleged to have committed the offence in respect of which the proceedings are taken at or about the time the person came to Canada is evidence of the age of that person, if the entry or record was made before the time when the offence is alleged to have been committed.

(3) In the absence, before the youth court, of any certificate, copy, entry or record mentioned in subsection (2), or in corroboration of any such certificate, copy, entry or record, the youth court may receive and act on any other information relating to age that it considers reliable.

(4) In any proceedings under this Act, the youth court may draw inferences as to the age of a person from the person's appearance or from statements made by the person in direct examination or cross-examination. 1980-81-82-83, c. 110, s. 57.

58. (1) A party to any proceedings under this Act may admit any relevant fact or matter for the purpose of dispensing with proof thereof, including any fact or matter the admissibility of which depends on a ruling of law or of mixed law and fact.

(2) Nothing in this section precludes a party to a proceeding from adducing evidence to prove a fact or matter admitted by another party. 1980-81-82-83, c. 110, s. 58.

59. Any evidence material to proceedings under this Act that would not but for this section be admissible in evidence may, with the consent of the parties to the proceedings and where the young person is represented by counsel, be given in such proceedings. 1980-81-82-83, c. 110, s. 59.

60. (1) In any proceedings under this Act where the evidence of a child or a young person is taken, it shall be taken only after the youth court judge or the justice, as the case may be, has

(*a*) in all cases, if the witness is a child, and

(*b*) where he deems it necessary, if the witness is a young person,

instructed the child or young person as to the duty of the witness to speak the truth and the consequences of failing to do so.

(2) The evidence of a child or a young person shall be taken under solemn affirmation as follows:

I solemnly affirm that the evidence to be given by me shall be the truth, the whole truth and nothing but the truth.

(3) Evidence of a child or a young person taken under solemn affirmation shall have the same effect as if taken under oath. 1980-81-82-83, c. 110, s. 60.

Appendix C

Constitution Act, 1982

SCHEDULE B

CONSTITUTION ACT, 1982

PART I

CANADIAN CHARTER OF RIGHTS AND
FREEDOMS

Whereas Canada is founded upon principles that recognize the supremacy of God and the rule of law:

Guarantee of Rights and Freedoms

1. The *Canadian Charter of Rights and Freedoms* guarantees the rights and freedoms set out in it subject only to such reasonable limits prescribed by law as can be demonstrably justified in a free and democratic society.

Fundamental Freedoms

2. Everyone has the following fundamental freedoms:
(*a*) freedom of conscience and religion;
(*b*) freedom of thought, belief, opinion and expression, including freedom of the press and other media of communication;
(*c*) freedom of peaceful assembly; and
(*d*) freedom of association.

Democratic Rights

3. Every citizen of Canada has the right to vote in an election of members of the House of Commons or of a legislative assembly and to be qualified for membership therein.

4. (1) No House of Commons and no legislative assembly shall continue for longer than five years from the date fixed for the return of the writs at a general election of its members.

(2) In time of real or apprehended war, invasion or insurrection, a House of Commons may be continued by Parliament and a legislative assembly may be continued by the legislature beyond five years if such continuation is not opposed by the votes of more than one-third of the members of the House of Commons or the legislative assembly, as the case may be.

5. There shall be a sitting of Parliament and of each legislature at least once every twelve months.

Mobility Rights

6. (1) Every citizen of Canada has the right to enter, remain in and leave Canada.

(2) Every citizen of Canada and every person who has the status of a permanent resident of Canada has the right

(*a*) to move to and take up residence in any province; and
(*b*) to pursue the gaining of a livelihood in any province.

(3) The rights specified in subsection (2) are subject to

(*a*) any laws or practices of general application in force in a province other than those that discriminate among persons primarily on the basis of province of present or previous residence; and

(*b*) any laws providing for reasonable residency requirements as a qualification for the receipt of publicly provided social services.

(4) Subsections (2) and (3) do not preclude any law, program or activity that has as its object the amelioration in a province of conditions of individuals in that province who are socially or economically disadvantaged if the rate of employment in that province is below the rate of employment in Canada.

Legal Rights

7. Everyone has the right to life, liberty and security of the person and the right not to be deprived thereof except in accordance with the principles of fundamental justice.

8. Everyone has the right to be secure against unreasonable search or seizure.

9. Everyone has the right not to be arbitrarily detained or imprisoned.

10. Everyone has the right on arrest or detention

(*a*) to be informed promptly of the reasons therefor;

(*b*) to retain and instruct counsel without delay and to be informed of that right; and

(*c*) to have the validity of the detention determined by way of *habeas corpus* and to be released if the detention is not lawful.

11. Any person charged with an offence has the right

(*a*) to be informed without unreasonable delay of the specific offence;

(*b*) to be tried within a reasonable time;

(*c*) not to be compelled to be a witness in proceedings against that person in respect of the offence;

(*d*) to be presumed innocent until proven guilty according to law in a fair and public hearing by an independent and impartial tribunal;

(*e*) not to be denied reasonable bail without just cause;

(*f*) except in the case of an offence under military law tried before a military tribunal, to the benefit of trial by jury where the maximum punishment for the offence is imprisonment for five years or a more severe punishment;

(*g*) not to be found guilty on account of any act or omission unless, at the time of the act or omission, it constituted an offence under Canadian or international law or was criminal according to the general principles of law recognized by the community of nations;

(*h*) if finally acquitted of the offence, not to be tried for it again and, if finally found guilty and punished for the offence, not to be tried or punished for it again; and

(*i*) if found guilty of the offence and if the punishment for the offence has been varied between the time of commission and the time of sentencing, to the benefit of the lesser punishment.

12. Everyone has the right not to be subjected to any cruel and unusual treatment or punishment.

13. A witness who testifies in any proceedings has the right not to have any incriminating evidence so given used to incriminate that witness in any other proceedings, except in a prosecution for perjury or for the giving of contradictory evidence.

14. A party or witness in any proceedings who does not understand or speak the language in which the proceedings are conducted or who is deaf has the right to the assistance of an interpreter.

Equality Rights

15. (1) Every individual is equal before and under the law and has the right to the equal protection and equal benefit of the law without discrimination and, in particular, without discrimination based on race, national or ethnic origin, colour, religion, sex, age or mental or physical disability.

(2) Subsection (1) does not preclude any law, program or activity that has as its object the amelioration of conditions of disadvantaged individuals or groups including those that are disadvantaged because of race, national or eth-

nic origin, colour, religion, sex, age or mental or physical disability.

[Note: This section became effective on April 17, 1985. See subsection 32(2) and the note thereto.]

Official Languages of Canada

16. (1) English and French are the official languages of Canada and have equality of status and equal rights and privileges as to their use in all institutions of the Parliament and government of Canada.

(2) English and French are the official languages of New Brunswick and have equality of status and equal rights and privileges as to their use in all institutions of the legislature and government of New Brunswick.

(3) Nothing in this Charter limits the authority of Parliament or a legislature to advance the equality of status or use of English and French.

17. (1) Everyone has the right to use English or French in any debates and other proceedings of Parliament.

(2) Everyone has the right to use English or French in any debates and other proceedings of the legislature of New Brunswick.

18. (1) The statutes, records and journals of Parliament shall be printed and published in English and French and both language versions are equally authoritative.

(2) The statutes, records and journals of the legislature of New Brunswick shall be printed and published in English and French and both language versions are equally authoritative.

19. (1) Either English or French may be used by any person in, or in any pleading in or process issuing from, any court established by Parliament.

(2) Either English or French may be used by any person in, or in any pleading in or process issuing from, any court of New Brunswick.

20. (1) Any member of the public in Canada has the right to communicate with, and to receive available services from, any head or central office of an institution of the Parliament or government of Canada in English or French, and has the same right with respect to

any other office of any such institution where

(*a*) there is a significant demand for communications with and services from that office in such language; or

(*b*) due to the nature of the office, it is reasonable that communications with and services from that office be available in both English and French.

(2) Any member of the public in New Brunswick has the right to communicate with, and to receive available services from, any office of an institution of the legislature or government of New Brunswick in English or French.

21. Nothing in sections 16 to 20 abrogates or derogates from any right, privilege or obligation with respect to the English and French languages, or either of them, that exists or is continued by virtue of any other provision of the Constitution of Canada.

22. Nothing in sections 16 to 20 abrogates or derogates from any legal or customary right or privilege acquired or enjoyed either before or after the coming into force of this Charter with respect to any language that is not English or French.

Minority Language Educational Rights

23. (1) Citizens of Canada

(*a*) whose first language learned and still understood is that of the English or French linguistic minority population of the province in which they reside, or

(*b*) who have received their primary school instruction in Canada in English or French and reside in a province where the language in which they received that instruction is the language of the English or French linguistic minority population of the province,

have the right to have their children receive primary and secondary school instruction in that language in that province.

[Note: See also section 59 and the note thereto.]

(2) Citizens of Canada of whom any child has received or is receiving primary or secondary school instruction in English or French in Canada, have the right to have all their children receive primary and secondary school instruction in the same language.

(3) The right of citizens of Canada under subsections (1) and (2) to have their children receive primary and secondary school instruction in the language of the English or French linguistic minority population of a province

(*a*) applies wherever in the province the number of children of citizens who have such a right is sufficient to warrant the provision to them out of public funds of minority language instruction; and

(*b*) includes, where the number of those children so warrants, the right to have them receive that instruction in minority language educational facilities provided out of public funds.

Enforcement

24. (1) Anyone whose rights or freedoms, as guaranteed by this Charter, have been infringed or denied may apply to a court of competent jurisdiction to obtain such remedy as the court considers appropriate and just in the circumstances.

(2) Where, in proceedings under subsection (1), a court concludes that evidence was obtained in a manner that infringed or denied any rights or freedoms guaranteed by this Charter, the evidence shall be excluded if it is established that, having regard to all the circumstances, the admission of it in the proceedings would bring the administration of justice into disrepute.

General

25. The guarantee in this Charter of certain rights and freedoms shall not be construed so as to abrogate or derogate from any aboriginal, treaty or other rights or freedoms that pertain to the aboriginal peoples of Canada including

(*a*) any rights or freedoms that have been recognized by the Royal Proclamation of October 7, 1763; and

(*b*) *any rights or freedoms that may be acquired by the aboriginal peoples of Canada by way of land claims settlement.*

(*b*) any rights or freedoms that now exist by way of land claims agreements or may be so acquired.

[Note: Paragraph 25(*b*) (in italics) was repealed and the new paragraph substituted by the *Constitution Amendment Proclamation, 1983* (No. 46 *infra*).]

26. The guarantee in this Charter of certain rights and freedoms shall not be construed as denying the existence of any other rights or freedoms that exist in Canada.

27. This Charter shall be interpreted in a manner consistent with the preservation and enhancement of the multicultural heritage of Canadians.

28. Notwithstanding anything in this Charter, the rights and freedoms referred to in it are guaranteed equally to male and female persons.

29. Nothing in this Charter abrogates or derogates from any rights or privileges guaranteed by or under the Constitution of Canada in respect of denominational, separate or dissentient schools.

30. A reference in this Charter to a province or to the legislative assembly or legislature of a province shall be deemed to include a reference to the Yukon Territory and the Northwest Territories, or to the appropriate legislative authority thereof, as the case may be.

31. Nothing in this Charter extends the legislative powers of any body or authority.

Application of Charter

32. (1) This Charter applies

(*a*) to the Parliament and government of Canada in respect of all matters within the authority of Parliament including all matters relating to the Yukon Territory and Northwest Territories; and

(*b*) to the legislature and government of each province in respect of all matters within the authority of the legislature of each province.

(2) Notwithstanding subsection (1), section 15 shall not have effect until three years after this section comes into force.

[Note: This section came into force on April 17, 1982. See the proclamation of that date (No. 45 *infra*).]

33. (1) Parliament or the legislature of a province may expressly declare in an Act of Parliament or of the legislature, as the case may be, that the Act or a provision thereof shall operate notwithstanding a provision included in section 2 or sections 7 to 15 of this Charter.

(2) An Act or a provision of an Act in respect of which a declaration made under this section is in effect shall have such operation as it would have but for the provision of this Charter referred to in the declaration.

(3) A declaration made under subsection (1) shall cease to have effect five years after it comes into force or on such earlier date as may be specified in the declaration.

(4) Parliament or the legislature of a province may re-enact a declaration made under subsection (1).

(5) Subsection (3) applies in respect of a re-enactment made under subsection (4).

Citation

34. This Part may be cited as the *Canadian Charter of Rights and Freedoms*.

PART II

RIGHTS OF THE ABORIGINAL PEOPLES OF CANADA

35. (1) The existing aboriginal and treaty rights of the aboriginal peoples of Canada are hereby recognized and affirmed.

(2) In this Act, "aboriginal peoples of Canada" includes the Indian, Inuit and Métis peoples of Canada.

(3) For greater certainty, in subsection (1) "treaty rights" includes rights that now exist by way of land claims agreements or may be so acquired.

(4) Notwithstanding any other provision of this Act, the aboriginal and treaty rights referred to in subsection (1) are guaranteed equally to male and female persons.

[Note: Subsections 35(3) and (4) were added by the *Constitution Amendment Proclamation, 1983* (No. 46 *infra*).]

35.1 The government of Canada and the provincial governments are committed to the principle that, before any amendment is made to Class 24 of section 91 of the "*Constitution Act, 1867*", to section 25 of this Act or to this Part,

(*a*) a constitutional conference that includes in its agenda an item relating to the proposed amendment, composed of the Prime Minister of Canada and the first ministers of the provinces, will be convened by the Prime Minister of Canada; and

(*b*) the Prime Minister of Canada will invite representatives of the aboriginal peoples of Canada to participate in the discussions on that item.

[Note: Added by the *Constitution Amendment Proclamation, 1983* (No. 46 *infra*).]

PART III

EQUALIZATION AND REGIONAL DISPARITIES

36. (1) Without altering the legislative authority of Parliament or of the provincial legislatures, or the rights of any of them with respect to the exercise of their legislative authority, Parliament and the legislatures, together with the government of Canada and the provincial governments, are committed to

(*a*) promoting equal opportunities for the well-being of Canadians;

(*b*) furthering economic development to reduce disparity in opportunities; and

(*c*) providing essential public services of reasonable quality to all Canadians.

(2) Parliament and the government of Canada are committed to the principle of making equalization payments to ensure that provincial governments have sufficient revenues to provide reasonably comparable levels of public services at reasonably comparable levels of taxation.

PART IV

CONSTITUTIONAL CONFERENCE

37. *(1) A constitutional conference composed of the Prime Minister of Canada and the first ministers of the provinces shall be convened by the Prime Minister of Canada within one year after this Part comes into force.*

(2) The conference convened under subsection (1) shall have included in its agenda an item respecting constitutional matters that

directly affect the aboriginal peoples of Canada, including the identification and definition of the rights of those peoples to be included in the Constitution of Canada, and the Prime Minister of Canada shall invite representatives of those peoples to participate in the discussions on that item.

(3) The Prime Minister of Canada shall invite elected representatives of the governments of the Yukon Territory and the Northwest Territories to participate in the discussions on any item on the agenda of the conference convened under subsection (1) that, in the opinion of the Prime Minister, directly affects the Yukon Territory and the Northwest Territories.

[Note: Part IV was repealed effective April 17, 1983 by section 54 of this Act.]

PART IV.1
CONSTITUTIONAL CONFERENCES

37.1 *(1) In addition to the conference convened in March 1983, at least two constitutional conferences composed of the Prime Minister of Canada and the first ministers of the provinces shall be convened by the Prime Minister of Canada, the first within three years after April 17, 1982 and the second within five years after that date.*

(2) Each conference convened under subsection (1) shall have included in its agenda constitutional matters that directly affect the aboriginal peoples of Canada, and the Prime Minister of Canada shall invite representatives of those peoples to participate in the discussions on those matters.

(3) The Prime Minister of Canada shall invite elected representatives of the governments of the Yukon Territory and the Northwest Territories to participate in the discussions on any item on the agenda of a conference convened under subsection (1) that, in the opinion of the Prime Minister, directly affects the Yukon Territory and the Northwest Territories.

(4) Nothing in this section shall be construed so as to derogate from subsection 35(1).

[Note: Part IV.1 was added by the *Constitution Amendment Proclamation, 1983* (No. 46 *infra*). By the same proclamation, it was repealed effective April 18, 1987. See section 54.1 of this Act.]

PART V

PROCEDURE FOR AMENDING CONSTITUTION OF CANADA

38. (1) An amendment to the Constitution of Canada may be made by proclamation issued by the Governor General under the Great Seal of Canada where so authorized by

(*a*) resolutions of the Senate and House of Commons; and

(*b*) resolutions of the legislative assemblies of at least two-thirds of the provinces that have, in the aggregate, according to the then latest general census, at least fifty per cent of the population of all the provinces.

(2) An amendment made under subsection (1) that derogates from the legislative powers, the proprietary rights or any other rights or privileges of the legislature or government of a province shall require a resolution supported by a majority of the members of each of the Senate, the House of Commons and the legislative assemblies required under subsection (1).

(3) An amendment referred to in subsection (2) shall not have effect in a province the legislative assembly of which has expressed its dissent thereto by resolution supported by a majority of its members prior to the issue of the proclamation to which the amendment relates unless that legislative assembly, subsequently, by resolution supported by a majority of its members, revokes its dissent and authorizes the amendment.

(4) A resolution of dissent made for the purposes of subsection (3) may be revoked at any time before or after the issue of the proclamation to which it relates.

39. (1) A proclamation shall not be issued under subsection 38(1) before the expiration of one year from the adoption of the resolution initiating the amendment procedure thereunder, unless the legislative assembly of each province has previously adopted a resolution of assent or dissent.

(2) A proclamation shall not be issued under subsection 38(1) after the expiration of three years from the adoption of the resolution initiating the amendment procedure thereunder.

40. Where an amendment is made under subsection 38(1) that transfers provincial legis-

240

lative powers relating to education or other cultural matters from provincial legislatures to Parliament, Canada shall provide reasonable compensation to any province to which the amendment does not apply.

41. An amendment to the Constitution of Canada in relation to the following matters may be made by proclamation issued by the Governor General under the Great Seal of Canada only where authorized by resolutions of the Senate and House of Commons and of the legislative assembly of each province:

(*a*) the office of the Queen, the Governor General and the Lieutenant Governor of a province;

(*b*) the right of a province to a number of members in the House of Commons not less than the number of Senators by which the province is entitled to be represented at the time this Part comes into force;

(*c*) subject to section 43, the use of the English or the French language;

(*d*) the composition of the Supreme Court of Canada; and

(*e*) an amendment to this Part.

42. (1) An amendment to the Constitution of Canada in relation to the following matters may be made only in accordance with subsection 38(1):

(*a*) the principle of proportionate representation of the provinces in the House of Commons prescribed by the Constitution of Canada;

(*b*) the powers of the Senate and the method of selecting Senators;

(*c*) the number of members by which a province is entitled to be represented in the Senate and the residence qualifications of Senators;

(*d*) subject to paragraph 41(*d*), the Supreme Court of Canada;

(*e*) the extension of existing provinces into the territories; and

(*f*) notwithstanding any other law or practice, the establishment of new provinces.

(2) Subsections 38(2) to (4) do not apply in respect of amendments in relation to matters referred to in subsection (1).

43. An amendment to the Constitution of Canada in relation to any provision that applies to one or more, but not all, provinces, including

(*a*) any alteration to boundaries between provinces, and

(*b*) any amendment to any provision that relates to the use of the English or the French language within a province,

may be made by proclamation issued by the Governor General under the Great Seal of Canada only where so authorized by resolutions of the Senate and House of Commons and of the legislative assembly of each province to which the amendment applies.

44. Subject to sections 41 and 42, Parliament may exclusively make laws amending the Constitution of Canada in relation to the executive government of Canada or the Senate and House of Commons.

45. Subject to section 41, the legislature of each province may exclusively make laws amending the constitution of the province.

46. (1) The procedures for amendment under sections 38, 41, 42 and 43 may be initiated either by the Senate or the House of Commons or by the legislative assembly of a province.

(2) A resolution of assent made for the purposes of this Part may be revoked at any time before the issue of a proclamation authorized by it.

47. (1) An amendment to the Constitution of Canada made by proclamation under section 38, 41, 42 or 43 may be made without a resolution of the Senate authorizing the issue of the proclamation if, within one hundred and eighty days after the adoption by the House of Commons of a resolution authorizing its issue, the Senate has not adopted such a resolution and if, at any time after the expiration of that period, the House of Commons again adopts the resolution.

(2) Any period when Parliament is prorogued or dissolved shall not be counted in computing the one hundred and eighty day period referred to in subsection (1).

48. The Queen's Privy Council for Canada shall advise the Governor General to issue a proclamation under this Part forthwith on the adoption of the resolutions required for an amendment made by proclamation under this Part.

49. A constitutional conference composed of the Prime Minister of Canada and the first ministers of the provinces shall be convened by the Prime Minister of Canada within fifteen years after this Part comes into force to review the provisions of this Part.

Amendment to the Constitution Act, 1867

[Sections 50 and 51 are omitted. They added a new s. 92A and a new Sixth Schedule to the Constitution Act, 1867.]

PART VII

GENERAL

52. (1) The Constitution of Canada is the supreme law of Canada, and any law that is inconsistent with the provisions of the Constitution is, to the extent of the inconsistency, of no force or effect.

(2) The Constitution of Canada includes

(*a*) the *Canada Act 1982*, including this Act;

(*b*) the Acts and orders referred to in the schedule; and

(*c*) any amendment to any Act or order referred to in paragraph (*a*) or (*b*).

(3) Amendments to the Constitution of Canada shall be made only in accordance with the authority contained in the Constitution of Canada.

53. (1) The enactments referred to in Column I of the schedule are hereby repealed or amended to the extent indicated in Column II thereof and, unless repealed, shall continue as law in Canada under the names set out in Column III thereof.

(2) Every enactment, except the *Canada Act 1982*, that refers to an enactment referred to in the schedule by the name in Column I thereof is hereby amended by substituting for that name the corresponding name in Column III thereof, and any British North America Act not referred to in the schedule may be cited as the *Constitution Act* followed by the year and number, if any, of its enactment.

54. Part IV is repealed on the day that is one year after this Part comes into force and this section may be repealed and this Act renumbered, consequentially upon the repeal of Part IV and this section, by proclamation issued by the Governor General under the Great Seal of Canada.

[Note: On October 31, 1987, no proclamation had been issued under this section.]

54.1 *Part iv.1 and this section are repealed on April 18, 1987.*

[Note: Added by the *Constitution Amendment Proclamation, 1983* (No. 46 *infra*).]

55. A French version of the portions of the Constitution of Canada referred to in the schedule shall be prepared by the Minister of Justice of Canada as expeditiously as possible and, when any portion thereof sufficient to warrant action being taken has been so prepared, shall be put forward for enactment by proclamation issued by the Governor General under the Great Seal of Canada pursuant to the procedure then applicable to an amendment of the same provisions of the Constitution of Canada.

[Note: On October 31, 1987, no proclamation had been issued under this section.]

56. Where any portion of the Constitution of Canada has been or is enacted in English and French or where a French version of any portion of the Constitution is enacted pursuant to section 55, the English and French versions of that portion of the Constitution are equally authoritative.

57. The English and French versions of this Act are equally authoritative.

58. Subject to section 59, this Act shall come into force on a day to be fixed by proclamation issued by the Queen or the Governor General under the Great Seal of Canada.

[Note: The *Constitution Act, 1982* was, subject to section 59 thereof, proclaimed in force on April 17, 1982 (No. 45 *infra*).]

59. (1) Paragraph 23(1)(*a*) shall come into

force in respect of Quebec on a day to be fixed by proclamation issued by the Queen or the Governor General under the Great Seal of Canada.

(2) A proclamation under subsection (1) shall be issued only where authorized by the legislative assembly or government of Quebec.

(3) This section may be repealed on the day paragraph 23(1)(*a*) comes into force in respect of Quebec and this Act amended and renumbered, consequentially upon the repeal of this section, by proclamation issued by the Queen or the Governor General under the Great Seal of Canada.

[Note: On October 31, 1987, no proclamation had been issued under this section.]

60. This Act may be cited as the *Constitution Act, 1982*, and the Constitution Acts 1867 to 1975 (No. 2) and this Act may be cited together as the *Constitution Acts, 1867 to 1982*.

61. A reference to the "*Constitution Acts, 1867 to 1982*" shall be deemed to include a reference to the "*Constitution Amendment Proclamation, 1983*".

[Note: Added by the *Constitution Amendment Proclamation, 1983* (No. 46 *infra*). See also section 3 of the *Constitution Act, 1985 (Representation)* (No. 47 *infra*).]

CANADIAN BILL OF RIGHTS

An Act for the Recognition and Protection of Human Rights and Fundamental Freedoms

8-9 Elizabeth II, c. 44 (Canada)

[Assented to 10th August 1960]

The Parliament of Canada, affirming that the Canadian Nation is founded upon principles that acknowledge the supremacy of God, the dignity and worth of the human person and the position of the family in a society of free men and free institutions;

Affirming also that men and institutions remain free only when freedom is founded upon respect for moral and spiritual values and the rule of law;

And being desirous of enshrining these principles and the human rights and fundamental freedoms derived from them, in a Bill of Rights which shall reflect the respect of Parliament for its constitutional authority and which shall ensure the protection of these rights and freedoms in Canada:

Therefore Her Majesty, by and with the advice and consent of the Senate and House of Commons of Canada, enacts as follows:

PART I

BILL OF RIGHTS

1. It is hereby recognized and declared that in Canada there have existed and shall continue to exist without discrimination by reason of race, national origin, colour, religion or sex, the following human rights and fundamental freedoms, namely,

(*a*) the right of the individual to life, liberty, security of the person and enjoyment of property, and the right not to be deprived thereof except by due process of law;

(*b*) the right of the individual to equality before the law and the protection of the law;

(*c*) freedom of religion;

(*d*) freedom of speech;

(*e*) freedom of assembly and association; and

(*f*) freedom of the press.

2. Every law of Canada shall, unless it is expressly declared by an Act of the Parliament of Canada that it shall operate notwithstanding the *Canadian Bill of Rights*, be so construed and applied as not to abrogate, abridge or infringe or to authorize the abrogation, abridgment or infringement of any of the rights or freedoms herein recognized and declared, and in particular, no law of Canada shall be construed or applied so as to

(*a*) authorize or effect the arbitrary detention, imprisonment or exile of any person;

(*b*) impose or authorize the imposition of cruel and unusual treatment or punishment;

(*c*) deprive a person who has been arrested or detained

(i) of the right to be informed promptly of the reason for his arrest or detention,

(ii) of the right to retain and instruct counsel without delay, or

(iii) of the remedy by way of *habeas cor-*

pus for the determination of the validity of his detention and for his release if the detention is not lawful;

(*d*) authorize a court, tribunal, commission, board or other authority to compel a person to give evidence if he is denied counsel, protection against self crimination or other constitutional safeguards;

(*e*) deprive a person of the right to a fair hearing in accordance with the principles of fundamental justice for the determination of his rights and obligations;

(*f*) deprive a person charged with a criminal offence of the right to be presumed innocent until proved guilty according to law in a fair and public hearing by an independent and impartial tribunal, or of the right to reasonable bail without just cause; or

(*g*) deprive a person of the right to the assistance of an interpreter in any proceedings in which he is involved or in which he is a party or a witness, before a court, commission, board or other tribunal, if he does not understand or speak the language in which such proceedings are conducted.

3. *The Minister of Justice shall, in accordance with such regulations as may be prescribed by the Governor in Council, examine every proposed regulation submitted in draft form to the Clerk of the Privy Council pursuant to the Regulations Act and every Bill introduced in or presented to the House of Commons, in order to ascertain whether any of the provisions thereof are inconsistent with the purposes and provisions of this Part and he shall report any such inconsistency to the House of Commons at the first convenient opportunity.*

3. *The Minister of Justice shall, in accordance with such regulations as may be prescribed by the Governor in Council, examine every regulation transmitted to the Clerk of the Privy Council for registration pursuant to the Statutory Instruments Act and every Bill introduced in or presented to the House of Commons, in order to ascertain whether any of the provisions thereof are inconsistent with the purposes and provisions of this Part and he shall report any such inconsistency to the House of Commons at the first convenient opportunity.*

3. (1) Subject to subsection (2), the Minister of Justice shall, in accordance with such regulations as may be prescribed by the Governor in Council, examine every regulation transmitted to the Clerk of the Privy Council for registration pursuant to the *Statutory Instruments Act* and every Bill introduced in or presented to the House of Commons by a Minister of the Crown, in order to ascertain whether any of the provisions thereof are inconsistent with the purposes and provisions of this Part and he shall report any such inconsistency to the House of Commons at the first convenient opportunity.

(2) A regulation need not be examined in accordance with subsection (1) if prior to being made it was examined as a proposed regulation in accordance with section 3 of the *Statutory Instruments Act* to ensure that it was not inconsistent with the purposes and provisions of this Part.

[Note: The original section 3 (the first text in italics) was repealed and a new section 3 substituted by section 29 of the *Statutory Instruments Act* 19-20 Eliz II, c. 38, and the section enacted by that Act (the second text in italics) was repealed and the present section 3 substituted by section 105 of the *Statute Law (Canadian Charter of Rights and Freedoms) Amendment Act*, 33-34 Eliz. II, c. 26.]

4. The provisions of this Part shall be known as the *Canadian Bill of Rights*.

PART II

5. (1) Nothing in Part I shall be construed to abrogate or abridge any human right or fundamental freedom not enumerated therein that may have existed in Canada at the commencement of this Act.

(2) The expression "law of Canada" in Part I means an Act of the Parliament of Canada enacted before or after the coming into force of this Act, any order, rule or regulation thereunder, and any law in force in Canada or in any part of Canada at the commencement of this Act that is subject to be repealed, abolished or altered by the Parliament of Canada.

(3) The provisions of Part I shall be construed as extending only to matters coming within the legislative authority of the Parliament of Canada.

. . . .

Glossary of Common Legal Terms and Phrases

A.

action Case, cause, suite, or controversy disputed or contested before a court.

actus reus Proof that a criminal act has occurred.

ad hoc For this (special) purpose.

ad idem At one.

adjudication Giving or pronouncing a judgment.

adversary proceeding One having opposing, contested parties.

adversary system The trial method used based on the belief that truth can best be determined by giving opposing parties full opportunity to present and establish their evidence, and to test the evidence presented by cross-examination.

affidavit Assertion under oath.

alternative dispute resolution Settling a dispute without the formality of a trial. Includes mediation, conciliation, arbitration, settlement, amongst others.

amicus curiae A friend of the court.

appeal A request by the losing party in a legal action that the judgment be reviewed by a higher court.

appellant The party who initiates an appeal to a "higher" (appellate) court.

arbitration A form of alternative dispute resolution, in which the parties bring their dispute to a neutral third party and agree to abide by his or her decision.

B.

bona fide In good faith.

burden of proof In the law of evidence, the necessity or duty of proving facts in dispute raised between the parties in an action. The responsibility of proving a point. For example, in a civil case the burden of proof rests with the plaintiff, who establish his or her case by such standards of proof as on the balance of probabilities.

C.

case law Law based on previous decisions.

causa causans Causing, cause.

certiorari A means of getting an appellate court to review a lower court's decision. An order requiring the lower court to convey the record of the case to the appellate court and to certify it as accurate and complete. If an appellate court grants a writ of certiorari, it agrees to take the appeal.

citation A reference to a source of legal authority.

common law Law arising from tradition and judicial decisions rather than from laws passed by legislatives. Also called case law.

consensus (ad idem) Agreement (in the same terms).

contra Against.

contra proferentum Against the proferror (i.e., one who prepared a document).

contributory negligence A legal doctrine that says that if the plaintiff in a civil action for negligence is also negligent, he or she cannot recover damages from the defendant for the defendant's negligence depending, of course, on degree.

corroborating evidence Supplementary evidence that tends to strengthen or confirm the initial evidence.

court costs The expenses of bringing or defending a lawsuit other than lawyer's fees. An amount of money may be awarded to the successful party (and recoverable from the losing party) as reimbursement for court costs.

D.

decision The judgment reached or given by a court of law.

de facto In fact, that is, actually occurring although not officially sanctioned.

defendant In a civil case, the person being sued, the person against whom relief is sought. In a criminal case, the person charged with a crime.

de jure In law, that is, occurring as a result of official action.

de novo Hearing or trying a matter anew, as if it had not been heard or tried previously.

discovery The pre-trial process by which one party discovers the evidence that will be relied upon in a trial by the opposing party.

dismissal The termination of a lawsuit.

dissent An appellate court's opinion of reasons setting forth the minority view and outlining the disagreement of one or more judges with the majority decision.

due process The right of all persons to receive the guarantees and safeguards of the law and the judicial process. Includes such requirements as adequate notice, the right to counsel, the right to remain silent, to a speedy and public trial, to an impartial jury, and to confront and secure witnesses.

E.

eiusdem generis Of the same class.

en banc All judges of a court sitting together. Often appellate courts hear cases in panels of three judges. If a case is heard by the full court, it is heard en banc.

equity Generally, justice or fairness. Historically, equity refers to a separate body of law developed in England in reaction to the inability of the common-law courts, in their strict adherence to rigid writs and forms of action, to consider or provide a remedy for every injury. The principle of this jurisprudence is that equity will find a way to achieve a lawful result when legal procedure is inadequate.

ex parte On behalf only of one party without notice to any other party.

F.

factum Act or deed.

H.

hearsay Evidence not within the personal knowledge of the witness but given to the witness by a third party. Hearsay evidence generally is not admissible in court, although there are many exceptions to this rule.

I.

ibid. In the same place.

idem (or id.) The same.

in camera In chambers, or in private. A hearing in camera make take place in the judge's office outside of the presence of the jury and the public.

in loco parentis In place of a parent, someone charged with the same rights, duties, and responsibilities.

in re In the matter (of).

infra Below, signifying a cross reference to a subsequent part of the document or chapter.

inter alia Among other things.

inter alios Among other persons.

inter vires Within the powers.

injunction An order of the court requiring a party to refrain or cease from doing a particular act or taking certain actions. A preliminary injunction may be granted provisionally, until a full hearing can be held to determine if it should be made permanent.

J.

joint and several liability A legal doctrine which makes each of the parties responsible for all of the damages awarded in a lawsuit if the other parties cannot pay.

judgment The final disposition of a lawsuit or official decision of a court of record.

judicial review Authority of a court to review the official actions of other branches of government.

justiciable Issues and claims properly examined in court.

L.

liable Legally responsible for.

limitations Statutes setting out times within which actions must be brought.

litigant A party to a lawsuit.

litigation A case, controversy, or lawsuit between two or more parties for the purpose of enforcing an alleged right or recovering money damages for a breach of duty.

M.

mala fides Bad faith.

mandamus A writ issued by a court ordering a public official to perform an act.

mediation A form of alternative dispute resolution, in which the parties bring their dispute to a neutral third party, who helps them agree on a settlement.

mens rea Guilty mind.

motion An application for a rule or order, made to a court or judge.

mutatis mutandis With necessary changes.

N.

negligence Failure to exercise that degree of care that a reasonable person would exercise under the same circumstances.

novus actus interveniens New act intervening (i.e., to break a chain of causation).

nunc pro tunc Now for then (i.e., retroactively).

O.

obiter By the way.

obiter dictum (plural dicta) Thing said by the way.

onus Burden.

P.

parens patriae Father of the country.

pari passu In equal step (i.e., equally).

pendente lite The lawsuit pending.

per By.

per se By itself.

plaintiff A person who brings a civil action against another party.

pre-trial hearing A meeting between the judge and parties or their lawyers involved in a lawsuit to narrow the issues, agree on what will be presented at the trial, and to make a further effort to settle the case without a trial.

prima facie At first sight, fact presumed to be true unless disproved by evidence to the contrary.

proximate cause The act which caused an event to occur. A person generally is liable only if an injury was proximately caused by his or her action or his or her failure to act when he or she had a duty to act.

R.

ratio decidendi Reason for deciding.

reasonable man A phrase used to denote a hypothetical person who exercises qualities of attention, knowledge, intelligence, and judgment that society requires of its members for the protection of their own interest and the interests of others. Thus, the test of negligence is based on either a failure to do something that a reasonable person, guided by considerations that ordinarily regulate conduct, would do, or on the doing of something that a reasonable and prudent person would not do.

Regina Queen.

remedy Legal or judicial means by which a right or privilege is enforced or the violation of a right or privilege is prevented, redressed, or compensated.

res Thing, matter, substance.

res gestae Things done, facts surrounding an incident.

res judicata Matter adjudicated.

respondent superior Theory whereby a master is held liable for the wrongful acts of his or her servant or employee if the servant or employee is acting within the scope of his or her employment.

Rex King.

S.

self defence Claim that an act otherwise criminal was legally justifiable.

settlement An agreement between the parties disposing of a lawsuit.

sine die Without a day (i.e., indefinitely).

sine qua non Without which not (i.e., essential).

stare decisis The doctrine that courts will follow principles of law laid down in previous cases. Similar to precedent.

status quo (ante) The original state.

statutory law Law enacted by legislatures as distinguished from case law or common law.

stay An order of the court halting a judicial proceeding.

sub judice Before the courts.

supra Above, signifying cross reference to an earlier part of the document or chapter.

T.

tort A theory of negligence involving an injury or wrong committed on the person or property of another. A tort is an infringement of the rights of an individual, not founded on contract. There must be a legal duty to the person harmed. There must be a breach of that duty and there must be damage to the person wronged as the proximate result of the breach.

U.

uberrimae fidei Of utmost good faith.

ultra vires Beyond the powers.

V.

verbatim Word for word.

versus Against.

viva voce With living voice (i.e., orally).

volenti non fit injuria Voluntary assumption of risk.